C O N F R O N T I N G

THE POWERS...

ARE YOU READY FOR BATTLE? IF YOU ARE, I BELIEVE THIS book will provide a solid launching pad for moving out against the enemy!

C. Peter Wagner

C. PETER WAGNER

CONFRONTING THE POWERS

**HOW THE NEW TESTAMENT
CHURCH EXPERIENCED THE
POWER OF STRATEGIC-LEVEL
SPIRITUAL WARFARE**

Regal Books
A Division of Gospel Light
Ventura, California, U.S.A.

Published by Regal Books
A Division of Gospel Light
Ventura, California, U.S.A.
Printed in U.S.A.

Regal Books is a ministry of Gospel Light, an evangelical Christian publisher dedicated to serving the local church. We believe God's vision for Gospel Light is to provide church leaders with biblical, user-friendly materials that will help them evangelize, disciple and minister to children, youth and families.

It is our prayer that this Regal book will help you discover biblical truth for your own life and help you meet the needs of others. May God richly bless you.

For a free catalog of resources from Regal Books/Gospel Light please contact your Christian supplier or call 1-800-4-GOSPEL.

All Scripture quotations are from *The New King James Version.* Copyright © 1979, 1980, 1982, 1992, Thomas Nelson, Inc. Used by permission.

Library of Congress Cataloging-in-Publication Data
Wagner, C. Peter.
    Confronting the powers / C. Peter Wagner.
        p. cm.
    Includes bibliographical references and index.
    ISBN 0-8307-1819-2
    1. Spiritual warfare. 2. Powers (Christian theology) I. Title.
    BT975.W24 1996   95-51972
    235'.4—dc20   CIP

1 2 3 4 5 6 7 8 9 10 11 12 / 02 01 00 99 98 97 96

Rights for publishing this book in other languages are contracted by Gospel Literature International (GLINT). GLINT also provides technical help for the adaptation, translation and publishing of Bible study resources and books in scores of languages worldwide. For further information, contact GLINT, P.O. Box 4060, Ontario, CA 91761-1003, U.S.A., or the publisher.

CONFRONTING

Contents

THE POWERS...

CONFRONTING

Part I: Understanding the Issues

THE POWERS...

Spiritual Warfare Yesterday, Today and Tomorrow

THE WORLDWIDE PRAYER MOVEMENT IS OUT OF CONTROL! Never since Pentecost itself has history recorded a level of prayer on six of the continents comparable to what is happening today. The Bible tells us that somewhere in heaven golden bowls are being filled with "incense, which are the prayers of the saints" (Rev. 5:8). Exactly when the bowls will be full to overflowing no one knows. But one thing is certain: The incense level in the bowls has never been higher and rising faster than it is today!

Many think the burgeoning prayer movement is a sign that the great revival for which generations of Christians have been hoping and praying is just around the corner. Four of my good friends have just written books on the subject. Bill Bright stresses the role that fasting plays in his *The Coming Revival* (New Life Publications). Robert Coleman's newest book is *The Coming*

World Revival (Crossways Books). Tom Phillips has just published *Revival Signs: Joining the New Spiritual Awakening* (Vision House), and David Bryant, chairman of the National Prayer Committee and convener of the Forum for National Revival, documents current trends as well as anyone in his *The Hope at Hand* (Baker Books). Bryant says, "God is stirring up his people to pray specifically, increasingly, and persistently for world revival....If God is stirring up the church to pray with this distinctive focus and consensus, he will not let us pray in vain. He has promised to hear and answer us fully. We can prepare for the answers with confidence."[1]

A favorite topic of pastors across the country and around the world is prayer. Not too long ago, prayer typically would appear far down on their priority lists. Today some of their churches are doing something few churches would have thought of in the past: They are adding line items to their budgets for prayer ministries! Thousands of churches have installed prayer rooms, tastefully furnished rooms that include a phone line or two and perhaps a fax machine or a computer for e-mail. These rooms are occupied by intercessors 24 hours a day. Some are bringing in outside speakers for special prayer conferences. A few have added full-time or part-time staff members who have the title "minister of prayer," "pastor of prayer" or "prayer coordinator."

Theological seminaries and Bible schools are introducing courses about prayer in their curricula. Not too many years ago Asbury Seminary was virtually the only seminary in the United States, at least that I knew of, that offered courses about prayer. Now a seminary *without* them would be regarded as antiquated.

RADICAL VARIETIES OF PRAYER

As would be expected, one of the consequences of the increasing popularity of prayer in the lives and ministries of Christian leaders is a growing awareness of the varieties of forms and functions of prayer. A number of these forms are coming as rather unwelcome surprises to some leaders, especially in cases where neither their training nor their experience has furnished them with theological hooks on which to hang some of the more radical concepts and practices seen today.

One of these newer varieties of prayer currently gaining wide attention among Christian leaders around the world is being called "strategic-level intercession." Very few of us, particularly in the United States and other nations of the Western world, had even so much as heard either this term or related ones such as "spiritual warfare," "territorial spirits," "prophetic acts," "remitting the sins of nations," "spiritual mapping," "warfare prayer", "tearing down strongholds" or "identificational repentance" during our seminary or Bible school days. Many of these terms have been coined in the 1990s. It is understandable, therefore, that such innovative concepts would require considerable processing, especially among those of more conservative temperaments. For some, the assimilation of new ideas requires more time than for others.

Certain highly respected leaders, I must report, have been stretched out of their theological comfort zones by some of the things I have recently been talking about, writing books and articles about and teaching in my classes at Fuller Theological Seminary. They have therefore become somewhat upset, and many of them have not hesitated to express their concerns in public. The result has been a rather heated controversy and, to use a term I first heard from my friend Tom White, I have involuntarily become a "lightning rod" toward which many have directed their fiery bolts of criticism.

By this I do not wish to imply that I am the only or even the principal spokesperson for advocating these newer and possibly radical varieties of prayer and strategic-level spiritual warfare. Throughout this book I will name the names of many others who have been teaching these things longer and much more profoundly than I. I have been greatly indebted to them and comforted by their willingness to join me in taking some risks and bearing the brunt of subsequent attacks. Together we sense a collegiality in what we agree is a highly significant contemporary development in the kingdom of God. We believe we are hearing some of the important things the Spirit is saying to the churches these days, although others may at the same time be hearing equally important, but different, words from the Spirit.

To be honest, I feel blessed that some would regard me as a lightning rod, and I see it as having some positive implications for me personally. My early life on a dairy farm in upstate New York made me thoroughly conversant about lightning rods. Every barn had several of them along the peak of the roof. When an electrical storm came, and many of them were ferocious, lightning in the vicinity of the barn would invariably strike the lightning rod. After the storm, both the barn and the lightning rod emerged intact. The only reason the lightning rod could have absorbed such an incredible amount of electricity and kept the barn from damage was that it was thoroughly grounded.

If God has given me the privilege of taking the heat of criticism that otherwise might be directed toward my friends, I can only remain intact if I am well grounded, both in my personal relationship with God and in His Word. The positive consequence is that it forces me to keep closer to Jesus than otherwise might be the case.

THE SEEDBED: THE LAUSANNE MOVEMENT

I have had the privilege of being involved in leadership circles of worldwide evangelical Christianity for more than 30 years. At this writing, my chief involvement is with the A.D. 2000 and

Beyond Movement. It may seem strange, but it is accurate for me to report that the A.D. 2000 Movement is the first one I have been associated with that gives prayer a high and central visibility. This is not to say that the other circles I have moved in are prayerless or fail to affirm that prayer is important. All have acknowledged that prayer is indispensable. In all candor, my observation is that previous emphases on prayer tended to be more toward rhetoric or tokenism compared to what we are seeing today.

How did we get from there to here?

Although an important preliminary meeting was held in Berlin in 1966, the Congress on World Evangelization held in Lausanne, Switzerland, in 1974 is regarded as the most historic watershed in the development of evangelical Christianity in our generation. From that gathering of some 4,000 invited delegates from all parts of the world came the Lausanne Committee for World Evangelization (LCWE), and what has become known as the Lausanne Movement. I was privileged to serve on the LCWE from its founding until the second major congress in 1989.

Prayer played a role in Lausanne I in Switzerland, but it was not given a prominent place other than the mandatory opening and closing of platform sessions with brief prayers, along with occasional prayer in small groups among delegates. Of 99 plenary addresses, devotionals, strategy papers, theology of evangelism expositions and presentations of functional groups, only one dealt with the subject of prayer. Bruno Herm's address, "Prayer in Evangelization," occupied less than 1 percent of platform time at the congress.

Vonette Bright and the World Prayer Assembly

The key person in heightening and sustaining a significant prayer emphasis in the Lausanne Movement was Vonette Bright, also a long-term member of the LCWE. Largely as a result of her vision, the World Prayer Assembly, the largest international prayer meeting that had ever been held, was convened in Seoul, Korea, in 1984. More than 20 speakers, many of whom are still household names in the prayer movement such as Evelyn Christenson, Glenn Sheppard, Wesley Duewel, Dick Eastman, David Bryant, Joy Dawson and others furnished the leadership. Their stirring addresses are published in *Unleashing the Power of Prayer* (Moody Press), edited by Vonette Bright and Ben A. Jennings.

Although I was not present at the World Prayer Assembly, it influenced me indirectly, as it did thousands of others. At that time prayer had a low position on my personal priority list. I would always be politely affirming to Vonette Bright, but I must admit, in an embarrassingly condescending way. Prayer, I thought, might have been OK for good women such as Vonette and for a few hyperspiritual men, but I preferred to concentrate my energies on "important" things such as teaching church growth principles and developing new strategies for world evangelization.

Imperceptibly at first, my attitude toward prayer began to change right around the time of the World Prayer Assembly. I was by then deeply involved with my mentor, John Wimber, in exploring the relationship between church growth and supernatural signs and wonders. At that time I also began hearing the voice of God telling me what my next major assignment would be, namely prayer and how it relates to evangelizing the lost.

My first reaction was to question God's wisdom in giving me such a boring assignment so near to what would inevitably be the closing years of my professional career. "Boring," because I must admit that my prayer experiences, both personal and corporate, had up to that time leaned definitively toward the boring side. How wrong I was! I began seriously to research, write and participate in the worldwide prayer movement in 1987, and the years since then have been by far the most exciting years of more than 40 years of ordained ministry!

One of the first things I did after my change was to sit down with Vonette Bright and sincerely apologize to her for the stupid condescending attitude I had exhibited toward her in all those years together in the Lausanne Committee. As it always had been, the fruit of the Holy Spirit was evident in her response, and she graciously forgave me and welcomed me into the worldwide prayer movement.

Lausanne II in Manila

I had been researching and teaching about prayer for two years when the next Congress on World Evangelization, called Lausanne II, was convened in Manila, Philippines, in 1989. By then, among other things, I had discovered the awesome power of personal intercession and I had recognized that some members of the Body of Christ had been given the spiritual gift of intercession by God. I had previously known that the gift existed, and I had also written about it in my book *Your Spiritual Gifts Can Help Your Church Grow* (Regal Books). Now, however, I had gone a step further and had begun experiencing the power of receiving personal intercession in my own life, seeing first-hand what a tremendous difference it could make. I later developed this in detail in my book *Prayer Shield* (Regal Books).

As I was participating in the program planning for Lausanne II in Manila, I sensed God saying to me that personal intercession should play a role in Lausanne II in Manila unlike anything previously included in international evangelical gatherings. *What would it be like,* I asked in a visionlike state of mind, *if a group of 50 widely respected intercessors might see their way clear to come to Manila at their own expense, bypass the intricate selection process for delegates, put up in the Philippine Plaza Hotel right across from the convention center where the meetings would be held, and pray 24 hours a day during the 11 days of Lausanne II in Manila?* My next thought was, *This must be the voice of God!*

My friends on the LCWE executive committee and the program committee thought it was an excellent idea, so they gave me the green light. Because I couldn't handle administrating such a project, I approached Ben Jennings, prayer leader of Campus Crusade for Christ and one of the key organizers, along with Vonette Bright, of the World Prayer Assembly held five years earlier. He was delighted to do it, and the 50 intercessors came and met together and prayed for the 11 days. It was the nearest thing to a spiritual nuclear power plant we had ever seen. About half were charismatics and half traditional evangelicals, knit together in Christian love, harmony and intimacy with the heavenly Father.

Ben Jennings's Lausanne II prayer team was seen by him and others as a direct answer to many of the prayers of the World Prayer Assembly in 1984. Its ripple effects are still being felt. For one thing, few high-visibility national and international Christian gatherings have since been planned without a similar team of intercessors praying either around the clock or at least during the times of the sessions themselves. And in Manila itself, the Lausanne II congress became a historic milestone, not only giving birth to the emerging A.D. 2000 Movement, but also serving as the seedbed for some of the initial concepts of strategic-level spiritual warfare that this book addresses.

THE A.D. 2000 UNITED PRAYER TRACK

Although it had not been a part of the intentional planning of the Lausanne II program committee, no fewer than five of the workshop speakers addressed issues related to what we had begun calling "territorial spirits." The level of interest in these workshops was striking. In contrast to anything that might have happened in Lausanne I, the best-attended optional track (series of workshops) was the Holy Spirit Track, the second was the Spiritual Warfare Track and the third the Prayer Track. Considerably fewer people elected to attend the other 45 tracks offered to the delegates. Observers commented that this in itself was one of the most dramatic differences between Lausanne I and Lausanne II. Clearly many Christian leaders from around the world were hearing things from the Holy Spirit they had not been hearing previously.

In the providence of God, a transition occurred after Lausanne II. It shifted the primary responsibility for catalyzing and coordinating the worldwide forces for evangelism from the Lausanne Movement to the A.D. 2000 Movement under the leadership of Thomas Wang and Luis Bush. As I have previously mentioned, prayer was a central focus of the A.D. 2000 Movement from the start. Its organizational structure was designed around 10 units called "tracks" or resource networks. Each has a coordinator who constitutes part of the middle management of the organization, and who is given a great deal of liberty and autonomy in developing the philosophy, programming, personnel and funding for the particular track. One of them is called the United Prayer Track.

The first candidate as coordinator of the United Prayer Track was David Bryant, who through the 1980s gained high visibility as one of evangelical Christianity's premier prayer leaders. He strongly developed the prayer ministry of Intervarsity Christian Fellowship, then branched out on his own as the founder of Concerts of Prayer International. As I mentioned before, he became influential in the U.S. National Prayer Committee, and was also one of the key leaders of the World Prayer Congress of 1984. His excellent books *In the Gap* (Regal Books), *Concerts of Prayer* (Regal Books) and *The Prayer Pacesetters Sourcebook* (Concerts of Prayer) were being widely circulated in the United States and around the world. As they prayed about this, however, David and his Concerts of Prayer International board

believed his gifts would be most useful for the kingdom of God
if he continued moving deeply into the concerts of prayer for
spiritual awakening rather than spreading himself more thinly
across the entire world prayer movement.

Peter Wagner was Luis Bush's next choice to coordinate the
United Prayer Track. By 1991, prayer had become my chief
area of research and writing, so I welcomed the opportunity to
build relationships with prayer leaders throughout the world.
My one condition was that if I accepted the leadership of the
United Prayer Track, I would also be allowed to bring with me
the Spiritual Warfare Network, which by then had taken shape.
Luis Bush readily agreed, realizing ahead of time that this
would attach the whole A.D. 2000 Movement to some of the
more radical forms of praying for the lost with which some
were experimenting.

THE SPIRITUAL WARFARE NETWORK

As I have said, Lausanne II was the seedbed for the subsequent
development of the Spiritual Warfare Network. While in Manila, the Lord spoke to me in a voice that, although not audible,
was almost as clear as if it had been: "I want you to take leadership in the area of territorial spirits."

When I told my wife, Doris, what I had heard, she said, "If
we accept that assignment, we will need much stronger personal intercession than we have now!" The upshot was that we
did accept it, God did upgrade our personal intercessors considerably and I became the coordinator of the International
Spiritual Warfare Network.

Because of the high priority the A.D. 2000 Movement gives
to prayer, the United Prayer Track has grown rapidly and has
become one of the more highly visible units within the organization. Although strategic level spiritual warfare is only one of
the many forms of prayer embraced and encouraged by the

Prayer Track, it is so new to many that considerable controversy has arisen around it. Dealing with this criticism precipitated a yearlong study process that resulted in publishing a 5,000-word document in 1994 called "The Philosophy of Prayer for World Evangelization Adopted by the A.D. 2000 United Prayer Track." The complete text of this remarkable statement is found in the appendix to this book, and I will refer to it from time to time in subsequent chapters.

The controversy that has developed in the 1990s should not be seen as questioning whether Christians should or should not engage in spiritual warfare. Indeed, the Lausanne Covenant, the widely publicized document that emerged from Lausanne I in 1974, states in Article 12 entitled "Spiritual Conflict": "We believe that we are engaged in constant spiritual warfare with the principalities and powers of evil who are seeking to overthrow the Church and to frustrate its task of evangelization." The question arises, however, whether the kind and intensity of spiritual warfare we are authorized by God to engage in has biblical limits.

Levels of Spiritual Warfare

In an attempt to clarify the issues involved, the Spiritual Warfare Network believed from the outset that it would be helpful to distinguish among three levels of spiritual warfare. Although all three relate to confronting spiritual beings in the same invisible world of darkness, and all three are unavoidably interrelated, we can see the picture more clearly when we use this terminology.

Ground-level spiritual warfare involves casting demons out of people. This ministry was practiced by Jesus and has been a part, to a lesser or greater extent, of Christian churches throughout the centuries. Although deliverance ministries have been common in Pentecostal and charismatic circles for many years, they are now strongly entering mainstream evangelical churches through leaders such as Neil Anderson, formerly a professor at Talbot School of Theology in Biola University, Charles Kraft of Fuller Theological Seminary, Tom White of Frontline Ministries and others.

Occult-level spiritual warfare deals with demonic forces released through activities related to Satanism, witchcraft, Freemasonry, Eastern religions, New Age, shamanism, astrology and many other forms of structured occultism. As those involved in ministering to people associated with such things well know, the demonic powers at work in such cases are significantly different from those operating on the ground level, and therefore other approaches are called for to deal with this kind of spiritual warfare.

Strategic-level spiritual warfare describes confrontation with high-ranking principalities and powers such as Paul writes about in Ephesians 6:12. These enemy forces are frequently called "territorial spirits" because they attempt to keep large numbers of humans networked through cities, nations, neighborhoods, people groups, religious allegiance, industries or any other form of human society in spiritual captivity. This level of warfare, also called "cosmic-level spiritual warfare," has precipitated most of the current controversy. Some believe that we overstep our divinely appointed boundaries if we engage the enemy on this level, and this book addresses such objections.

PRAYER AS A MEANS TO AN END

The A.D. 2000 United Prayer Track was established to mobilize prayer for the completion of the task of world evangelization encapsulated in the motto: "A church for every people and the gospel for every person by the year 2000." This particular kind of prayer is clearly a means to an end rather than an end in itself.

This needs some explanation because prayer can also be

and often is an end in itself. Biblical prayer comes in a variety of forms. The essence of prayer is a personal relationship with God, and from that viewpoint all prayer could be seen as an end in itself. Communication with the Father—speaking to Him and hearing from Him—is foundational to every one of the varied forms of prayer. This is an end in itself because it pleases God.

It is important to recognize that prayer is not a way for humans to manipulate God. If this were the case, Christian prayer would not differ from magic or sorcery. Christian prayer brings us into such intimacy with God that we are able to tune in to His love, grace, will, purpose and timing and then adjust our own planning accordingly.

Prayer makes a difference. As Richard Foster says, "We are working with God to determine the future. Certain things will happen in history if we pray rightly."[2] Although our prayers do not change the nature or character of God, they can have a direct influence on what God does or does not do. Our sovereign God has established a law of prayer. This means He has made certain things He wishes to do in human affairs contingent on the prayers of His people. If God's people are obedient and faithful in prayer, God's "Plan A" so to speak, will go into effect. If not, we can expect a less desirable "Plan B." Asking for Plan A does not violate our obedience to God—just the opposite. It reflects our obedience to God and our mutual desire for His perfect will to be done.

This approach to the theology of prayer opens the door for Walter Wink to make his classic statement: "History belongs to the intercessors."[3]

Contemplative Prayer

Not all pray-ers are called to pray for evangelizing the lost as a primary focus of their prayer activity. Through the centuries many saints of God, and we have been blessed by the biographies of several, have been called to dedicate their lives to "practicing the presence of God." They have felt God's leading to a lifetime of personal waiting on God and bringing Him pleasure through praise and worship. Their examples of piety constantly remind us all of the awesome holiness and magnificence of God.

Prayer for the Church

Other prayer leaders have been called to mobilize prayer for revival or spiritual awakening among believers and their churches. This is essential because the work of God in the world will not be done in the way that God wants if churches have left their first love and find themselves in a powerless state. A desperate need of the hour is for massive spiritual renewal within the churches throughout the nations.

Inherent in authentic prayer for revival is a desire for reaching the lost, on the premise that truly revived Christians will tune in to the heart of God for the salvation of souls. Experience has shown, however, that this association is not automatic. We could cite many examples of apparent spiritual renewal in recent decades that had little or no evangelistic effect. We must recognize the danger of what some have called the "bless me syndrome." Believers can easily become so enthralled with their immediate spiritual experiences that they neglect the broader demands of the kingdom of God. When this happens, it is something less than true revival.

As an example, the Evangelical Association of New England took a survey of 325 pastors in 1994, asking their frank opinions of how well they were doing on issues that are generally of high concern to churches. Out of 11 issues, they felt the best about "worship and music experience." Following that, eight other issues were positive, but in decreasing degrees. Only two of the issues concerning churches were negative: "prayer" and "community outreach," the focal points of this book! This is not to say that New England churches have all entered the "bless me syndrome," but it does show that in real life the tendency could easily be in that direction.[4]

Praying for the Lost

Partly to help redirect the kind of revival that tends to neglect evangelism, God has raised up a company of believers whose primary emphasis in prayer is to pray for the salvation of the lost. They join those engaged in contemplative prayer and prayer for revival in the churches as members of the same Body of Christ, but like hands, eyes and ears, they have different functions for the benefit of the whole.

Two fundamental biblical premises underlie current emphases on prayer directed at winning nations, unreached people groups or cities to Christ. First is Paul's statement in 2 Corinthians 4:3,4: "But even if our gospel is veiled, it is veiled to those who are perishing, whose minds the god of this age has blinded, who do not believe, lest the light of the gospel of the glory of Christ, who is the image of God, should shine on them." The devil directly and explicitly attempts to obstruct the evangelization of the lost in certain ways. Can these obstructions be removed?

I believe that God has provided ways and means for His people to remove many of these obstacles to evangelization. This is the second biblical premise. Prayer is number one among the weapons of spiritual warfare God has provided. Paul says: "For the weapons of our warfare are not carnal but mighty in God for pulling down strongholds, casting down arguments and every high thing that exalts itself against the knowledge of God" (10:4,5). This premise marries prayer for the lost with spiritual warfare because our number one spiritual weapon is prayer.

We need to understand up front that prayer and spiritual warfare do not in themselves save the lost. No one was ever saved through pulling down strongholds or binding the strong-man. Only the preaching of Christ and Him crucified, followed by repenting and experiencing personal faith in Jesus as Savior and Lord can bring the new birth and life eternal. Prayer and spiritual warfare, however, can play strategic roles in removing obstacles the devil erects in his attempts to keep people on the road to hell.

Innovative Prayer for the Lost
In this context, praying people and prayer movements through-out the world have been actively developing innovative ways of praying for the lost. Up until recently, most prayer leaders and books about prayer have emphasized praying in the church, whether in local congregations, in home groups or in several churches combining for concerts of prayer. This kind of prayer is basic. It must not only be continued, but it must also

---

"Revival will come when we get the walls down between the church and the community!"

---

be increased if God's kingdom is going to spread in our cities and nations. Prayer, however, should not be limited to praying in the church.

In recent years, God has been showing His people that great spiritual power is released when believers pray *in the community*. Awhile ago I heard Pastor Jack Graham of Prestonwood Baptist Church in Dallas say something I have taken ever since as a prophetic word of God for the church today: "Revival will come when we get the walls down between the church and the community!" Accompanying that is a prophetic

Scripture I have heard leaders in many parts of the world affirming they believe is just as applicable today as it was when God first said it to Joshua thousands of years ago: "Every place that the sole of your foot will tread upon I have given you" (Josh. 1:3). I think we should take this literally, believing that an important part of taking our cities for God is to get the physical soles of our feet, accompanied with our whole persons, into the community along with our major weapon of spiritual warfare—prayer.

Having this in mind, God has given us four ways of praying in the community that seem to stand out above the others. All four were virtually unknown to the majority of Christians before the 1990s, although some pioneers had been experimenting with them through the years. I have written a chapter about each of the four ways in my book *Churches That Pray* (Regal Books), so here I will only list them and mention other important resources for those who desire more information.

1. Praise marches. These, most commonly taking the form of Marches for Jesus, focus primarily on cities. A key source for understanding the rationale and the methodology for praise marches is Graham Kendrick's book *Public Praise* (Creation House).

2. Prayerwalking. Increasing numbers of believers are gathering in small groups and walking the streets of their neighborhoods praying for God's blessing in every way on what they see or what God brings to mind as they move along. Steve Hawthorne has teamed with Graham Kendrick in the best book on the subject, *Prayerwalking* (Creation House).

3. Prayer journeys. Prayer teams travel as a group to certain places previously targeted through spiritual mapping to pray that God's kingdom will come in all its fullness to that place. A key resource for this is John Hanna's how-to manual, *Prayer Journeys* (Caleb Project, 10 West Dry Creek Circle, Littleton, CO 80120). To understand more of the background for this kind of prayer, I also recommend *Winning the Prayer War* by Kjell Sjöberg (New Wine Press).

4. Prayer expeditions. In prayer expeditions, teams travel from one geographical point to another, usually over a period of time, to pull down strongholds over regions and pray that God's purposes for the people of the region will be fulfilled. Many will walk for days or weeks, but other forms of transportation and a variety of time frames are also appropriate. As yet we do not have a book about prayer expeditions, but much can be gleaned from the prayer diaries used by John Presdee and his teams in recent expeditions from London to Berlin, from Berlin to Moscow and from Berlin to Paris.

WORLDWIDE PRAYER INITIATIVES

In conjunction with the United Prayer Track, several significant worldwide prayer initiatives have taken place to get massive prayer for the lost into our communities or target areas. Many, but not all, of these events have been focused on the 10/40 Window, a piece of geography between 10 degrees and 40 degrees north latitude, stretching from North Africa over to Japan and the Philippines. More than 90 percent of the least-evangelized peoples of the world live in this area:

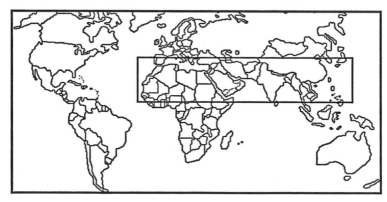

To illustrate how praying for the lost is being practiced by many today, here are some of the initiatives that have recently occurred or are planned at this writing:

• **Praying Through the Window I.** In October 1993, more than 20 million Christians prayed and fasted for 2 of the 62 nations of the 10/40 Window each day of the month, while more than 250 prayer-journey teams actually traveled to the nations to pray "on site with insight."

• **Praying Through the Window II.** In October 1995, 30 million Christians did home-based praying for the 100 gateway cities of the 10/40 Window in a synchronized way, and up to 100 intercessors made one-week prayer journeys to each one of the cities. This means a total of up to 10,000 intercessors moved across national and regional boundaries to pray specifically for the lost.

• **Praying Through Ramadan.** The spiritual highlight of the year for committed Muslims is their 30-day fast called Ramadan. In 1995, some 2 million Christians prayed and fasted through the 30 days, asking God to answer the Muslims' prayers that God would reveal Himself to them through visions and dreams. They followed a 30-day prayer guide published by Youth With a Mission (YWAM). In one small church in Houston, Texas, called Houston House of Prayer, 11 intercessors led by my friend and personal intercessor Alice Smith, went on a water-only fast for the entire 30 days. It is expected that the number of pray-ers will double in 1996.

• **The Day to Change the World.** June 25, 1994, saw between 10 and 12 million Christians out on their city streets in Marches for Jesus in 168 nations of the world. That year, believers in São Paulo, Brazil, mobilized 800,000 marchers on their streets, and in 1995 their March for Jesus totaled 1.2 million believers!

SPIRITUAL TECHNOLOGY FOR THE 1990S

From what has been said, and from much other evidence, it is plain that the decade of the 1990s is not normal times for the Church of Jesus Christ. Considering that light is appearing at the end of the Great Commission tunnel for the first time in history, and the exceptional depth of entrenchment of the enemy within the 10/40 Window, the challenges have never been greater. As I observe the ways in which the spiritual battle is being engaged in our decade, I am impressed with five "musts" for Christians who are attempting to hear what the Spirit is saying to the churches these days. Note that attached to each one of these "musts" is a technical term coming into general use only in the 1990s.

1. We must hear the Lord: prophecy. We need the practice as well as the theory that prayer is two way—we speak to God and we hear God's voice. Many of us need to be more finely tuned in understanding how the biblical gift of prophecy is being used today.

2. We must engage the enemy: strategic-level spiritual warfare. It is time to stop allowing Satan free reign over our cities and neighborhoods. Principles of strategic-level spiritual warfare need to be employed to clear the way for God's kingdom.

3. We must target our prayers: spiritual mapping. We know that when praying for individuals, the more specific and pointed our prayers can be, the more effective they are. The same applies to our communities, and our prayers now can be more precisely targeted through skillful spiritual mapping. Kjell Sjöberg encourages us in this by saying, "Individuals exist today with a gift for prophetic espionage. Certain people who have experience of God's holiness and his steadfast love, while in worship before him, have been given a hunting instinct to track down the enemy's manipulations."[5]

4. We must remit corporate sins: identificational repentance.

Warfare praying for our communities invariably involves a great deal of repentance. New insights about corporate or identificational repentance are allowing us to get to the roots of many present-day social and spiritual sicknesses and deal with causes rather than just symptoms. John Dawson's *Healing America's Wounds* (Regal Books) is a key resource.

5. *We must invade the community: prayer evangelism*. New strategies for citywide evangelism include such things as saturation church planting and prayer outside the churches, elements conspicuously absent from more traditional models. The use of prophetic acts after the style of Isaiah and Ezekiel is becoming more common. On the Day to Change the World in

---

Social scientists propound what they call "diffusion of innovation theory" in which they explain that whenever new ideas are introduced into social networks, a predictable process is set into motion.

1993, for example, YWAM and others recruited and deployed prayer journey teams that traveled to the 24 cardinal points of the world (the northernmost, southernmost, easternmost and westernmost points of six of the continents) to pray that the strongholds over the continents would be pulled down and the fullness of God's kingdom would come.

LIGHTS ARE FLASHING EVERYWHERE

As one could predict from this brief description of new and innovative ways of doing prayer and spiritual warfare, reactions from the Christian public are varied. Many are flashing green lights and saying, "Hey, let's move ahead! Why didn't we know about these things sooner?" Others are flashing yellow lights and saying, "You may have a point, but much more study is needed before we take the risks of committing to something this new." Red lights are also flashing. Some have reached the conclusion that strategic-level intercession should not be practiced at all, much less advocated for Christians on six of the continents.

It is not unusual to observe this kind of reaction. Social scientists propound what they call "diffusion of innovation theory" in which they explain that whenever new ideas are introduced into social networks, a predictable process is set into motion. Four kinds of sequential responses usually follow the initiatives of the innovators. They are called (1) early adopters, (2) middle adopters, (3) late adopters and (4) nonadopters. This happens in the Christian community as well as in society in general. Few today recall that when the Sunday School movement was proposed by an innovator, Robert Raikes, strong criticism was directed against him from many directions. I mention that because we now live in a generation in which it would be extremely rare to find a Christian leader opposed to the Sunday School on principle.

The most intense controversy takes place during the period of the early adopters, which is exactly where the ideas revolving around strategic-level spiritual warfare find themselves today. I have been through several of these cycles of diffusion of innovation during my 45 years of ordained ministry. In the 1970s, many were attacking the Church Growth Movement, uncomfortable with our emphases on numbers, on consecrated pragmatism, on the priority of evangelism and on the homogeneous unit principle. These don't seem to be hot issues anymore. Then in the 1980s, John Wimber and I took a great deal of flack about power evangelism and our teachings on divine healing, miracles and casting out demons. Strong voices that still object to these on principle are now few and far between.

I welcome the sometimes energized discussions we have been experiencing about strategic-level spiritual warfare, and our emphases on such things as spiritual mapping, identificational repentance, the gift of prophecy and prophetic acts. Those engaged in dialogue, from whichever side, are sincerely expressing various opinions, exposing weaknesses, suggesting mid-course corrections, and through it all arriving at more and more consensus. I do not enjoy criticism, but at the same time I am open to it because I want to be sure my conclusions have been thoroughly tested. Above all, I maintain a large degree of confidence that we will reasonably soon move into the middle adopter stage in which the controversy will begin to subside.

ACADEMIC DIALOGUE

One of the encouraging signs is that the discussion of strategic-level spiritual warfare is beginning to enter the forums of academic dialogue. Ordinarily, new ideas generated through frontline ministry are experimented with for a minimum of 10 years or so before a serious theological dialogue finds a place on the agendas of academicians. This was the case, for example, with church growth and power evangelism. But it is happening much more quickly with spiritual warfare.

As an example, I think of my friend Ralph Winter, founder of the U.S. Center for World Mission. I know Ralph well—we were colleagues on the faculty of the Fuller Seminary School of World Mission for years. Ralph is a cautious person who evaluates new ideas carefully. He never became an advocate of power ministries, although he was not one of the critics either. From a heart totally committed to world evangelization, however, Winter wrote a new book, *Thy Kingdom Come*, which was distributed to each of the 4,000 delegates to the A.D. 2000

Global Consultation on World Evangelization in Seoul, Korea, in 1995. In it, he says things such as the following:

• "Satan holds whole people in bondage. We can't wrestle a single soul out of his hand without challenging his authority in that particular people group."[6]

• "In groups where no real breakthrough has occurred, the contest is still a 'power encounter' between the Spirit of God and the powers of darkness. This is why the front line is prayer. This is why Asian evangelists say they must first 'bind the strongman' before entering a village that sits in darkness waiting for the great light."[7]

• "We must remember that taking light into dark places will meet fierce resistance. In the Bible the concept of *darkness* is not merely the absence of light but the presence of a malignant, destroying person. That is why the kingdoms of this world will not easily yield."[8]

WHY I'M WRITING THIS BOOK

When I accepted the responsibility of coordinating the Spiritual Warfare Network and the United Prayer Track in the early 1990s, I fully realized that some of our ideas might provoke a bit of controversy, but I did not think I would ever be called upon to write a book-length apologetic for our experiments in many parts of the world. My desire was *not* to do such a thing because since 1980 I had received a clear directional mandate from God not to engage in any more polemics, and those familiar with my writings know I have obeyed that mandate to the best of my ability.

Because I have now become a chief lightning rod for the criticism of what has become an important matter for many Christian leaders, I have acquired a responsibility I did not seek. My task has now become to produce a book that presents a cogent rationale for the ministry of strategic-level intercession without engaging in polemics. My dictionary defines a polemic as "a person who argues in opposition to another." This is what I hope to avoid. I have no taste for attempting to prove that someone else is wrong in order to make me look right. Therefore I will avoid as much as possible citing people with whom I disagree. At the same time, I will be conscientious in representing opposing positions fairly and accurately. I will not be dealing with personalities, but with issues.

I fully realize this will not be an easy task. I do not consider myself exempt from the warning Walter Wink so eloquently gives us: "It is axiomatic in religious polemic that people tend to evaluate their own religious position in terms of its best exemplars, and the religions they wish to attack by their worst."[9] I once heard Ed Silvoso say that we tend to judge ourselves by our *intentions*, while we judge those who disagree with us by their *actions*. I will try not to do that.

WAR GAMES AND MY THEOLOGY

A good deal of emotion is wrapped up in what some of the critics have been saying. One suggests that we may not be proposing spiritual warfare, but rather playing "war games." Another sees us dealing more with "mythology" than theology. Some think that by advocating strategic-level spiritual warfare we do great discredit to God and the glory of the gospel. We are seen as taking a "magical" approach, subverting the power of Christ and glorifying the power of Satan. Some accuse us of ending up with "missiological syncretism" because we choose to work from an "animistic paradigm" rather than a biblical paradigm. We are accused of operating from a faulty epistemology and for engaging in extremely irresponsible scholarship.

Through the discussions of the past few years, several key issues have emerged. Those are the issues I will try to address in this book. A key difference of opinion lies in the question of how much authority Jesus has given us as His disciples. Some believe that all the authority we have been given for certain is to confront demonic powers attached to individual persons, and that we overstep our boundaries when we suggest doing spiritual warfare against territorial spirits. I, on the other hand, take a more literal view of Jesus' statement in Luke 10:19: "Behold, I give you the authority...over all the power of the enemy." Behind my conclusions, as well as the conclusions of those who disagree with me, lie serious questions of epistemology, hermeneutics, history and biblical evidence.

The rest of this book will deal with these central issues.

A CONCILIATORY WORD

Before addressing the issues themselves, I want to make sure I am clearly understood regarding a sensitive matter. Many have taken a position against strategic-level spiritual warfare because they think they are being coerced to become like those of us who advocate it. They do not want to be poured into our mold against their wills. They think they have heard us say that first-class Christians are those who go to the front lines and do warfare prayer, but those who don't will find themselves in a lower category. I must admit, if I thought someone else were treating me that way I would oppose them as well.

I am a firm believer in the diversity of gifts in the Body of Christ, as readers of my book *Your Spiritual Gifts Can Help Your Church Grow* (Regal Books) well know. The whole Body cannot be an eye. Furthermore, "those members of the body which seem to be weaker are necessary" (1 Cor. 12:22). God loves those whom He calls to the front lines and He loves those whom He calls to undergird the front-line troops in prayer and support.

This fits well into the Old Testament law of warfare. As God was preparing His troops to take the Promised Land, He invited those who had just built a house, who had just planted a vineyard, who had just become engaged to a woman and who were fearful of the battle to stay at home (see Deut. 20:1-8). Those who guarded the military equipment and provisions were to be just as highly regarded as those who went to war. As King David later said, "As his part is who goes down to the battle, so shall his part be who stays by the supplies; they shall share alike" (1 Sam. 30:24).

I realize I have not always been as careful about saying this as I should be. At times my enthusiasm for pushing back the enemy so that more souls will be saved has exceeded my tact and my need to show respect and honor to those whose callings and ministries in the Church are different from mine, and for this I ask pardon. A friend of mine says that his church is called to the *bedroom* (intimacy with God) and not to the *battlefield* (confronting the powers). I want to bless those who are called to the bedroom as much as those who are called to the battlefield.

As I attempt in this book to justify strategic-level spiritual warfare as one of the legitimate contemporary ministries of the church, my prayer is that unity and mutual respect will prevail. After all, Jesus set a high standard for us when He prayed to the Father "that they all may be one, as You, Father, are in Me, and I in You; that they also may be one in Us, that the world may believe that You sent Me" (John 17:21).

■ REFLECTION QUESTIONS ■

1. Consider the idea of a team of intercessors praying together on-site while an important Christian gathering is taking place. Have you experienced this in your cir-

cles in the past? Would you suggest it for the future?
How could it happen?

2. How feasible do you think it would be to have traditional evangelicals and charismatics pray together regularly in your community?

3. Name and discuss the three levels of spiritual warfare
until you are confident you understand the differences.

4. In what sense can we say that sometimes prayer is an
end in itself and sometimes it is a means toward an end?

5. List the four methods of praying outside the church in
the community. Then name as many examples of each
as you can.

Notes

1. David Bryant, *The Hope at Hand* (Grand Rapids: Baker Books, 1995), p. 231.
2. Richard J. Foster, *Celebration of Discipline* (San Francisco: HarperSanFrancisco, 1988),
p. 35.
3. Walter Wink, *Engaging the Powers* (Minneapolis: Fortress Press, 1992), p. 298.
4. This survey was reported in a 1994 paper, "Church Leadership Services New England
Pastoral Survey," from the Evangelical Association of New England, Boston, Mass.
5. Kjell Sjöberg, *Winning the Prayer War* (Chichester, England: New Wine Press, 1991),
p. 60.
6. Ralph D. Winter, *Thy Kingdom Come* (Pasadena: William Carey Library, 1995), p. 11.
7. Ibid., p. 12.
8. Ibid.
9. Walter Wink, *Cracking the Gnostic Code* (Atlanta: Scholars Press, 1993), pp. 42-43.

How Do We Know What We Know? Evaluating Epistemology

I REALIZE THAT THE SIX-SYLLABLE WORD "EPISTEMOLOGY" needs a bit of explanation for most.

Everyone of us has a built-in system to sort out what is true from what is not. We do not believe everything we hear, but how does that discernment system work? How do we know when something is really true? How do we know what we know? Most normal people worldwide tap into that inborn system of discerning what should be believed and what should not every day of their lives without so much as giving thought to whether it is there, much less how it works. This is just like telling time from your watch without knowing or caring how the insides of the watch are able to function day after day. We do it constantly.

To most people, therefore, it doesn't make much difference. To philosophers, however, it makes a great deal of difference, so they have coined the label "epistemology," which means, in nonphilosophical language, trying to figure out how we know what we know.

ACCURATE INFORMATION ABOUT THE INVISIBLE WORLD

If we are going to do warfare prayer and confront the powers of darkness in the invisible world, it is essential that we have accurate information about the nature and function of these powers.

This raises crucial questions in the minds of thinking Christians. Is such knowledge available? If it is, where does it originate? How do we access it? How can we tell what is true from what is false? How do we know if something is real; if it is a clever deception of Satan, or if it is merely a figment of our imaginations?

My purpose in this chapter is to get to the bottom of such questions in a clear and practical way. I realize that whole books in the field of philosophical theology have been written on the subject of epistemology, but few Christians who are on the front lines of strategic-level spiritual warfare around the world will ever see such books, much less take time to explore and master their rather intricate reasoning. Therefore, I would not attempt to write a philosophical chapter in this book even if I possessed the credentials to do so, which I openly admit I do not.

The questions revolving around how we know what we know about the invisible world, however, cannot be ignored by responsible Christians. Predictably, much of the criticism I have received against my views about strategic-level spiritual warfare has been focused on issues of epistemology. Many believe that I and others like me are getting a good deal of our information from the wrong sources and therefore our conclusions cannot be trusted. It goes without saying that I, on the other hand, believe our information comes from reliable sources. How, then, can we tell the difference?

Let me try to explain it in some detail.

GROUND RULES FOR THEOLOGY

As I have said, I am writing this book to address the major issues that are being raised by my critics. All of them, I think, would agree with me that we are not enemies. We would agree that as Christian leaders our discussions, whether verbally or in writing, must be permeated by the fruit of the Spirit. I would hope we could agree on the ground rules for dealing with the theological issues underlying our views about strategic-level spiritual warfare, the nature of the invisible world and our authority in Christ to confront the powers of darkness. If we don't have such ground rules, we will simply be passing each other like ships in the night, resolving few of our mutual concerns.

Can we first agree on a definition of theology? This would be an excellent starting point. If so, it must be a definition that goes to the core, and to which any number of details may later be added according to individual conviction. The simplified definition of theology I have been using for years and that I would hope we could agree on is as follows:

Theology is a human attempt to explain God's Word and God's works in a reasonable and systematic way.

If we do agree on this definition, it will make a difference in our attitudes. It helps us maintain the humility, before the Lord and before each other, that all of us desire. Through such a definition we become acutely aware that our findings have limitations because they are mere *human* positions, as opposed to something divinely inspired. Furthermore, we become aware that we are at best engaged in an *attempt* that by nature welcomes future revision, as opposed to a dogmatic conclusion forever set in concrete.

At this point, we also acknowledge the obvious fact that theology differs from the Scriptures (see Matt. 5:17-19; John 10:35b; 2 Tim. 3:16; 2 Pet. 1:20,21). The Scriptures are not *human* in their construction and content, but rather they are the divinely inspired Word of God. By this, I am not ignoring the reality that the books of the Bible were also written by human beings, but I do believe that the biblical writers were so uniquely directed by the Holy Spirit that their writings fall into an entirely different category from even the best of our theologies.

GROUND RULES ABOUT ATTITUDES

I would also hope we could agree that our theological conclusions can be spread over what we might call a "conviction spectrum," running from the nonnegotiable to the things that are abhorrent. Without such a spectrum, there would be no such thing as heresy. I believe that all of us engaged in this debate about spiritual warfare agree that such a thing as heresy does exist, and that we are mutually committed to avoid it. Furthermore, the spectrum will remind us that not all of our theological notions are of equal importance.

My friend Ted Haggard says this as well as anyone. In his excellent book *Primary Purpose* (Creation House), Haggard gives us guidelines on which Christian leaders in any city should base their spiritual unity, picturing differing theological ideas by drawing three concentric circles. In the center circle he writes *absolutes*, in the middle circle he writes *interpretations*, in the outer circle he writes *deductions*, and then outside the three circles he writes *subjective opinions, personal preferences, feelings* and *cultural norms.*[1]

Those of us coming to grips with some of the relatively new and at times somewhat radical ideas surrounding strategic-level spiritual warfare, spiritual mapping, identificational repentance and other such issues agree fairly well on the theological *absolutes*, many of which are verbalized in the Apostles' Creed. Moving toward the outside of the circle, we mutually recognize that however we might differ on our theological *deductions* (such as how and when to apply water in baptism) is a relatively minor matter. We are primarily concerned with the middle area of theological *interpretations*, and which I am addressing in this book.

"One fundamental thesis will control this discussion—the thesis that ministry precedes and produces theology, not the reverse."

Realizing this will help the tone of our discussion a great deal. We may, and in many cases do, have strong convictions emerging from one theological interpretation or another, and these cannot be entirely divorced from our personal feelings and emotions. If we constantly remind ourselves that we are not dealing with the theological *absolutes* of revealed truth, however, we can much better love and respect those who might disagree with our theological *interpretations.* I must confess, I often have held such strong convictions about my theological interpretations that when I read a refutation of some of my ideas I find myself thinking, *How could so-and-so be so stupid?* Then on my good days, I become convicted of my ungodly attitude and ask the Lord for forgiveness. He then reminds me that in almost every case, my critic is at least as intelligent and loves God at least as much as I do.

MINISTRY GENERATES THEOLOGY

My friend and colleague Ray Anderson, a highly respected theologian, says in an introduction to one of his books, "One fundamental thesis will control this discussion—the thesis that ministry precedes and produces theology, not the reverse."[2]

At first glance, this may not seem like a significant point. It has, however, become an issue of much debate among professional theologians. The opposite camp believes that theology must be correct in order to precede and produce correct ministry. I, however, agree with Ray Anderson. Though good theological understanding informs good ministry, I believe that ministry ordinarily comes first and then theology follows.

Take the apostle Paul as an example. Ray Anderson and I both would see Paul as a task theologian rather than as a philosophical theologian. Paul's theology was much more rooted in what he *experienced* and what he *did* than in his rabbinical training. What, for example, was the source of Paul's Christology, his doctrine of Jesus Christ? Did he arrive at his conclusions by a systematic exegesis of the messianic Scriptures of the Old Testament, which, as a learned rabbi, he knew very well? No. Paul's Christology was rooted in his *experience* with Jesus Christ Himself on the Damascus road. Only then did the messianic Scriptures begin to make sense to him.

Or take a later example—William Carey. Many of us date the beginning of the modern missionary movement to 1793, the year Carey went from England to India as a missionary. As the story goes, Carey was a shoemaker whom God called to become a pioneer missionary. This was an innovation; a radical idea in British church circles in those days. When William Carey shared his vision with some of the clergy of the church in his day, they forthrightly rejected his suggestion by saying words to the effect: "Young man, if God wants to save the heathen in India, He will do it without your help or ours; please be seated." The clear implication was that their theology, reflective of much of the theological "wisdom" of the day, had led them to believe that the ministry of foreign missions was unnecessary. They had what they considered to be "correct theology." They may even have added, as many of my critics do, "Your ideas are not biblical!"

William Carey has since become a hero to many of us because he decided to go to India even though the theologians told him he shouldn't. As a result of Carey's ensuing *ministry* in India, not only do we have some of the beginnings of the whole modern missionary movement, but we also have the subsequent development of a detailed and complete theology of mission that is subsumed under the rubric "missiology." Many missiologists today find the theological conclusions of the British theologians in 1793 obsolete and irrelevant. My point is that the change was triggered not by astute theological reasoning, but by ministry experience. That is not denying that the Holy Spirit used Carey's study of the Scriptures and of history for his spiritual formation. In the case of the development of missiology during the past 200 years, however, mission theology gradually emerged from mission ministry.

I am aware that some could conclude from my remarks that I disparage theology per se. Such is not the case. William Carey's decision to go to India was based on his reinterpretation of the then traditional understanding of the Great Commission, by which I am saying that he must have had a theology on which he based his actions. It is never one or the other in the final analysis because the process is circular with ministry provoking theology and the new theology provoking subsequent ministry. My point is that over the long haul, what we do and what we see God do through our ministry is more frequently a starting point for the subsequent development of theological analysis, particularly at hinge points of Christian history, rather than the other way around.

WE DO NOT LIVE IN NORMAL TIMES

When I look at the 1990s, I see the Christian Church in a decade of much challenge and change. As I mentioned in chapter 1, we now live in a time when Satan is backed up against the wall of the 10/40 Window and when the potential fulfillment of Jesus' Great Commission is in realistic sight for the first time in history. Since, in agreement with George Otis Jr. and others, I am personally convinced that Satan is more deeply entrenched in the 10/40 Window than he ever has been in any other part of the world, it seems that our missionary task has never been more formidable. We should not consider it unusual, therefore, that God would see fit to provide His people with tools that they might not have been aware of previously.

This provision has been happening, particularly in the decade of the 1990s, although its roots go back for many years in certain segments of the Church. *I believe that God is now giving His missionary force the greatest power boost it has had since the time that William Carey went to India in 1793.* The key elements of this power boost that have so far emerged are strategic-level spiritual warfare, spiritual mapping and identificational repentance.

Because these concepts for many are so new, theologians and missiologists are inevitably raising some legitimate questions:

1. Are these new ideas biblically justified?
2. Are they theologically sound?
3. Do they have antecedents in the history of the Church?

These are the questions I hope to address in this book.

PETER WAGNER'S LIMITATIONS

We are dealing here with *interpretations*, as Ted Haggard would say, and not with the *absolutes* of our faith, so we need to admit that a great deal of subjectivity necessarily enters the picture. I would like to think I am always totally objective in arriving at my conclusions, but it would be dishonest to claim this. I frankly admit that I have strong biases and limitations. Because my theology reflects my ministry experiences and the theology of my critics also reflects theirs, we should not think it strange that we might find ourselves differing on certain points.

What, then, are my biases and limitations? Let me detail some of them.

My lifetime calling is to *world evangelization*, not to philosophy or theology. My profession is that of a *missiologist*, not that of a pastor. My specialization as a missiologist is *church growth*, not mission history or mission theology or missionary anthropology. I see strategic-level spiritual warfare as important to all of these aspects of my life and ministry. Those who, unlike me, may be primarily pastors, philosophers, theologians, historians, anthropologists or whatever else might not see strategic-level spiritual warfare in the same light at all. Consequently, we might well disagree on some points.

By nature I find myself more goal oriented than process oriented. Application seems more important to me than theory. The theories I like the best are, frankly, the ones that work. Although I have been criticized for this position, I try to be as pragmatic in my ministry as the apostle Paul, who said, "I have become all things to all [people], that I might by all means save some" (1 Cor. 9:22). I agree with John Wesley who once said, "I would observe every punctilio or order, except where the salvation of souls is at stake. Then I prefer the end to the means."[3]

I will not compromise *absolutes*, but my *interpretations*, I freely admit, are greatly influenced by what they may or may not produce in advancing the kingdom of God.

Finally, I am more prophetic than pastoral. Some pastors I know have objected to strategic-level spiritual warfare because engaging in it might open its practitioners to counterattacks of the devil. They are concerned about the well-being of their flocks, and this is a proper concern. As I mentioned in the last chapter, they have said they want their churches to be more like *bedrooms* where believers experience intimacy with God rather than *battlefields* where their people confront the enemy. If I were a pastor, I might well join them, but, as I have said, this is not my calling. Their awareness of possible backlash is accurate because every known war has involved casualties, and strategic-level spiritual warfare is no exception.

I make it a practice in my teaching and ministry to help reduce the casualties of spiritual warfare to a minimum, but I am not under an illusion that we can reduce them to zero. Our enemy is indeed formidable, and I would not be among those who make the mistake of underestimating his wrath and his power to harm God's people. Furthermore, the Bible tells us that among those who lead the way in overcoming the forces of evil are those who "[do] not love their lives to the death" (Rev. 12:11). From one viewpoint we regret that, according to David Barrett, probably some 156,000 martyrs' deaths for Christ will occur this year. From another viewpoint, however, we might rejoice that these will constitute 156,000 setbacks for Satan and his evil cause!

WE ARE MOLDED BY OUR CULTURE

No one has helped those of us who come from Western churches understand our cultural biases more than Charles H. Kraft. His milestone book *Christianity with Power* has helped thousands go through what he calls a "paradigm shift," which unshackles them from rationalistic/scientific ways of thinking and allows them to understand the reality of the modus operandi of the invisible world.

Regardless of where we are born and raised, every one of us is immersed in a particular culture and its accompanying worldview. Not all people see the world around them the way others do. People who have different worldviews give different interpretations and meanings to exactly the same events, behavior patterns, objects or mores with which they come into contact. This obviously also applies to Christians who may understand the same biblical passage in different ways because they have been molded by different cultures.

Charles Kraft brings to our attention the concept that in many ways people who have been molded by Third World cultures have an inherent ability to understand some biblical teachings more accurately than those of us who have been shaped by Western cultures. He says, "Biblical peoples were much more like contemporary non-Western peoples than like Euro-Americans."[4]

This gives me an important clue about why I find relatively little criticism of strategic-level spiritual warfare in my frequent journeys to Third World nations. Most non-Westerners who have chosen to raise criticisms are those who have taken theological training in the West or in institutions whose theological paradigms have been strongly influenced by Western missionaries uncritical of their own cultural assumptions. Predictably, most of the criticism has come from those who live in the West or those who have been shaped to some degree by a Western worldview.

Why is this? It comes back to epistemology, the subject of this chapter. How do we know what we know?

THREE KINDS OF KNOWLEDGE

Charles Kraft tells us about three kinds of knowledge: intellectual knowledge, observational knowledge and experiential knowledge. He says, "In Western societies, it is information at the purely *intellectual* level that we are most aware of when we think of knowledge."[5] Tracing his own paradigm shift, or shift in perspective, in coming to believe that the power of God to heal the sick is alive and well today, Kraft says he never could have come to that conclusion through *intellectual* knowledge alone. He began to change his thinking first by *observing* John Wimber and others minister physical healing and having undeniably positive results. Only as he moved into *experiential* knowledge, however, was the shift completed. He was forever convinced that supernatural power is operative today only when he himself prayed for the sick and saw them miraculously healed by the power of God.[6]

Some Western theologians became very upset when Kraft began teaching that our interpretations of the Bible can be biased by our worldviews or shaped by what we have observed or by what we have experienced. One of them, whose name I choose not to mention, wrote a whole book, which was titled *Is Charles Kraft an Evangelical?* His conclusion, needless to say, was that Kraft's ideas had carried him beyond the boundaries of established Western evangelical Christianity. The critic apparently could not accept the idea that others, because of their worldviews, might have tools to interpret parts of the Scripture more accurately than he and his Western colleagues.

Ramsay MacMullen, a historian, in his outstanding work *Christianizing the Roman Empire*, tells us that most pagans who converted to Christianity between the years A.D. 100 and 400 did so not because they acquired what Kraft would call *intellectual* knowledge, but rather through *observational* and *experiential* knowledge. He argues that the motivation that largely led to a change in religious adherence came primarily through "So-and-So believed such-and-such, *because he saw...*" or "So-and-So did thus-and-such, *and therefore* other people...["]7

THE WORD OF GOD

By and large, the criticisms of strategic-level spiritual warfare revolving around the issues of epistemology reflect a fear that my colleagues and I may be in danger of watering down the authority of the Bible as the Word of God. Some things we hear seem to imply that we could be advocating "magical" and "animistic" notions of spirit power that contradict pure biblical teaching. Our ideas are seen to be false because we allegedly use an "animistic" rather than a biblical paradigm as a basis for our conclusions about some of the realities of the invisible world.

In response, let me state for the record that I hold a high view of biblical authority. I agree with the Lausanne Covenant, which states, "We affirm the divine inspiration, truthfulness, and authority of both Old and New Testament Scriptures in their entirety as the only written word of God without error in all they affirm, and the only infallible rule of faith and practice" (Article 2).

Although I wouldn't want to identify with some distorted literalism and though I recognize differing theological nuances are associated with the term, I have always seen myself as a biblical inerrantist. I want it to be clear that I agree with my critics in affirming that nothing we do or teach as believers in

Christ should in the least contradict or violate any direct or indirect teaching of the Bible. We are not dealing with the question of ultimate authority of the Old Testament and the New Testament. As far as I am concerned, this falls into Ted Haggard's category as an *absolute.* On the other hand, our *interpretations* of the Bible may and undoubtedly will differ from time to time, as I have already said.

LOGOS AND *RHEMA*

Two Greek terms are used in the New Testament to describe the word of God: *logos* and *rhema.* Although biblical scholars tell us we cannot draw an absolute distinction between the way they are used, because at times the two words are used interchangeably, a somewhat different meaning seems to be attached to each word. In simple terms, *logos* most frequently refers to the *written* Word of God (an exception being a reference to Jesus in John 1:1), and *rhema* most frequently refers to the directly *spoken* word of God.

By way of illustration, during His power encounter with Satan in the desert, Jesus used the *logos,* the written Word of God in the Old Testament, as a spiritual weapon by which He defeated the enemy in strategic-level spiritual warfare. He repeatedly said to the enemy, "It is written" (see Matt. 4:1-11). On the other hand, when Paul was engaged in a similar power encounter with the sorcerer Elymas (or Bar-Jesus) in Cyprus, he used a *rhema* word from the Lord: "And now, indeed, the hand of the Lord is upon you, and you shall be blind, not seeing the sun for a time" (Acts 13:11). Paul could not have found this word from God in any book of the Old Testament, so he did not say "It is written" as Jesus did.

Both forms of the word of God, *logos* and *rhema,* are valid sources of knowledge, and both should be used, as God directs, to confront the enemy in spiritual warfare. In Ephesians 6:17, where Paul makes reference to "the sword of the Spirit, which is the word of God," he uses *rhema*.

EVANGELICALS ARE USED TO *LOGOS*

One of the more high-profile paradigm shifts in recent years was experienced by Professor Jack Deere of Dallas Theological Seminary. A major distinctive of Dallas Seminary since its founding has been the so-called doctrine of "cessationism." This doctrine states that those spiritual gifts called "sign gifts," though fully operative in the days of the apostles, ceased when the age of the apostles and those on whom the apostles laid hands had ended. Consequently, the faculty of that seminary has taught that in our day it is not biblical to claim or to use gifts such as those of healings, miracles, tongues, interpretation of tongues, prophecy and others, depending on who is making the list. Jack Deere, a biblical scholar, taught cessationism in Dallas Seminary for years with deep conviction, as did his colleagues.

The story of Jack Deere's paradigm shift is told in great detail in his remarkable book *Surprised by the Power of the Spirit*. Incidentally, Deere sees himself as an exception to the rule that ministry produces theology. He says, "This shift in my thinking was not the result of an experience with any sort of supernatural phenomena. *It was the result of a patient and intense study of the Scriptures*" (emphasis his).[8] Be that as it may, of all the supernatural phenomena Jack Deere had previously rejected, but has now come to accept, hearing a *rhema* word from God turned out to be the most formidable barrier he had to cross.

As Deere puts it, "The most difficult transition for me in my pilgrimage was not in accepting that Scripture teaches that God heals and does miracles today through gifted believers. The thing I resisted the most, was most afraid of, and which took the most convincing was accepting that God still speaks today."[9]

I can fully identify with this. When I was converted as an adult, I cut my spiritual teeth on *The Scofield Reference Bible* and believed that cessationism reflected sound Christian doctrine. I served for 16 years as a missionary to Bolivia with mission boards that would accept only cessationists as missionaries. I earned graduate degrees from two prestigious theological seminaries—Fuller Seminary and Princeton Seminary—and in them was taught three things related to the matter of hearing directly from God.

1. When the New Testament speaks of the gift of "prophecy," it means doctrinally sound biblical preaching.
2. There is no such thing as "present day revelatory activity of God." This meant that God's complete revelation to humans is contained in the 66 books of the Bible. Anything purporting to be the word of God not found in the Scriptures is labeled "extrabiblical revelation," and must therefore be rejected as an authentic and trustworthy source of spiritual knowledge.
3. In light of these two issues, it is considered unacceptable to say such things as "I am doing such-and-such because God told me to." God does not speak to us directly apart from Scripture, and polite Christians do not claim that He does.

Needless to say, both Jack Deere and I now believe that God does speak to His people directly today and that He always has. In my paradigm shift, I was helped most of all by my good friend Cindy Jacobs, who has put her excellent teachings about prophecy into a recent book titled *The Voice of God*

(Regal Books). Deere says, "Today, after years of practical experience and intense study on the subject of God's speaking, I am
convinced that God does indeed speak apart from the Bible,
though never in contradiction to it."[10] Jack Deere's newest book
at this writing is a whole treatise about how the gift of prophecy operates today: *Surprised by the Voice of God* (Zondervan).

**The Bible remains the only final and
authoritative litmus test for divine revelation. The 66 books of the Bible constitute a
closed canon.**

Jack Deere and Peter Wagner are just two traditional evangelicals and former cessationists among rapidly increasing numbers of others who believe that a valid source of divine knowledge comes through what some would call "extrabiblical
revelation." I daresay that the standard-brand evangelical doctrine of "*logos* only" that we were taught might now find a place
on an "endangered doctrines" list, about to become extinct. As
always, I would not fail to reemphasize that any purported
extrabiblical revelation that contradicts or violates the written
Word of God *ipso facto* must be rejected by faithful Christians.
The Bible remains the only final and authoritative litmus test for
divine revelation. The 66 books of the Bible constitute a closed
canon.

CAN WE LEARN FROM GOD'S WORKS?

So far we have seen that we receive valid knowledge about
God and about the invisible world from the written Word of

God and from hearing the voice of God as He communicates His thoughts directly to us as individuals, frequently confirming them to us through groups with which we maintain ongoing prayer fellowship. Can we also obtain accurate information about the supernatural by observing or experiencing God's *works?*

This is a question often raised by my critics. Some of them think it may be acceptable to relate an anecdote about something God has done to illustrate a teaching previously derived from Scripture, but we should not expect to learn anything new about the invisible world simply by observing God at work.

When I proposed my definition of theology at the beginning of this chapter as "a human attempt to explain God's Word and God's works in a reasonable and systematic way," I purposely implied that I *do* think God's works are important sources of valuable information. I like what Paul Hiebert says in his well-known essay "The Flaw of the Excluded Middle." He begins it by reminding us that when the disciples of John the Baptist began to doubt whether Jesus was really the Messiah, "Jesus answered, not with logical proofs, but by a demonstration of power in curing the sick and casting out evil spirits."[11] Jesus didn't perform a new set of miracles to convince John's disciples; He simply referred them to some He had already performed. To put it another way: Jesus pointed to anecdotes, perhaps better described as narratives.

Jesus was not the only one who used narrative proof to verify important truths; the Gospel writers used them as well. Much of the validity of Christianity, including the Resurrection itself, is predicated on narrative accounts. The fact that such narratives are verified by their inclusion in the written Word of God is an important observation, but it does not thereby nullify the validity of other works of God that have not been reported in the Bible.

Consider, for example, the conclusion of Jack Voelkel, a veteran missionary to Latin America. He discusses the question of whether or not Christians can be demonized. This is a substantial issue today, and good Christian leaders are lining up on both sides. Voelkel's position is that Christians indeed *can* be demonized. Where does he get this information? In a recent essay about spiritual warfare, Voelkel frankly admits that neither his position nor that of his opponents can be proven by any clear teaching from the Bible. He naturally, therefore, turns to sources outside the Bible. Jack Voelkel says, "Since space limits a full discussion of this complex issue, let me note simply that my personal experience and observation generally has been that those practicing a ministry of [deliverance] have no doubt that Christians can be 'demonized' and need to be delivered."[12]

Voelkel's epistemology would agree with that of Charles Kraft. Both would see validity in *experiential* knowledge and *observational* knowledge. Voelkel establishes a theological point, namely that Christians can be demonized, by what I would refer to in the definition of theology I proposed earlier as "explaining God's *works* [in this case] in a reasonable and systematic way." In the broad sense of the word, Jack Voelkel draws a theological conclusion from extrabiblical revelation, although his conclusion does not *contradict* biblical teaching.

VERIFYING NARRATIVES

It goes without saying that some narratives are true and some are false. Obviously we can learn valid things about the works of God only through the true ones. How, then, can we tell the difference?

Members of the well-publicized Jesus Seminar spend a lot of time amassing quasischolarly evidence in an attempt to prove that the narratives found in the New Testament are false. They see no reason to believe in the reality of Jesus' miracles or His resurrection because their worldview does not permit the intrusion of the supernatural into the material world. Those of us engaged in current discussions of strategic-level spiritual warfare, however, would agree that the fact that these narratives, or accounts of the works of God, are accepted as valid by the biblical writers, under the inspiration of the Holy Spirit, is evidence enough for us that they are true.

When Jesus cast out a certain demon, two opposite reactions came from those who saw Him. The common people were amazed and attracted to Jesus and His power. The Pharisees, on the other hand, because of their prior theological and social commitments, concluded that Jesus must have done it by the power of Beelzebub (see Matt. 12:22-24). Notice that the question here is not so much whether miracles happen, but how they are interpreted. For Jesus Seminar professors, the events at face value simply could not have happened; for the common people and the Pharisees, the key question was: What is the source of the miraculous power? The Scriptures teach that Satan can do honest-to-goodness miracles. In the book of Revelation we are told that he empowers the beast who "performs great signs" (13:13). Not all miracles are from God. When some told Jesus they had done "many wonders in Your name," Jesus replied, "I never knew you" (see Matt. 7:22,23).

Fortunately, we have many resources to determine whether a given narrative is a valid account of God's works from which we can learn something more about God or whether it is a counterfeit. Negatively, I should point out that relying on scientific proof for testing the validity of such accounts will usually turn out to be a dead-end street, not convincing many skeptics. By the strict laws of scientific proof, we cannot so much as prove that any prayer at all has ever been answered or that God is our Creator or that God *exists* to the satisfaction of "scientific" skeptics.

Credible Witnesses

How, then, do we do it? In the final analysis, we validate the authenticity of reported narratives on the basis of the credibility of those who observe them or experience them. For example, beginning in the early 1970s I suffered severe headaches for 10 consecutive years. It was so bad that at one point I had no relief from the pain at all for 70 days and 70 nights. No available pain killer could stop the headaches. Then in 1983, John Wimber received a *rhema* word from God that the root cause of my headaches had been a demon and that I was to drive it out myself rather than ask someone else to do it for me. I obeyed. I cast out the demon in the name of Jesus, and I have not suffered any such headaches since that day.

For the last several years I have traveled frequently to Argentina and Brazil. I have talked to many people who have had their teeth filled by the power of God, including some who have had old bridges removed and replaced and some who have seen new teeth grow into places where former teeth have been extracted. I have personally looked into enough mouths and cross-examined enough people who have experienced divine dental work to be completely convinced, beyond any doubt, that this miracle has happened and is happening with considerable frequency in those two nations.

Most mouths I have looked into in Brazil have had teeth miraculously filled—not with a white substance such as in Argentina, but with gold! Pastors such as Pablo Deiros, a Baptist Ph.D. whom we have recently added to our faculty at the Fuller Seminary School of World Mission, tell almost as a matter of routine that many in their congregations have had teeth filled. It is no more unusual to them than seeing God heal broken marriages or of sinners being born again.

A book published not too long ago, which made the best-seller list for many weeks, referred specifically to my reports of tooth fillings and declared that such reports are "preposterous." The same person might also have regarded the story of the demon causing my headache as equally "preposterous." What can I say?

The New Birth Is a Miracle

This critic, whom I know personally, believes in the omnipotence of God just as strongly as I do. He would never deny that God has the power to get rid of a headache demon or to fill teeth. Why then would he wish to discredit these reports as "preposterous"? For one thing, it is probably significant that he is still a cessationist and therefore finds himself uncomfortable with stories of contemporary miracles relating to the sign gifts.

Curiously, however, this critic strongly believes in equally dramatic miracles associated with the gift of evangelist. If a hypothetical new convert in his church would stand up in public and report, "I used to get drunk and be unfaithful to my wife, but six months ago I accepted Jesus Christ as my Lord and Savior and since then I have been sober and God has reestablished my marriage," this critic would certainly say, "Praise the Lord for His wonderful power!"

Let's look at this. Is this new convert more honest than Peter Wagner? Is he more spiritual? Is he better educated and does he have more degrees in theology? Is he holier? Does he have more spiritual discernment? Does he have a longer track record of walking with the Lord? Knowing this particular critic, I am reasonably sure he would answer no to each of these hypothetical questions.

If so, why am I seen as "preposterous," but the new convert regarded as a credible witness?

One explanation might be that my critic has never, to my knowledge, personally experienced or observed a healing miracle. He is regarded as one of the best Bible students in America, but his study of the Bible has apparently not provided him the theological equipment to assimilate the kind of narratives Peter Wagner and many others are reporting. They just don't fit into his theology.

Believing Is Seeing
In a chapter called "The Myth of Pure Biblical Objectivity," Jack Deere wrestles with attitudes characteristic of such critics and concludes: "Christians do not disbelieve in the miraculous gifts of the Spirit because the Scriptures teach these gifts have passed away. Rather they disbelieve in the miraculous gifts of the Spirit because they have not experienced them."[13]

To put it another way, seeing is not always believing. Frequently the opposite is the case: *believing is seeing.* In other words, accurately learning from or interpreting or explaining certain works of God, whether physical healing or the new birth, is only possible for those who first believe such things are indeed possible and not preposterous. In the final analysis, it is a matter of faith.

THE FALL OF THE GODDESS OF MERCY

On a trip in 1993 to the island of Penang, Malaysia, I observed something I might have considered "preposterous" if the people who told me the story were not respected, credible witnesses—indeed, if I had not seen it myself. I might not have taken it seriously had I not by then developed a theological framework through which to understand it.

The Kek Lok Si Temple in Penang is the largest Chinese temple in Malaysia. It has been there for hundreds of years. In 1986 the temple authorities, dedicated to serving the Chinese Goddess of Mercy, agreed to attempt to increase her control of the island by erecting a gigantic statue, 100 feet high, on a mountain above the temple. This, for those who have eyes to see, constituted an aggressive act of spiritual warfare.

Some members of our Spiritual Warfare Network in Penang did have eyes to see. In a prayer meeting in their church, they were directed to target their warfare prayers into the center of the island where the temple and the statue were located. Receiving a *rhema* word from God, the Holy Spirit told them to pray Isaiah 47, substituting the Goddess of Mercy for the biblical "virgin daughter of Babylon" named in verse 1. As the power of the Spirit came upon them, they fervently prayed that:

- She would "sit on the ground without a throne" (v. 1).
- She would "take off the skirt and uncover the thigh" (v. 2).
- She would "no longer be called the Lady of the King-doms" (v. 5). At this point they also prayed that tourists would stop visiting the site.
- "Evil would come upon her and she should not know from where it arises" (see v. 11).
- "No one should save her" (see v. 15).

Humanly speaking, the chances that these prayers could be answered literally would be far less even than the chances of winning the Malaysian lottery!

Amazingly enough, within a week, the newspapers reported that a mysterious crack had appeared on the cement skirt of the idol! Despite frantic efforts to repair it, the crack kept increasing day after day, and within a month the entire skirt—tons of concrete—fell to the ground, exposing only the ugly column of reinforced concrete that formed the structural core of the statue.

Subsequent efforts by the temple authorities to repair and rebuild the statue have come to naught. Later in 1993, the statue actually caught fire, and now is an ugly, charred eyesore. The only tourists who have made their way there in years are

Christians eager to see with their own eyes the tangible results of warfare prayer against the attempted glorification of one of the chief demonic principalities over Malaysia.

The fall of this Goddess of Mercy was a work of God. Good theology will attempt to explain it in a reasonable and systematic way. Some current evangelical theologies, however, lack categories or vocabulary to deal with such phenomena. One solution many therefore use is to classify such a narrative as "preposterous," and to move from there to more comfortable theological territory.

CRITERIA FOR VERIFICATION

How can we tell the true from the spurious? I know of no fail-safe methodology. Indeed, I for one have been guilty of drawing some mistaken conclusions on more than one occasion, but I always try to be as accurate and as responsible as I can. I have developed a checklist of seven items that, to a considerable degree, can be used to maintain integrity in reporting the works of God through narratives and case studies.

1. It neither contradicts Scripture, nor would it violate any general biblical principles.
2. It brings glory to the triune God—Father, Son and Holy Spirit.
3. It conforms to the known will of God.
4. It blesses the people who have been touched by the event.
5. It measurably advances God's kingdom here on earth.
6. It is affirmed by at least two or three credible witnesses.
7. The conclusion merits agreement by responsible and like-minded colleagues.

WHAT CAN WE LEARN FROM THE WORLD OF DARKNESS?

We can learn valuable information from the totally reliable written Word of God, from the spoken or *rhema* word of God and from accurately analyzing and interpreting the works of God. As we move down this list of other possible sources of valid knowledge, the number of objections and criticisms increases, but the largest number of objections by far is attached to this final section—the possibility of learning from the world of darkness.

A frequent criticism suggests that I tend to work from an *animistic* worldview rather than from a *Christian* worldview. Related to that has been the accusation that I allow myself to buy too deeply into the dualism of my Indo-European ethno-linguistic heritage and that I am in danger of naively accepting the Indo-European mythology of eternal conflict between good and evil.

Briefly responding to the latter accusation, I must say that as a Christian I could never subscribe either explicitly or implicitly to a philosophical dualism, because I believe in "God the Father almighty, Maker of heaven and earth," as the Apostles' Creed states. This means that the devil himself as well as every principality and power and demonic being inhabiting the invisible world of darkness are creatures brought into being and subject to the almighty God and Father of the Lord Jesus Christ who "must reign till He has put all enemies under His feet" (1 Cor. 15:25). For biblical Christians, there is no such thing as an eternal conflict—only God is eternal.

Having said this, I have no problem in affirming a *limited* dualism, because Satan and his forces of evil are not yet all under Jesus' feet as they will be sometime in the future. Our sovereign God has, for His own reasons, permitted dark angels to exercise their power to steal, kill and destroy. He has likewise provided for us the weapons of warfare needed to serve

Him as "a good soldier of Jesus Christ" (2 Tim 2:3). The conflict between good and evil is not merely a figment of our imaginations, or a reversion to ancient mythology, but it accurately describes the spiritual reality in which we live and minister in the world of today.

The "Animistic Paradigm"

What about the "animistic paradigm"? When I read that Peter Wagner is suspected of subscribing to an animistic paradigm, I am not sure we agree on the fundamental definition of "animism." William A. Smalley, a highly respected missionary anthropologist, offers this definition: "Animism is the belief in personalized supernatural power. As such it contrasts with impersonal power (*mana* and related phenomena). Its manifestations range from one God as the only spirit being, through orthodox forms of the great monotheistic religions (including angels, demons, souls of the dead, and other forms of spirits), to innumerable ghosts, ancestor spirits, spirits in natural objects, and other phenomena characteristic of many 'primitive' religions."[14]

I must confess that I do believe, quite firmly, in personalized supernatural power with respect to God, angels and demons because the Bible affirms their existence. If I did not believe in personalized supernatural power, I could not simultaneously affirm that I accept the Bible as my ultimate authority. The Bible teaches clearly that the only true God is a person (in fact, three persons), and so are Satan, demons and angels.

I also understand that "animism" is often used today in a narrower sense than we find in Smalley's definition. Leafing through Patrick Johnstone's *Operation World*, for example, one will find that in many nations a percentage of *Christians* is given as opposed to a percentage of *animists*. In Smalley's terms I would gladly receive the label "animist" for myself, but in Johnstone's terms I would reject it. I think my critics are warning me against becoming a Johnstone kind of animist—a person whose *allegiance* is not to Jesus Christ alone, but to other supernatural forces.

How Can We Discern What Is True?

It seems to me that in contemporary non-Christian animism we find a mixture of truth, spiritual deception and many stages in between. I think it would be wise not to reject all forms of animism or all Indo-European mythology on an assumption that anything those systems or similar non-Christian systems affirm have absolutely *no validity*.

For example, many cultures have explicit creation myths. Almost all of them describe an original world confined to a disk of land mass in which a paradise has been made to function. This knowledge, having varying degrees of distortion, is common to almost all of humanity. In this case the general validity of creation myths is confirmed, as far as Christians are concerned, by the biblical revelation of the Garden of Eden.

Humanity as a whole tends to recognize God's creation and its subsequent history. Some details of this, but not all of them, have been revealed to us in Scripture. When they are so revealed, any deviation from the biblical record in any given cultural tradition is to be regarded by faithful Christians as inaccurate. As I have said, our final authority must remain the Word of God.

When Scripture itself does *not* provide us with divinely revealed glimpses of reality, the validity of any extrabiblical claim to reality must obviously be confirmed or rejected on the basis of criteria other than biblical exegesis. It would be a mistake to assume that *all* oral history transmitted through various cultural streams is *per se* invalid. Rather, it seems more reasonable to assume that each tradition might reflect *some* true aspects of reality, but have varying degrees of distortion.

Our criteria for evaluating this material should not be limited to the five senses or to what we have come to regard as scientific laws, although these are indispensable. Undoubtedly some parts of reality are primarily *spiritually* discerned, and therefore do not lend themselves to *scientific* analysis.

As an example, let's consider the new birth. I am aware of no scientific methodology that could verify that a given person has ever been regenerated by the supernatural power of the Holy Spirit and has become a new creature in Christ. We Christians believe that it really happens, but our knowledge of this comes only through faith and spiritual discernment. It is true that the fruit of regeneration can be cited as evidence of the new birth, but comparable changes in human behavior can also be explained by certain physical and psychological causes. Attitudinal and behavioral modifications do not *in themselves* constitute sufficient scientific proof that a personal supernatural being called the Holy Spirit has or has not done anything in a given case. In the final analysis, no *scientific* evidence can be cited that proves any reality that the Holy Spirit exists.

It is important also to recognize that spiritual insight, which receives information directly from the spirit world, is not an exclusive faculty of those who have been born again. Spiritual discernment certainly constitutes at least some dimension of the image of God in which all human beings, Christian or non-Christian, have been created. If this is correct, then human beings, whether Indo-Europeans, Melanesians, Amerindians or whatever they may be, can and often do possess valid information about the spirit world. At the same time, some of the information they possess is clearly distorted and invalid. Often, I suppose, this information is derived from misinformation intentionally introduced by the forces of darkness to keep a given people group in spiritual captivity.

TESTING ALL THINGS

Our task, therefore, is to "Test all things; hold fast what is good" (1 Thess. 5:21). How do we do that? We rely on the enlightenment the sovereign God chooses to give us as believers. For example:

- We have the Holy Spirit—the third Person of the Trinity—in us, and we can and should live lives filled with the Holy Spirit.
- We are invited to enter into daily intimacy with the Father in prayer, speaking to Him and hearing His voice. God has been known to communicate with humans in an audible voice, through inner impressions, in visions, in dreams, through prophets and by personal appearances.
- We are not to operate as lone individuals, but as members of the Body of Christ. When we deal with truths about the spirit world, we look for the agreement of others and we welcome accountability to them for testing the validity of our conclusions.
- Some have been given the spiritual gift of discernment of spirits (see 1 Cor. 12:10). This means God has given them an extraordinary ability to help us discern what is valid from what is invalid. They have what could be likened to a spiritual Geiger counter that has a special capacity, through the Holy Spirit, to detect demonic presence, often revealing surprisingly detailed and accurate knowledge of its identity and intentions.
- In dealing with knowledge of the invisible world, all of us need great humility, frankly recognizing that we may not be full *enough* of the Holy Spirit, that we may not be intimate *enough* with the Father or that we may not be open *enough* to receive input from our

peers on any given occasion. This means at times we may not be as accurate as we could wish in discerning which knowledge of the invisible world is valid and which knowledge is to be rejected. We rarely err by admitting this and by always being tentative in our conclusions.

From this perspective, and considering these disclaimers, it becomes evident that some non-Christians, whether animist shamans, gurus, lamas, philosophers or whatever, may be able to communicate to us some information about the reality of the spirit world in which they have gained considerable expertise. These non-Christian sources, of course, must be evaluated with much prayerful scrutiny and caution. Still, we must keep in mind that the spirit world to which they are dedicated is a real world, not the figment of their "heathen" imaginations. Therefore, some things about it can be accurately known. A particularly important source of credible information may be those occult practitioners who have been born again and filled with the Holy Spirit. Not everything former occultists say may be true, but with biblical discernment certain insights can be gained.

Some have raised the question of whether we can receive valid information from demons themselves. Demons are portrayed in the Bible as beings who have personalities and intelligence, and as beings who can and do speak. They are also portrayed as deceivers. It must therefore be concluded that they do possess some valid information. The question then becomes: Does any of this valid information get communicated to us when they speak? Obviously so, but discernment is needed to process whatever we hear from them in order to separate truth from falsehood. I once heard Ed Murphy point out this very interesting fact: *Every time the words of a demon are recorded in the New Testament, they speak the truth!* Is this not biblical evidence that we can indeed get valid information from the world of darkness?

THE ISSUE OF ALLEGIANCE

The larger question is not whether the operative modality of the spirit world is a part of total reality, but what we, as servants of the most high God, choose to *do* with this information. Committed animists have chosen to submit themselves to the power and authority of demonic spirits. They have chosen to give their allegiance to the *creature* rather than to the *Creator.* Christians, on the other hand, have decided to renounce all allegiance to the hosts of wickedness and to give their full allegiance to the Son of God. Make no mistake about it: This is a difference of great magnitude.

If understanding the reality of this invisible world, in whatever amount of detail, is regarded by some as following an "animistic paradigm," informed Christians will share it. The demons themselves "believe—and tremble" (Jas. 2:19). If, however, an "animistic paradigm" implies *allegiance* to forces of darkness or *worship* of the creature rather than the Creator, informed Christians should strenuously reject it.

SUMMARY

How do we know what we know?

The primary source of knowledge about God and the spiritual realm is the Bible—the written Word of God. This, however, is not our exclusive source. When we have proper safeguards and are under the anointing of the Holy Spirit, we can also receive valuable information from the *rhema*—or spoken Word of God—from careful observation and analysis of the works of God in the world, and from representatives of the world of darkness whether in human or spiritual form, although they must always be approached and evaluated as hostile witnesses. As we know, hostile witnesses do not have a reputation for reliability.

■ REFLECTION QUESTIONS ■

1. Have you ever thought of whether theology usually emerges from ministry or whether ministry usually comes from theology? Discuss your opinions.
2. Do you think that intellectual knowledge, observational knowledge and experiential knowledge are equally valid? Which is most important in your daily life?
3. Is it possible for us to hear God's voice? Has God ever communicated directly with you? What was it like? How did you know it was God?
4. Can we learn anything from observing God's works, even when He seems to do something that is not directly mentioned in the Bible? How can we tell that it is really God?
5. Some think that occult practitioners or even demons can provide us valid information about the spirit world. Others would regard their information as falsehood or deception. What do you think?

Notes
1. Ted Haggard, *Primary Purpose* (Orlando, Fla.: Creation House, 1995), p. 58.
2. Ray Anderson, *Theological Foundations for Ministry* (Grand Rapids: William B. Eerdmans Publishing Co., 1979), p. 7.

3. Wesley is cited in *And Are We Yet Alive?* by Richard B. Wilke (Nashville: Abingdon Press, 1986), p. 58.
4. Charles H. Kraft, *Christianity With Power* (Ann Arbor: Vine Books, 1989), pp. 87-88. Also see Charles H. Kraft and Marguerite G. Kraft, "Communicating and Ministering the Power of the Gospel Cross-culturally," *The Kingdom and the Power,* ed. Gary S. Greig and Kevin N. Springer (Ventura, Calif.: Regal Books, 1993, pp. 345-356.
5. Ibid., p. 94.
6. Ibid., pp. 95-96.
7. Ramsay MacMullen, *Christianizing the Roman Empire (A.D. 100-400)* (New Haven, Conn.: Yale University Press, 1984), p. 62.
8. Jack Deere, *Surprised by the Power of the Spirit* (Grand Rapids: Zondervan Publishing House, 1993), p. 23.
9. Ibid., p. 212.
10. Ibid., p. 214.
11. Paul G. Hiebert, "The Flaw of the Excluded Middle," *Anthropological Reflections on Missiological Issues* (Grand Rapids: Baker Books, 1994), p. 189.
12. Jack Voelkel, "Spiritual Warfare: Just What Is It and What Does the Bible Say?" *Church Planter's LINK* (Fourth Quarter 1994 & First Quarter 1995): 34.
13. Deere, *Surprised by the Power of the Spirit,* p. 55.
14. William A. Smalley, "Animism," *Concise Dictionary of the Christian World Mission,* ed. Stephen Neill, Gerald H. Anderson, and John Goodwin (Nashville: Abingdon Press, 1971), p. 24.

Back to the Bible: Consistency in Hermeneutics

NE OF MY FRIENDS WHO DISAGREES WITH ME, ALTHOUGH not in a critical spirit, believes in the pervasive influence of principalities and powers over human societies of all kinds, but he does not believe the powers are personal supernatural beings such as literal demons. He believes they are superhuman powers that have been generated by deeply rooted social sins such as oppression, greed, lust for control, war, racism and other forms of collective evil. Once they are generated, they then go beyond the possibility of human control, and only the intervention of God, released primarily through faithful intercession, can overcome their power to perpetuate human misery.

CAN WE LEARN FROM PERETTI?

My friend, somewhat playfully, hints that my viewpoint

may have been derived from novelist Frank Peretti, whose best-selling books *This Present Darkness* and *Piercing the Darkness* describe in much detail how he imagines demons and angels go flapping around, slicing off each others' wings with swords.

It should go without saying that neither one of us, in more sober moments, would want to draw important conclusions from the fantasies of a novelist. I have said many times, however, that I am grateful for Frank Peretti who, through his fiction, raised many important questions in the minds of Christians across the theological spectrum in the 1980s. I believe that God providentially used him to prepare the way for the insights about strategic-level spiritual warfare that are now coming from such nonfiction authors as John Dawson, Cindy Jacobs, Francis Frangipane, Dick Eastman, Charles Kraft, George Otis Jr., Ed Silvoso and many others who have been writing in the 1990s.

On at least one essential matter, I think Peretti is correct. Peretti and I would agree that demons and angels are personalities. My friend sees them as the corporate personality or the driving spirit of social institutions, not as something literally existing above and outside of society.

I am not raising this issue here in an attempt to prove my friend wrong. I simply want to point out that we come to different conclusions about the nature of the powers largely because we differ in our opinions about the inspiration and authority of the Scriptures. My friend would not be as comfortable as I in subscribing to the Lausanne Covenant, which affirms that the Scriptures are "without error in all they affirm," nor would he accept the label of "biblical inerrantist" for himself.

As I said in the last chapter, I accept the Bible as the written Word of God, and the final authority for testing the validity of any of our conclusions relating to Christian faith and practice in general and relating to the realities of the invisible world more specifically. It is because I embrace a high view of Scripture that I come to the conclusion that spirit beings have personalities and names, that they think and talk, that they have wills and that they act upon decisions they make. They are created by God, but they are not created in the image of God as human beings are. All this is clearly stated in both the Old Testament and the New Testament.

Fortunately, the critics I am primarily dealing with in this book would, by and large, agree with Frank Peretti and me that demonic beings are indeed personalities and not simply socially generated forces, as my other friend would argue. We also see eye to eye about the inspiration and authority of the Bible. Why, then, would we still disagree?

INTERPRETING THE BIBLE

Our disagreement is based on the way we choose to *interpret* the Bible. We find ourselves taking differing positions on what theologians call "biblical hermeneutics." We also have some divergent viewpoints about how we receive information and form conclusions about issues that may be only *implicitly* rather than *explicitly* taught in the Bible. I'll try to make this clear as we move along.

Many of my critics say they hope I become more "balanced" in the things I teach, meaning they want me to agree more with them. The fact of the matter is that, in religious discussion, we most often suppose we are the ones who occupy the middle ground, and our task is to avoid what we see as extremes on the left and extremes on the right. I think the most frequently used quote regarding balance in our views of the demonic comes from C. S. Lewis, who said: "There are two equal and opposite errors into which our race can fall about the devils. One is to disbelieve in their existence. The other is to believe, and to feel an excessive and unhealthy interest in them."[1]

It is easy to agree with C. S. Lewis. Virtually all my critics and I do. Few of us, however, are prepared to admit that we, in contrast to our opponents, fall into either of the errors. For example, I think many of my critics are terribly naive in their underestimation of the power demonic spirits have and use. They, on the other hand, think my views are excessive and unhealthy as well as dangerous.

During the past 20 years or so, a lot of discussion has revolved around questions of worldview. Because all of us tend to consider our particular culture and our particular worldview as "normal," it follows that those who deviate from our viewpoint to one degree or another would be considered "abnormal." It would help if we realized that a considerable amount of our reluctance to accept the reality of the invisible world can be traced to the so-called Enlightenment of the eighteenth century.

INFLUENCED BY THE ENLIGHTENMENT

The best contemporary account of how the Enlightenment has influenced the worldview of most of us Westerners, particularly in our attitude toward the supernatural, can be found in Charles Kraft's book *Christianity with Power*. Thinkers such as Kant, Newton and Voltaire created the intellectual environment for the birth and development of modern science, for which we are grateful. The trade-off was a rejection of supernaturalism in place of rationalism. If our human reasoning or our five senses cannot verify a certain reality, it cannot be considered reality, according to the way many people in our culture think. This, of course, applies directly to the invisible world. Kraft says, "Because such Enlightenment influence has become so strong in our societies, modern Westerners—both non-Christian and Christian—now find it extremely difficult to believe in angels, Satan, demons, and even God."[2]

Does our worldview influence our hermeneutics or how we interpret the Bible? Of course it does. Our worldview implants in each of us a certain mental grid through which we process *all* information that comes our way. A story has been told that two or three hundred years ago the Dutch ambassador to Siam was having dinner with the King of Siam. The king, whose worldview had been formed while living exclusively in the tropics, loved the ambassador's stories about life in Europe until he claimed that in the winter, water in a lake would get so hard that elephants could walk on it. The king concluded that such a thing was preposterous and that the ambassador must be a liar!

We chuckle at this story, but if we're honest, we admit we are as limited by our worldviews as the King of Siam, although using different applications. Although we wish it were not true, our understanding of Scripture is also limited to one degree or another by our worldview. Charles Kraft says, "Even though there is often a wide discrepancy between the teachings of Scripture and [our] common Western assumptions...we often find ourselves more Western than scriptural."[3]

At this point, I want to be as fair as I can to my critics. Since the publication of Charles Kraft's book, most evangelical leaders, particularly missiologists, have been making every effort to disassociate themselves from the Enlightenment worldview. It has become almost a personal insult to infer that someone's interpretation of the Bible is influenced by the Enlightenment. Although we recognize this, Charles Kraft and I both conclude that many of the differences in the way we interpret the Scriptures, in contrast to the way our critics interpret the same Scriptures, are that we have been able to distance ourselves further from the Enlightenment worldview than they have. We also see this as one of the reasons we receive much less criticism of strategic-level spiritual warfare from our Third World Christian colleagues than we do from our Western colleagues. The Enlightenment had little influence, for example, in the Himalayas or in the Amazon basin.

THE APOSTLES' BIBLE: THE OLD TESTAMENT

The only Bible that Peter, Paul and James, to say nothing of Jesus, had was the Old Testament. In considering the biblical teaching about strategic-level spiritual warfare, we must not only take into account the teachings of the Old Testament, but we must also recognize that the ministry of the apostles in the New Testament era *assumed* that the teaching of the Old Testament was normative. I stress *assumed,* to bring to mind that many of the things that were taught and practiced by the apostles would not have been mentioned either in the accounts of

> Just because the virgin birth is not mentioned in any of the Epistles, should not lead us to conclude that the apostles did not believe in it or that they would not have their converts believe in the virgin birth of Christ. Not all important events are found in the Epistles.

their ministry in the Gospels and Acts or in the Epistles they later wrote because the authors took them for granted.

At least one person I have read recently says that because he does not find the apostles recommending casting out demons to the churches to which they wrote Epistles, he therefore would not recommend it today. This is curious because neither do we find them telling the churches to conduct prayer meetings for the salvation of the lost or to be sure that they witness to their neighbors about Jesus. Just because the virgin birth is not mentioned in any of the Epistles, to use another example, should not lead us to conclude that the apostles did not believe in it or that they would not have their converts believe in the virgin birth of Christ. Not all important events are found in the Epistles.

For example, a growing number of us believe that identificational repentance is an extremely vital ingredient in effective strategic-level spiritual warfare. When we look for the biblical justification for this, however, we find relatively little about it in the New Testament. We may find bits and pieces here and there, such as the analogy of Jesus' substitutionary atonement, Peter accusing Jews who were not on site at the time of crucifying Jesus (see Acts 2:36) or some hints in Stephen's speech in Acts 7. Some stress the first person plural of the Lord's Prayer and argue that "forgive us *our* sins" could refer to corporate sins. Still, the fact remains that the New Testament contains no outright or explicit teaching about identificational repentance.

The Old Testament, however, contains abundant amounts of material about the principles and practice of identificational repentance. Important books about the subject, such as John Dawson's *Healing America's Wounds* (Regal Books) and Cindy Jacobs's *Possessing the Gates of the Enemy* (Chosen Books), will confirm this. My purpose here is not to argue the merits of identificational repentance, but rather to point out that the apostles, as biblical believers, must have been thoroughly familiar with David remitting the sins of Saul against the Gibeonites (see 2 Sam. 21), Nehemiah confessing the sins of his fathers (see Neh. 1:6) or that the iniquities caused by the sin of one generation can pass on through subsequent generations (see Exod. 20:5).

The fact that the apostles did not reiterate this teaching in the Epistles is an important, but, in my opinion, not a *crucial* observation. I would say the same thing to the noninstrumental Churches of Christ that refuse to use musical instruments in their services because the apostles gave no teaching in the New Testament that Christians should do so. If we assume, which we should, that the apostles were following their Bible—the Old Testament—we could well conclude that musical instruments would have been freely used in worship in the early churches.

None of this is to deny that Jesus came with a new covenant. Certain Old Testament practices, such as the sacrifice of animals for the atonement of sins, we no longer do. This, however, was explicitly *changed* by the New Testament, which puts it into a different category from those things simply not mentioned.

I should also point out that times changed conclusively with the coming of Jesus Christ, the Messiah, and that New Testament days *since* Jesus' coming are dramatically different from Old Testament days *before* Jesus came. This is particularly true concerning our relationship with the invisible world, because along with Jesus came the invasion of the kingdom of God into territory over which Satan previously had a virtually exclusive franchise. For example, we see little in the Old Testament relating to power given to God's people to cast out demons, but there is substantial material about spiritual warfare in the New Testament. I will provide more details about this in chapter 5.

Open to New Things

The apostles apparently did not adhere so closely to their Bible that they refused to be open to the new things God desired to do through them. On the Day of Pentecost, Peter interpreted the events that took place as fulfilling what Joel had prophesied (see Acts 2:16-21). Checking through Joel 2, however, we find nothing that could indirectly be understood as speaking in tongues. On the grounds of not finding it in Joel or the other prophets or any place else in their Bibles, the apostles did not reject the new phenomenon of tongues. People later flocked to

Peter who was healing people by merely casting his shadow on them (see 5:15). Nothing in the Old Testament is a precedent. Paul did not find casting out demons with handkerchiefs in the Bible he carried, yet he did it by the power of the Holy Spirit (see 19:12). Although all this is true, the apostles would not have accepted anything that would have *violated* Old Testament principles, except what Jesus had specifically changed as a part of the new covenant.

The apostles would not have accepted anything that would have violated Old Testament principles, except what Jesus had specifically changed as a part of the new covenant.

In summary, we do not find the apostles saying, as some of my critics do, "We will not do so-and-so because we do not find it in the Bible." Along those lines, I recently read an entertaining quote from Billy Graham. I would presume he did not mean it to be taken literally, but in response to a question from reporters about his possible retirement, Billy Graham was said to reply, "I do not find any place in the Bible where anybody retires."[4] If he had meant it literally or offered it as a doctrinal principle, he would have been in deep trouble with the AARP, to say nothing of his many Christian friends who have retired long ago! As I read it, I mentally put my tongue in my cheek and wondered if anyone had reminded Mr. Graham recently that he would have an equally difficult time finding where the Bible mentions citywide crusade evangelism or preaching in stadiums.

The Apostles' Example Principle of Hermeneutics

Although other questions have surfaced as well, the major part of the criticism of strategic-level spiritual warfare that has come in during the last few years has revolved around issues of hermeneutics, and much of it is based on the same line of reasoning. To make this section as accurate as possible, I will not paraphrase the criticisms, but rather quote them verbatim under the names "Critic A" and "Critic B." I will not mention their names, but I will say that they are both personal friends of mine and that, although we may disagree on this point, we have the highest mutual respect for each other. Both are outstanding, well-respected Christian leaders.

Here is what each has written to me personally as we have had dialogues about the validity of strategic-level spiritual warfare:

- **Critic A:** "There is no model in Scripture of anyone doing what you are encouraging people to do. How can strategic-level spiritual warfare be God's clearly biblical method when the apostles themselves are not seen exercising that prerogative?"
- **Critic B:** "I have to confess that I remain unconvinced of the fundamental concept of *strategic-level* spiritual warfare. I say this because I find no warrant for the strategy of discerning, naming and praying against demonic spirits over cities and nations either in Scripture or illustrated in the history of the Christian Church. On the other hand, there is much teaching, both in Scripture and in church history, about *personal-level* spiritual warfare."

I could cite several others who use essentially the same argument for rejecting strategic-level spiritual warfare. Let's call it, for convenience, the "apostles' example principle of hermeneutics." If it is a correct hermeneutical principle that we reject any form of Christian ministry if we do not find precedent in the teachings of Jesus or in the lives and writings of the apostles, we then must also reject many other forms of Christian behavior, not only strategic-level spiritual warfare.

In my opinion, the "apostles' example principle" is not a valid hermeneutical principle, and I will give my reasons for saying that in the following paragraphs.

Before I do, however, let me say that more New Testament evidence for strategic-level spiritual warfare exists than Critics A and B would think. The second part of this book will offer some of that evidence, but meanwhile, before we get to the biblical material itself, we need to examine our hermeneutical principles.

LET'S BE CONSISTENT

It is good if we do find the apostles giving us clear examples of certain forms of ministry. When they don't, however, we should not reject them unrestrained. If the "apostles' example principle" is a true principle, it should then be applied rigorously across the board. By this I do not mean there could *never* be an exception to the rule, but I do mean there should not be *frequent* exceptions to the rule.

A principle of Christian ministry is especially weak if it lends itself to selective application. If its proponents choose to apply it to one set of circumstances, but then choose *not to apply it* to another parallel set of circumstances, the validity of the principle itself is in question.

I will examine a list of common Christian teachings and practices that enjoy a rather wide consensus among Christian leaders today, although in each one I will mention some who disagree. Practically all of the critics of strategic-level spiritual warfare with whom I am in dialogue will embrace practically all of the items on this list, both teaching them and practicing them. Strangely enough, none of them could pass the test of the "apostles' example principle" of hermeneutics. Could it be that those who *make* the rules do not always *play* by their rules?

• *Using the label "Trinity" to refer to God.* Behind this is the doctrinal teaching that God is "three persons in one essence." I myself have taught this throughout more than 40 years of ordained ministry, and I continue to teach it, but not because I have found it stated explicitly by any of the apostles. Later I will mention some of the guidelines that make me comfortable teaching such things as God is a Trinity. Meanwhile, I highly respect my friends in the United Pentecostal Church, for example, who take a so-called "modalistic" view, believing that God has only *one* personality and that He sometimes chooses to operate as Father, sometimes as Son and sometimes as Holy Spirit—three different "modes."

• *Freeing the slaves.* Slavery was a deeply established social institution in the time of the apostles. Slaves are mentioned from time to time in the writings of the apostles, but no *explicit* teaching suggests that the institution of slavery itself should be done away with or that slaves should be freed by their masters. I personally agree with the ethical principle that slavery is an evil institution and should not be tolerated by Christians, but my conviction comes from sources other than the example of the apostles.

• *A canon of 66 books.* If you ask me, the Bible contains 66 books, no more and no less. I disagree with the Roman Catholics who contend that we should include the apocryphal books in our canon of Scripture. This, to me, is a crucial item for Christian life and witness. Do I get it from the apostles? No comment needed.

• *Sunday as the primary day of worship.* Ask Messianic Jews or Seventh-day Adventists if you think the case for Sunday worship is open-and-closed. They will remind you that there is no evidence that such was the custom of the apostles, all of whom were practicing Jews. Most of us still worship on Sundays, but we have other reasons for doing so than our "apostles' example principle."

I will not prolong the list, although it could go on almost indefinitely by mentioning less significant practices such as celebrating Christmas or Easter, establishing Sunday Schools, erecting church buildings, organizing denominations, addressing the Holy Spirit in prayer or any number of other common practices not advocated by Jesus or the apostles.

I do want to add one more item, however, that is directly relevant to spiritual warfare, and that I happen to know is believed and practiced by both Critics A and B.

• *Christians can be demonized.* I agree with Critics A and B and many others that Christians not only can be, but also frequently are, demonized. We have formidable opponents about this issue—among them, for example, the Assemblies of God denomination, no less. Some years ago they issued a position statement: "Can Born-Again Believers Be Demon-Possessed?" In this statement they advised their pastors against casting demons out of Christians. More recently 10 of their leading scholars produced a book titled *Power Encounter: A Pentecostal Perspective.* One of these scholars, Morris Williams, says, "We do not believe for a moment that a believer can be demonized."[5]

Although there is considerable discussion about nuances of terms such as "possessed," "afflicted," "invaded" or "oppressed," the bottom line is that the ministry of casting demons out of Christians is not recommended. In summary, two arguments stand out to support their position:

1. We have no model in Scripture of the apostles casting demons out of Christians.
2. None of the apostles taught the believers in their churches to cast demons out of each other. "For this reason," Morris Williams says, "it is unscriptural to lay hands on believers to cast out demons."[6]

The question we now face is: Where do I, along with Critics A and B, get the information that Christians can indeed be demonized and that we should cast demons out of Christians when they are present? Our answers will be similar to the answer Jack Voelkel gave to the same question in the last chapter:

- Our personal ministry experience has led us to believe that Christians can be invaded by demons.
- We have arrived at a consensus that this is true from many others who have ministered in the area of deliverance.
- We have seen many positive, even dramatic, results in the lives of those Christians who have been delivered from demons. I could start with my own headache demon I described in the last chapter.
- None of the previous three *contradicts* any explicit biblical teaching.

BIBLICAL "CONCEPTS" VERSUS BIBLICAL "PROOF"

If we don't have specific examples from the apostles, or explicit teaching about the things we have listed, we can agree that advocating and doing these things is "biblical," but in a somewhat broader sense of the term. Although we might not have biblical *proof* for doing them, we can cite enough biblical *concepts* to make us comfortable. For example:

- The Bible does not *prohibit* activities such as celebrating Christmas as it does prohibit, for example, homosexuality.
- A systematic collation of biblical data will provide for us the *concepts* we need to formulate a doctrine such as that of the Trinity. It took the Early Church a couple of hundred years of debate to formulate the orthodox doctrine of the Trinity.
- God is glorified by the results of some things we do as Christians, such as freeing slaves. On the other hand, we might not celebrate Halloween because it does not glorify God.

Although such is not the case, as I will show later, even if we had little by way of the apostles' examples for strategic-level spiritual warfare, we could still believe in it and do it on the basis of these principles. I would not want to claim biblical "proof" for my position, but I am convinced I can find an abundance of biblical "concepts" that will lead us to believe strategic-level spiritual warfare is valid.

EVALUATING OUR CONCLUSIONS

Suppose I do not have airtight proof that strategic-level spiritual warfare should be practiced in confronting the powers? How then do I evaluate what evidence I do have? How much evidence do I need to establish a hypothesis strong enough to justify ministry in that area?

When Robert Raikes advocated the Sunday School movement more than 100 years ago, he encountered strong opposition. The major criticism he heard was, "This is not biblical."

Today we would rarely, if at all, hear that objection. Why? In this case, evidence of the value of the Sunday School and the blessings God has poured through it have accumulated enough through the years to reduce the objections to zero.

Such is not the case with all things. Take baptism as an example. Almost all Christians would agree that our views about baptism are important. Some would also argue that our salvation depends on these views. Others would have varying degrees of conviction. If we took a random sampling of Christian leaders to discuss baptism, we would find widely differing viewpoints, such as:

- Quakers and Salvation Army officers would argue that biblical baptism is a *spiritual baptism* and that water is not necessary.
- Presbyterians would expound *covenant theology* and argue that parents should baptize their infants because they are included in God's covenant.
- Lutherans and Episcopalians would stress *sacramental grace* and argue that through baptism we can be born again.
- Baptists would say that each person's decision to follow Christ is the turning point, and that only those old enough to *believe in Christ* should be baptized.

ABOUT WHAT ISSUES SHOULD WE ARGUE?

The reason I raise these issues, which most of us have known for some time, is to point out that among committed Christians today, baptism does not seem to be an issue about which we desire to argue. People were willing to give their lives for these issues in generations past, but such is not the case today. We rarely find books or papers written attempting to refute what others believe about baptism or say with any degree of hostility that those who disagree with us are "not biblical."

That is not to say we lack convictions about baptism. My personal conclusion is that it is dangerous to baptize infants because it can lead to false conclusions that the application of water and the use of certain words saves souls, which in turn can reduce the urgency for adult decisions to accept Christ as Lord and Savior. But I also join the majority of Christian leaders I know in agreeing that differing positions about baptism should not be regarded as heresy, that there is sufficient biblical evidence (although not proof) to support varying positions, that personal convictions are appropriate and that polemics against those who disagree with us are not the order of the day.

I regard strategic-level spiritual warfare in a category similar to baptism. We have differing positions accompanied with measures of conviction that our position is the correct and most biblical one. But we are not dealing with heresy, and we have enough biblical evidence to support varying positions, especially considering that we might interpret the same Scriptures in different ways.

In this book, I am not claiming biblical *proof* for the validity of strategic-level spiritual warfare, spiritual mapping or identificational repentance. I will, however, claim that we do have sufficient biblical *evidence* to warrant:

1. At the *least,* a working hypothesis that we can field test, evaluate, modify and refine;
2. At the *most,* a significant, relatively new spiritual technology God has given us to meet the greatest challenge to world missions since William Carey went to India more than 200 years ago. If this is the case, refusing to use it on the part of some might be to run the risk of unfaithfulness to the Master.

■ REFLECTION QUESTIONS ■

1. Have you read Frank Peretti's books? To what extent do you think they are biblically accurate? Do you agree that demons are actual personalities?
2. Discuss how our modern scientific or humanistic worldviews might influence the way we interpret the Bible, especially the parts that tell of miracles.
3. Do you agree that God can and does do "new" things that we might not find explicitly taught in the Bible?
4. You probably agree that slavery is not the will of God. How can you make that case from what we read about slavery in the Old Testament and the New Testament?
5. In light of your answer to number 4, discuss your understanding of the differences between biblical "concepts" and biblical "proof."

Notes
1. C. S. Lewis, *The Screwtape Letters* (New York: Macmillan, 1962), p. 3.
2. Charles H. Kraft, *Christianity with Power* (Ann Arbor: Vine Books, 1989), pp. 25-26.
3. Ibid., p. 26.
4. *National and International Religion Report* (April 3, 1995): 4.
5. Morris Williams, "Can Demons Invade Believers?" *Power Encounter: A Pentecostal Perspective,* ed. Opal L. Redden (Springfield, Mo.: Central Bible College Press, 1989), p. 184.
6. Ibid., p. 182.

Probing History: "Nothing New Under the Sun"

FOUR

SEVERAL TIMES I HAVE REFERRED TO STRATEGIC-LEVEL spiritual warfare, spiritual mapping and identificational repentance as new "spiritual technology" God seems to be giving to the Church for completing the Great Commission in our generation.

No sooner do we refer to something in the life of the Church as "new," then a knee-jerk reaction frequently sets in, asking (1) Whether it is *really* new or, (2) If it *is* new, could it therefore be valid? Undoubtedly, Solomon's words in Ecclesiastes 1:9 come to mind: "There is nothing new under the sun."

Let's flash back for a moment to Critic B whom I quoted in the last chapter. He said he could not accept strategic-level spiritual warfare "because I find no warrant for the strategy of discerning, naming and praying against demonic spirits over cities and nations either in Scripture or *illustrated in the history of the Christian church.*" In that chapter I dealt with the hermeneutical issue of whether something must be explicitly taught in the Bible for Christians to accept it. In this chapter I want to look at some of the questions of history that my friend, very appropriately, raises.

FIVE PRINCIPLES FOR PROBING HISTORY

For us to take a serious look at the possibility of finding examples of strategic-level spiritual warfare in the history of the Church, it is necessary first to delve into some obvious characteristics of history itself, every one of which will have direct influence on how we understand the issues raised by Critic B. Following are five important principles we need to keep in mind whenever we attempt to probe history:

Principle One. *Not everything that happens is recorded.* You and I can't remember everything that happened yesterday, to say nothing of last year or 10 years ago. As individuals, as families and as entire societies we have inbuilt filters that enable us to select, to a significant degree, what we choose to remember and then to discard the rest.

For us Christians, the history of Jesus and the apostles is of utmost importance. Yet we know from the Bible itself that the biblical authors employed this same filter, although in their case, under the inspiration and guidance of God Himself. When the apostle John finished writing his Gospel, he said, "There are also many other things that Jesus did, which if they were written one by one, I suppose that even the world itself could not contain the books that would be written" (John 21:25).

I did some calculations when I wrote my recent commentary on Acts, *Blazing the Way,* Volume 3 (Regal Books), examining Luke's account of the pastors' seminar Paul conducted in Miletus for the pastors of Ephesus and Asia Minor. The event is significant because it is the only example we have in all of Acts of Paul's teaching to Christians. To the average reader, Acts

19:18-35 may seem like a lot of material. On the unlikely supposition that Paul taught only a one-day seminar, however, Luke would have chosen a mere one-half of one percent of Paul's teaching to record in his history book. Our historical knowledge of this event, like most other events of history, is clearly limited because not everything that happens is recorded in written history or remembered in oral history.

Principle Two. *Not everything written has been preserved.* Many historical records have been trashed because their value was considered dubious or harmful by someone or other. Some documents have been destroyed out of malice toward enemies. In various periods of history, conquering armies would, as a matter of sealing their military victory, burn the libraries of those whom they had vanquished. Hernando Cortez, for example, destroyed many of the historical records of the Aztecs during his conquest, much to the dismay of contemporary Mesoamerican archaeologists and historians.

Principle Three. *Not everything preserved has been found.* One of the things that keeps historians busy is uncovering historical records that have been concealed for one reason or another. In our lifetime, one of the most amazing examples of this was the discovery of the Dead Sea Scrolls in 1947.

Principle Four. *Not everything found is available.* Another task of historians is to make known historical documents available to fellow historians and to the general public through translating, editing and publication. The more user friendly historical material can become, the more it can benefit society. For those of us not professionally involved in historiography, large quantities of material may be available about subjects that interest us, but the material is beyond our reach. I personally experienced this limitation as my research assistant, Janice Wheeler, and I attempted to find material for this chapter. I am certain that much more on the subject of strategic-level spiritual warfare is available than we were able to find, given our limited time and our limited skills as historians.

Principle Five. *Not everything available is interpreted in the same way.* Historians, like all other human beings, have personal paradigms—special lenses through which they choose to read history. I will come back to this and develop it in some detail later, because I suspect this may be a primary reason we do not currently have as much available historical data about strategic-level spiritual warfare as we might wish. Dealing with the invisible world is simply out of bounds in the minds of some historians, both Christian and non-Christian.

THREE SCENARIOS

If we keep these five principles in mind while we look into the relationship between history and strategic-level spiritual warfare, we will have gone a long way in understanding the real issues. Once we begin to probe history, three possible scenarios could develop:

Scenario A: We find no clear examples from history.
Scenario B: We find an abundance of examples from history.
Scenario C: We find only a few examples from history.

In my opinion, it does not matter much whether we actually end up with Scenario A or Scenario B or Scenario C. In any one of the three cases it is still possible to justify the validity of strategic-level spiritual warfare, keeping in mind the five principles listed earlier. Let's explore.

SCENARIO A: NO HISTORICAL EXAMPLES

Suppose we examine the nineteen hundred years of the history of the Church following the age of the apostles and we fail to arrive at anything that could reasonably be interpreted as an example of our forebears' practicing what we now call strategic-level spiritual warfare or spiritual mapping or identificational repentance. This, from the viewpoint of those of us who support these things, is what we would see as a worst-case scenario.

Although this does not happen to be the real situation, as we shall soon see, even if it were we would need to keep two important things in mind.

First, we would need to admit that the absence of available material doesn't *prove* that no one in the past did strategic-level spiritual warfare. Maybe they were doing spiritual warfare, but it wasn't recorded, or maybe it was recorded but subsequently lost. The ways and means of doing historical research are constantly improving, and new historical information keeps surfacing. We may well know a good deal tomorrow that we do not yet know today.

Second, even if we did agree with the hypothetical conclusion that strategic-level spiritual warfare was never done in the past, we are then faced with another crucial question: *Can God do a new thing?* Or, better put, *would* God do something new in the 1990s that He has not done, in a worst-case scenario, in any previous generation of Christians?

Few people I know, whether they agree or disagree with strategic-level spiritual warfare, would deny that God might very well decide to do something new in our generation. Nothing we know about the nature of God would preclude that. In Isaiah we read that God said, "Behold, I will do a new thing" (Isa. 43:19). He said on another occasion, "Behold, the days are coming,...when I will make a new covenant with the house of Israel and with the house of Judah" (Jer. 31:31). The time is also coming in the future when He will "make all things new" (Rev. 21:5).

It is not impossible, then, to imagine that God might well decide to provide us with new spiritual technology for completing the Great Commission in our generation. Whether this actually would include strategic-level spiritual warfare or spiritual mapping or identificational repentance is still a matter of debate. I personally think it does include them, and as far as the historical perspective is concerned, I have become convinced that God does indeed initiate new things in different generations. The best example I have found of this has come through my intensive study of spiritual gifts.

DISCOVERING THE MINISTRY OF ALL BELIEVERS

During the past three decades I have developed a degree of expertise in the field of spiritual gifts. Of all the books I have written, *Your Spiritual Gifts Can Help Your Church Grow* (Regal Books) has by far been the best-seller. As I have researched the history of spiritual gifts, I have come up against a Scenario A. So far I have found virtually no historical examples of the teaching that the ministry in local congregations should be done, not primarily by the clergy, but by the laypeople through the spiritual gifts God has given them.

This comes as a surprise to many. The acceptance of the phenomenon of the ministry of the whole Body of Christ cannot be traced back much further than the early 1970s. Ray Stedman's book *Body Life* (Regal Books), published in 1972, was a pioneer document. Some might imagine that the Pentecostal movement, which began in the early 1900s, had introduced this teaching, but that is not entirely accurate. The Pentecostal movement certainly brought some spiritual gifts to the attention of the Church as a whole. Its list, however, was largely limited to the nine gifts cataloged in 1 Corinthians 12, including the more spectacular sign gifts such as tongues, interpretation of tongues, prophecy, healings and such. Furthermore, Pentecostal leaders did not necessarily teach that these gifts, along with the other 18 spiritual gifts, were the ordinary means for every believer to do his or her part in carrying out the day-by-day ministry of the local church. The early classical Pentecostal movement was surprisingly clerical, and some of it still is.

Martin Luther has become a theological hero for almost all Protestants because, among other things, he rediscovered the priesthood of all believers. This was a new thing as far as the history of the sixteenth century was concerned—altogether as new for them as strategic-level spiritual warfare is today. It brought to the attention of Christians that it was not necessary to go through an ordained priest to communicate with God, as the church had been teaching, but that every believer could go directly to the Father and through intercession could bring others to the Father as well. Although Martin Luther taught the *priesthood* of all believers, he never went beyond it to develop the *ministry* of all believers. Subsequent Lutheranism, like classical Pentecostalism, became highly clerical, operating on the assumption that the primary ministry of the local congregation was to be done by the clergy who had been employed for such a reason.

Some earlier reactions against clericalism and toward lay ministry could be found in such radical movements as the Quakers, the Plymouth Brethren and the Restoration Movement developed by Alexander Campbell and Barton W. Stone. With a few exceptions, these movements did not stress either expositionally or operationally the need for believers to discover, develop and use the more than two dozen specific spiritual gifts mentioned in the New Testament. Only since the 1970s have we seen a growing consensus across the whole Body of Christ that every believer has been given spiritual gifts to do ministry and that a major role of the pastor is to help the people discover what gifts they have, and then to release the laity for the ministry to which God has called them.

My point is that here we have an example of a relatively new thing God is doing and that currently enjoys wide agreement, despite the fact that we have very little historical precedent. Could the same not be the case with strategic-level spiritual warfare? Quite possibly, God *could be* doing another new thing!

SCENARIO B: ABUNDANT EXAMPLES

If we had abundant examples of Christians throughout history engaging in strategic-level spiritual warfare, I might not even be writing this book. Historical tradition goes a long way in making up for a perceived lack of biblical precedent. I personally think we *do* have plenty of biblical precedent for strategic-level spiritual warfare. We have many more examples than we do for celebrating Christmas and Easter, for worshiping primarily on Sunday, for constructing church buildings or for claiming a biblical canon of 66 books. These practices have no direct biblical precedent, but are nevertheless common to many committed believers today.

Not many critics are going around these days and complaining that Christmas and Easter or church buildings are wrong and that we should not advocate them. Few people would want to spend the time reading a book explaining why we should not have more or less than 66 books in our Bibles. Although these things are not taught explicitly in the Bible, we don't hear people becoming upset and saying, "That is not biblical!" as many are saying about strategic-level spiritual warfare. Why?

The answer to this relates to the advantage of a Scenario B. If we find enough historical tradition, we then do not seem to be as concerned as we might otherwise be about whether or not we find a certain thing in the Bible, providing the Bible does not clearly *prohibit* it. At the same time, we must recognize that historical tradition has its own limitations. We have plenty of Christian tradition for placing graven images in our churches, for example, but I, for one, would not accept this in my church because the Bible *prohibits* it. Even so, tradition is quite powerful.

When we honestly think about it, we Protestants may be surprised at how much we allow tradition, rather than Scripture, to influence our beliefs. Evangelicals in particular hate to

---

> **"Our environment, our theological traditions, and our teachers have much more to do with what we believe than we realize. In some cases they have much more influence over what we believe than the Bible itself."**

---

admit this, but it is true. One evangelical who has written clearly about it is Jack Deere. Deere gives the hypothetical example of a student who, let's say, has no personal position on the millennium. If the student decides to attend Westminster Seminary in Philadelphia, chances are that he or she would become a convinced amillennialist. But if the same student were to enroll in Dallas Seminary, he or she would probably graduate as an equally convinced premillennialist.

Deere says, "Our environment, our theological traditions, and our teachers have much more to do with what we believe than we realize. In some cases they have much more influence over what we believe than the Bible itself."[1]

Having said this, I would be the first to admit that examples from history relating specifically to strategic-level spiritual warfare are not abundant enough to convince many that it matters little whether we find it explicitly taught in the Bible or not. In this case we do not have the luxury of a Scenario B. This by no means, however, should be taken to imply that historical examples are *absent*. All it means is that the scenario we are mainly dealing with in this book is a Scenario C.

SCENARIO C: WE HAVE A FEW EXAMPLES

Ramsay MacMullen is a credentialed historian, the Dunham Professor of History and Classics at Yale University. As a professional historian, MacMullen has chosen the Roman Empire as his principal field of concentration. Few have researched the primary and secondary sources relating to the history of the Roman Empire more thoroughly than Ramsay MacMullen. He backs his conclusions with extensive footnotes from works in Greek, Latin, Syriac, German and French, as well as English.

Any professional historian specializing in the Roman Empire must attempt to analyze and explain an extremely significant historical phenomenon: How was it that the Roman Empire, which was totally pagan (with the exception of pockets of Jews here and there), became Christian over a period of about 300 years? Ramsay MacMullen has done this and he reports his findings in his remarkable book *Christianizing the Roman Empire A.D. 100-400*. Not knowing MacMullen personally, I have no information about his personal faith or religious convictions. For that reason, I refer to him as a "secular historian" in the sense that I have no reason to suppose he examines the data from any agenda other than a desire to analyze the situation with accuracy and historical integrity.

It is important to know this because MacMullen's conclusions are rather amazing. Although he lists several factors that contributed to the Christianization of the Roman Empire, all other factors are seen as secondary to the overwhelming significance of *casting out demons*. MacMullen's major point of departure is remarkably similar to mine.

MacMullen says, "My interest focuses only on how non-Christians were won over to the church."[2] Toward the end of his book, he "sums up and sharply delineates a great deal that has been discussed in the preceding pages: emphasis on miraculous demonstration, head-on challenge of non-Christians to a test of power, head-on confrontation with supernatural beings inferior to God, and contemptuous dismissal of merely rational...paths toward true knowledge of the divine."[3]

Head-to-Head with the Powers

I want to stress that the phrase "head-on confrontation with supernatural beings inferior to God" refers, as any reader of MacMullen's work will immediately see, to exactly what we call in the terminology of the 1990s *strategic-level spiritual warfare*. MacMullen's work also contains substantial material about other aspects of power ministries such as ground-level spiritual warfare and occult-level spiritual warfare, healings, miracles and prophecies. The historical questions we are examining at the moment, however, relate to intentional confrontation with principalities, powers and territorial spirits. Ramsay MacMullen argues that there is a *great deal* of this in history—much more, he supposes, than we can find in the relatively few written sources historians have available at the present time.

In a section relating to Paul and John's ministry in confronting Diana of the Ephesians, which I will detail in chapter 9, MacMullen says that the power of Christianity was confirmed in Ephesus, "demonstrated head-on in the riven altar [of Diana]."[4] He goes on to explain: "Driving all competition from the field head-on was crucial. The world, after all, held many dozens and hundreds of gods. Choice was open to everybody. It could thus be only a most exceptional force that would actually displace alternatives and compel allegiance; it could only be the most probative demonstrations that would work. We should therefore *assign as much weight to this, the chief instru-*

ment of conversion, as the best, earliest reporters do" (emphasis mine).[5]

Some, I know, will be surprised by this conclusion of a secular historian. They may wish Ramsay MacMullen would have told them that the pure preaching of justification by faith, raising up the cross of Jesus Christ, persuasively arguing the sovereignty of God, the sacrifice of Jesus Christ, the purity of Christian ethics and the testimonies of lives changed through the new birth would have been the chief reasons for the conversion of the pagans inhabiting the Roman Empire. Such reasoning needs to be considered. MacMullen specifically points out, "It was not the church's liturgy, nor morals, nor monotheism, nor internal organizations...that seemed to non-Christians much different from other people's."[6]

What was it, then? Rather, says MacMullen, "the one point of difference that seems most salient was the antagonism inherent in [Christianity]—antagonism of God toward all other supernatural powers."[7] In language that would outdo almost any member of the Spiritual Warfare Network today, MacMullen describes the aggressiveness in spiritual warfare of the early Christian evangelists and missionaries toward the powers of darkness: "The manhandling of demons—humiliating them, making them howl, beg for mercy, tell their secrets, and depart in a hurry—served a purpose quite essential to the Christian definition of monotheism: it made physically (or dramatically) visible the superiority of the Christian's patron Power over all others."[8]

In modern missiological terminology, this describes classic power encounters. I define a power encounter as: *A visible, practical demonstration that Jesus Christ is more powerful than the spirits, powers or false gods worshiped or feared by the members of a given people group.*[9] Just as it was in the first few centuries, the power encounter can be an important key to effective evangelism today in cities and countrysides around the world. In my opinion, we should be using it much more.

Let's see how this played out in the third, fourth, sixth and eighth centuries.

GREGORY THE WONDERWORKER

How would you rate the following for missionary work in the third century?

A child named Gregory is born and raised in a thoroughly animistic home where evil spirits are honored and served as the lords of every phase of family life. At 14 he makes a trip with his brother to Caesarea Philippi, meets a famous Christian teacher named Origen, masters dialectics, philosophy, geometry, astronomy, morals, physics, ancient literature, Grecian philosophy, biblical science and theology, and in the process accepts Jesus Christ as his Lord and Savior. He becomes a missionary to his hometown of Neocaesarea, described as "rich and populous, deeply buried in vice and idolatry."[10]

Kenneth Scott Latourette, a historian, reports: "When he died, about A.D. 270, after approximately thirty years in office, it is said that in contrast with the seventeen Christians whom he found on his accession to the episcopal see, only seventeen of the populace remained pagan."[11] What missionary wouldn't love that kind of a track record?

What could have stimulated and nurtured such a classic people movement? Gregory was no flake. He describes his learning under Origen by saying, "He filled our minds with a rational, instead of an irrational, wonder at the sacred economy of the universe and the irreprovable constitution of all things."[12] Gregory was highly regarded by his peers for "humility, self-distrust, and practical sense...a man of singular force of character and weighty judgment."[13] Having earned all these credentials, his main thrust of spreading the gospel gained him the name that has come to us through history: Gregory Thaumaturgus or, being translated, Gregory the Wonderworker.

Gregory's first convert came when, traveling through the countryside, he took lodging one night in a notable pagan shrine dedicated to the honor of Apollo. That evening Gregory found himself engaged in spiritual warfare, joined in a fierce battle against the principality who had long ago been invited to occupy that temple. When the shaman or temple priest in charge arrived at the temple the next day, he was surprised that he could get no response from the demon who was usually there. That night the demon himself appeared to him in a dream and said that he could only return to the temple with Gregory's permission. The shaman found Gregory and explained his situation, whereupon, according to one historian, Gregory "wrote an order for him: 'Gregory to Apollo, I give you leave to return to your place, and to do as you have done.' The priest put the letter by the image and forthwith the demon returned."[14]

Power Can Win Souls

Although it may sound strange to us today that Gregory might have given the demon permission to return, that is not the point. The point is that, in the eyes of the shaman and others who worshiped at the temple of Apollo, the Christian missionary had possessed extraordinary power over what was presumably a well-known territorial spirit, and the spirit had been the first one to acknowledge it. The result? "The priest's faith in the god was shattered. Returning to St. Gregory, he became a catechumen, and subsequently, by holiness of life, proved worthy to succeed the saint as bishop."[15]

As an interesting footnote, at least one of the records of this notable incident recounts that the occult practitioner seemed to have had unusual difficulty in accepting Gregory's teaching of the doctrine of Jesus' incarnation. Gregory, therefore, determined to persuade him. According to the source, "So [Gregory], by a prayer, caused a great rock to move from one spot to another. Thus overcoming his doubts, he bore off the servant of the gods as a captive of the Faith."[16]

Such incidents were common in the life and ministry of Gregory the Wonderworker, and Ramsay MacMullen includes several of them in his epochal book. In one case MacMullen tells of Gregory casting out a demon. Without using the term itself, MacMullen concludes that this had been a territorial spirit. He says, "And the [demon] himself, being enraged by the *territory conquered from him* by the bishop [Gregory], where once *both countryside and chief city were in the grip of demons,* inspires a woman to defame him. She is a prostitute, and accuses him of being one of her lovers, but he exorcizes the evil spirit from her also" (emphasis mine).[17]

To what I suppose might be the consternation of some of my critics who suggest that proclaiming the gospel, rather than power ministries, is the only missionary activity really necessary to evangelize pagans, MacMullen says of Gregory the Wonderworker: "He succeeded perhaps in part through speaking publicly to groups. He is shown speaking like that, but confirming or instructing. No conversions are said to result. Rather, and expressly, conversions result from his supernatural acts; by implication and by position in the narrative, they are presented as the cause of the whole grand picture of his success in his campaigns *against demonic hosts*" (emphasis mine).[18]

Spiritual warfare, including the strategic-level variety, was not an incidental, but a chief part of Gregory's enormously successful missionary and evangelistic work in the third century.

MARTIN: PIONEER MISSIONARY TO FRANCE

He is known as Martin of Tours. He has gone down in history as the most famous pioneer missionary to France, then called

Gaul. He was renowned for his piety, his compassion, his generosity, his simple lifestyle and his extraordinary spiritual authority.

As a part of his missionary strategy for reaching the animistic peoples of France, Martin used strategic-level spiritual warfare. He had the advantage of ministering in the fourth century, after the Emperor Constantine had become a Christian in 312, and after the persecution of Christians had ceased. Martin and his peers could therefore spread the gospel wherever they desired under the protection, instead of the opposition, of the government.

Ramsay MacMullen explains how the change in government opened the way for more aggressive strategic-level spiritual warfare. In the post-312 world, he says, the missionaries "carry forward earlier impulses into greatly altered settings. They can act in the open and go on the offensive....Where once they had driven devils only from poor souls possessed [ground-level spiritual warfare], now they can march into the holiest of shrines and, with spectacular effect before large crowds, *expel the devils from their very homes* [strategic-level spiritual warfare]" (emphasis mine).[19]

The Spirit in the Pine Tree

One of these spectacular demonstrations of God's power has been preserved in the records of the life of Martin of Tours. In a certain village he had cast the territorial spirit or spirits out of the chief temple and had demolished the temple itself, as was his custom. But curiously this did not seem to bother the pagans there as much as it had in other places. The reason soon became clear when he discovered that the chief dwelling place of the territorial spirit was a nearby pine tree, not the temple itself. When Martin started to cut down the pine tree, the people then rose up against him.

Martin informed them that because the tree had been dedicated to the demon, it had to be destroyed. Once he had said that, a spokesperson for the group confronted Martin and said, "If you have any trust in thy God, whom you say you worship, we ourselves will cut down this tree, and be it your part to receive it when falling; for if, as you declare, your Lord is with you, you will escape all injury."[20] Martin gladly accepted this challenge to enter into visible battle against the demonic spirit who had been holding these people in captivity for who knows how long and who had been greatly enjoying their sacrifices and worship.

I have participated in many events involving strategic-level spiritual warfare during the past few years, but never have I seen one of this magnitude. The non-Christians had determined they would be willing to destroy their pine tree if by doing so the missionary who had been spreading the claims of a God superior to their own could be destroyed along with it. They knew as well as Martin that their battle was not with flesh and blood or with objects such as trees, but rather with principalities and powers.

It so happened that the pine tree had been growing decisively in one certain direction, so there could be no doubt where it would fall when cut. The crowd demanded that Martin stand alone on the spot where it would certainly fall, which he did. Martin's biographer, Sulpitius Severus, says that the pagans "began, therefore, to cut down their own tree with great glee and joyfulness...there was at some distance a great multitude of wondering spectators...the monks at a distance grew pale...expecting only the death of Martin."[21]

But Martin, trusting confidently in the power of God, waited peacefully until the huge tree made a loud cracking noise and began to crash. He then raised his hand against it, acting in the authority Jesus Christ had given him. Severus says, "Then, indeed, after the manner of a spinning top (one might have thought it driven back), it swept round to the opposite side, to such a degree that it almost crushed the rustics who had taken their places there in what was deemed a safe spot."[22]

The unbelievers were amazed at the power of the true God against the evil spirit whom they had served and honored for so long. The monks wept for joy. The name of Jesus Christ was exalted by all. "The well-known result was that on that day salvation came to that region. For there was hardly one of that immense multitude of heathens who did not express a desire for the imposition of hands, and, abandoning his impious errors, made a profession of faith in the Lord Jesus."[23] Not only that village, but the whole region was soon filled with churches and monasteries.

Is there much doubt that through the bold and aggressive strategic-level spiritual warfare initiated by the missionary Martin, the territorial spirit was dislodged and the blessings of the kingdom of God were then showered upon that people group? MacMullen comments that when the demons encountered by Martin of Tours were so intimidated that they would even reveal their names, as Mercury did on one occasion, "That was the kind of theological demonstration that was irrefutable."[24]

SAINT BENEDICT

Benedict of Nursia is the founder of Western Christian monasticism. His *Benedictine Rule* became the textbook not only for his order, but also for many other orders that followed through the ages. Benedict ministered in the sixth century throughout Italy. He wrote his famous *Rule* in a monastery he had built on the top of Monte Cassino, a mountain that had been given to him as a gift by a person of some political importance. Much of what we know of St. Benedict comes from Pope Gregory the Great who wrote his biography about 50 years after Benedict's death.

Benedict faced a formidable challenge when he accepted

the gift of the mountain on which to build his monastery. Although Italy was mostly Christian by then, Monte Cassino was known far and wide as a center of pagan rituals, sacrifices and worship, very possibly a seat of Satan for the whole region. At least six separate shrines had been established there for worship of some of the more influential principalities of the day: Apollo, Jupiter, Mithra, Venus and more. Pagan worship was illegal, but, as Theodore Maynard says in his biography of Benedict, "a certain amount of pagan worship was still being practiced, for the peasantry in outlying parts was still largely addicted to the ancient gods, despite the legal interdiction."[25]

Taking on the Powers at Monte Cassino

When Benedict arrived on Monte Cassino, he prepared for serious spiritual warfare with a 40-day fast. He then began to do power ministries and to preach to the people until a number of them had been born again. He was now ready to take on the powers that had, perhaps for millennia, claimed that area as their spiritual territory. The major shrine honored Apollo, and it was surrounded by a forest throughout which the other places of wicked sacrifice were located, and that were at the time enjoying a high level of spiritual activity. Hugh Edmund Ford's account of Benedict's approach is among the more graphic: "The man of God, coming hither, beat in pieces the idol [of Apollo], overthrew the altar, set fire on the woods, and in the temple of Apollo built the oratory of St. Martin....On this spot, the saint built his monastery."[26]

Maynard's comment indicates that this aggressive assault on the forces of the enemy had territorial, not just personal, significance: "Every last vestige of paganism was eradicated from the plateau that towered over the district." The powers of darkness that had held that region in captivity for ages had been decisively broken. We are not given the details of the warfare, nor are we told where the powerful spirits went after Benedict was through with them. One thing we do know: The god of this age was no longer able to blind the minds of the unbelievers of that part of Italy, chiefly because Saint Benedict was willing to go to war.

Satan did not take this defeat lightly. Time and again he counterattacked, trying to bring Benedict down. Some of his biographers suggest that at Monte Cassino he on more than one occasion might have come face to face with Satan himself and not only with high-ranking demons. Gregory the Great describes him as ministering with such power that miracles were virtually a part of his everyday life.

On one occasion in morning prayers Benedict received the prophetic word that "Today Satan will pull one of his tricks." So he sent a word of warning to those who were working to construct the monastery: "Be careful, brethren, because the devil is coming to you." Sure enough, the wall they were working on collapsed, and a monk standing under it was crushed, mangled and killed.

Benedict, continuing in prayer, ordered the battered and deformed corpse to be brought to him. As Cardinal Schuster describes it, "They fetched it on the blanket and deposited it in the little room on the ground floor of the tower on the mat where the Abbot was accustomed to prostrate himself in prayer. After dismissing them, the saint, heavy of heart, closed the door and continued his prayer more fervently....Suddenly the dead man rose from the mat and announced that he was cured. St. Benedict spoke words of encouragement to him, gave him his blessing, and sent him back straightway to continue his work."[27] Apparently there was no allowance for sick leave in the *Benedictine Rule!*

BONIFACE AND THOR'S OAK TREE

In the eighth century an English missionary, Boniface, was sent to the pagan peoples of Germany by Pope Gregory II. He spent three years being mentored by another British missionary, Willi-brord, learning from him how to do spiritual warfare, including power encounters provoked by the physical destruction of pagan temples. After that, he set out to evangelize the region of Hesse. Here is how a historian, Kenneth Scott Latourette, describes the German religion Boniface encountered: "There was a belief in spirits and in gods. The latter were a part of the personifications of earth, water, fire, storm, the sun, the moon, and other forces and objects which affected the physical well-being of people. Certain springs and trees were held sacred, and temples for the gods were maintained."[28] This sounds very much like a battlefield requiring spiritual warfare.

When Boniface arrived in Hesse, he discovered that a prin-cipal power point for keeping the people there in spiritual darkness generation after generation was an ancient oak tree in Geismar. Here was a setup for a strategic-level spiritual encounter. Much to the horror of a large multitude of pagans, Boniface publicly issued a head-on challenge to the territorial spirit named Thor, a powerful principality who had used that tree as a base for deeds of perversion for longer than anyone in Hesse could remember. Boniface personally took on the task of felling the tree.

Many of the spectators expected beyond the shadow of a doubt that the missionary would quickly perish under the wrath of the mighty Thor. Quite the contrary! Even before he had cut the tree through, a fierce wind burst on the scene and sent the tree crashing to the ground, breaking it into four distinct sec-tions! No question remained in anyone's mind that they had seen none other than the hand of the true God. Thor was embarrassed and thoroughly defeated. Through the courageous ministry of Boniface, the strongman over the territory had been bound, and the way was then open for evangelism and church planting.

Latourette tells it like this: "The pagan bystanders, who had been cursing the desecrator, were convinced of the power of the new faith....The Geismar episode may well have proved decisive evidence in terms which the populace could understand of the superior might of the God of the Christians."[29] Much fruit

---

Historians have paradigms, too. They form subjective judgments, evaluating the validity of what they find in their sources according to previous mental constructions they have developed.

---

resulted, for very rapidly the entire Hessian people group became Christian, rejecting its allegiance to Thor and his cohorts.

HISTORIANS HAVE PARADIGMS, TOO

I have tried as hard as I can to probe more deeply some of our Christian history to find examples of strategic-level spiritual warfare being used for world evangelization. I can imagine many readers saying, "Amazing! I never knew that our forebears such as Gregory and Martin and Benedict and Boniface and undoubtedly many others understood and practiced strategic-level spiritual warfare just as dedicated people in Youth With a Mission or Generals of Intercession or churches in Argentina are doing today!" I can also imagine some saying, as they did when I reported tooth filling in South America, "Preposterous! Things like this never could have nor should we gullibly believe that they ever did really happen!"

It is possible to find church history books that might mention these people, but that, when they do, choose not to tell any of the stories I have just told. Other history books might mention the stories, but interpret them in a different way. Historians have paradigms, too. They form subjective judgments, evaluating the validity of what they find in their sources according to previous mental constructions they have developed. Some undoubtedly would argue that Boniface's oak tree, for example, was nothing but an ordinary oak tree, and that any significance it might have had beyond that was only a figment of the primitive and untutored imagination of the Hessian people.

An Attempt to Ignore the Demonic

Some historians check historical sources with a previous assumption that no such things as personal demons inhabit the invisible world, much less powerful ones named Thor. They explain that people who lived in those days might have naively believed they were facing actual demons by relegating their uninformed mentality to some prescientific age of credulity. Those ancient people were considered so gullible that they could believe and say just about anything, so it becomes the historian's job today to decide which part of what they believed was actually true and which part must have been mere superstition, disassociated from reality.

The same thing applies to the way some study and understand the Bible itself, which is also a historical document. In the nineteenth century, for example, numbers of liberal European scholars had bought so heavily into the humanism and rationalism and positivism of the Enlightenment that they concluded, among other things, that miracles were impossible. Not only couldn't miracles have really occurred in the lives of such as Gregory or Martin, but neither could they have occurred in the life of Jesus. Entire books were subsequently written to prove that Jesus couldn't have been born of a virgin, that he couldn't have turned water into wine and that he couldn't have been raised from the dead. This so-called "biblical scholarship" subsequently spread from Europe to other parts of the world and, I am sorry to say, it exists in some circles today.

Those who deny that Jesus was raised from the dead would, *ipso facto*, disbelieve the story of Benedict raising from the dead the monk who had been killed when the wall collapsed on him. Some would assume that death, by definition, is final and therefore it is impossible for anyone truly dead ever to be raised. That explains the difference in interpretation of the reports coming out of Indonesia during the revival of 1965-1970 when many spectacular miracles, including raising of the dead, were widely reported.

In my book *How to Have a Healing Ministry in Any Church*, I document how intelligent, spiritual Christian leaders, who actually went to Indonesia to do research on site, went with differing assumptions and therefore interpreted the same information in opposite ways. Some said yes, the dead had been raised, while others said no, they were not dead at all, but they had just fainted. The same thing happens with people who are employed as professional historians.

Speaking of professional historians, Ramsay MacMullen is acutely aware of what I have just said. He, unlike some of his more skeptical colleagues, reads history with the assumption that the Greco-Roman world affirmed that demons do, in fact, inhabit the invisible world just as God does, and that overt, intentional power encounters between these forces was the chief contributing cause for the Christianization of the Roman Empire. MacMullen's discussion of these very issues is extremely enlightening, coming from a secular historian.

Our Christian "Limited Dualism"

For one thing, MacMullen does not hesitate to address the dualism common in all of pagan human society in pre-Christian times. In chapter 2, I mention that some of my critics accuse me of being overly influenced by the dualism of my Indo-European ethnolinguistic tradition. To this I reply that I cannot accept a *philosophical* dualism, but I can accept a *limited* dualism reflected in the spiritual battles between the forces of God and the demonic forces of Satan. Along the same lines, Mac-Mullen explains how the gospel was spread in the early centuries: "In a tradition that reached back to its very roots, Christianity in the person of its most electric figures *lit up the dualism* they preached on the local level, as we may call it, before specific gatherings, and so dramatized Christian confrontation with the enemy—be it error or demons—through visible acts"[30] (emphasis mine).

Not all historians see eye to eye with MacMullen. He quotes P. Brown as saying, "Historians...of the church have declared that such phenomena [ground-level spiritual warfare and strategic-level spiritual warfare] 'are more problems of crowd psychology than of Christian piety.' In so doing, they have declared the study of exorcism, possibly the most highly rated activity of the early Christian church, a historiographical 'no-go' area."[31] Explaining it away as "crowd psychology" is a clear function of paradigm, and a major reason some have too hastily concluded that history is silent concerning strategic-level spiritual warfare.

Citing evidence to the contrary, MacMullen draws on some of the best and most authentic earliest reporters of the spread of Christianity. For example:

- **Justin** boasts: "How many persons possessed by demons, everywhere in the world and *in our own city*, have been exorcised by many of our Christians."[32]
- **Irenaeus** asserts: "Some people *incontestably and truly* drive out demons, so that those very persons become believers."[33]
- **Tertullian** says: "Let a man be produced *right here*

before your court who, it is clear is possessed by a demon, and that spirit, commanded by any Christian at all, will as much confess himself a demon in truth as, by lying, he will elsewhere profess himself to be a god."[34]

- **Cyprian:** Relating more directly to strategic-level spiritual warfare, Cyprian addresses the phenomenon of demons in idols who "when they are adjured by us in the name of the true God, yield forthwith and confess, and admit they are forced also to leave the bodies [objects] they have invaded."[35]

Does History Help?

My hope is that when Critic B reads this chapter he will decide to modify his statement that he must reject strategic-level spiritual warfare because he has not found it illustrated in the history of the Christian Church. I realize, of course, that not everyone will. Some will still say, "Preposterous!" After researching and writing this chapter, the first of its kind that I am aware of, my own faith in the power of God has been greatly strengthened, as has my confidence that those of us who believe that strategic-level spiritual warfare is a valuable tool for enabling us to complete the Great Commission in our generation may well be on the right track.

■ REFLECTION QUESTIONS ■

1. Suppose we find no examples in history of something like strategic-level spiritual warfare. Would this, in itself, make such ministry invalid?
2. Can you name two or three things we do in our

churches primarily out of following traditions as opposed to biblical commands to do them?

3. The historian Ramsay MacMullen tells of how the gospel spread through "head-on confrontations with supernatural beings inferior to God." What do you think some of those confrontations might have looked like?

4. Martin of Tours would go right into pagan temples and command the demons to leave. Do you think missionaries should do that today? Why or why not?

5. Do historians have biases? Is that reflected in some history books in our schools today? How might that influence our understanding of the ministry of spiritual warfare in church history?

Notes

1. Jack Deere, *Surprised by the Power of the Spirit* (Grand Rapids: Zondervan Publishing House, 1993), p. 47.
2. Ramsay MacMullen, *Christianizing the Roman Empire A.D. 100-400* (New Haven, Conn.: Yale University Press, 1984), p. 87.
3. Ibid., p. 112.
4. Ibid., p. 27.
5. Ibid.
6. Ibid., p. 19.
7. Ibid.
8. Ibid., p. 28.
9. C. Peter Wagner, *How to Have a Healing Ministry in Any Church* (Ventura, Calif.: Regal Books, 1988), p. 150.
10. Michael Walsh, *Butler's Lives of Patron Saints* (San Francisco: HarperSanFrancisco, 1987), p. 205.
11. Kenneth Scott Latourette, *The First Five Centuries* (Grand Rapids: Zondervan Publishing House, 1970), p. 89.
12. William Smith and Henry Wace, ed., *A Dictionary of Christian Biography*, Vol. II (London, England: John Murray, 1880), p. 731.
13. Ibid., p. 730.
14. W. Telfer, "The Latin Life of St. Gregory Thaumaturgus," *The Journal of Theological Studies*, No. 31 (1929-1930): 152-153.

15. Ibid.
16. Ibid.
17. MacMullen, *Christianizing the Roman Empire,* p. 60.
18. Ibid., p. 61.
19. Ibid., p. 113.
20. Sulpitius Severus, *Life of St. Martin, Classics of Christian Missions,* ed. Francis M. DuBose (Nashville: Broadman Press, 1979), pp. 121-122.
21. Ibid., p. 122.
22. Ibid.
23. Ibid.
24. MacMullen, *Christianizing the Roman Empire,* p. 62.
25. Theodore Maynard, *Saint Benedict and His Monks* (London, England: Staples Press Limited, 1956), p. 37.
26. Hugh Edmund Ford, "Benedict of Nursia," *The Catholic Encyclopedia,* Charles G. Herbermann, et. al., ed., Vol. II (New York: Robert Appleton Company: 1907), p. 471.
27. Idlephonse Cardinal Schuster, *Saint Benedict and His Times* (London, England: B. Herder Book Co., 1951), pp. 186-187.
28. Kenneth Scott Latourette, *The Thousand Years of Uncertainty,* Vol. 2 of *A History of the Expansion of Christianity* (Grand Rapids: Zondervan Publishing House, 1938; revised edition, 1966), p. 88.
29. Ibid., p. 92.
30. MacMullen, *Christianizing the Roman Empire,* p. 62.
31. Ibid., p. 27.
32. Ibid.
33. Ibid.
34. Ibid.
35. Ibid.

Part II:
Biblical Evidence

Spiritual Warfare in Jesus' Ministry

FIVE

J ESUS LED A RELATIVELY PEACEFUL LIFE UNTIL HE WAS BAP-
tized by John the Baptist in the Jordan River and was
filled with the Holy Spirit. Then, as many would say
today, "all hell broke loose!" The Bible records that the
very first thing that happened after God said in an audible voice "This is My beloved Son, in whom I am well
pleased" (Matt. 3:17) was that "Jesus was led up by the
Spirit into the wilderness to be tempted by the devil"
(4:1).

Jesus' public ministry began with an eyeball-to-eyeball power encounter with Satan himself! This is an
account of the highest level of spiritual warfare ever
recorded in history. Is there any doubt that this power
encounter set the tone and the pattern for Jesus' entire
ministry, not only here on earth, but also after Jesus left
the earth? The most serious, and ultimately fatal, blow
that Jesus dealt to Satan was His death on the cross, but

that did not end the war. Now that Jesus is at the right hand of God the Father the war continues, and it will, "for He must reign till He has put all enemies under His feet," and then "He delivers the kingdom to God the Father" (1 Cor. 15:24,25).

THE BATTLE IS ON!

We live in that time period starting with the showdown between the Son of God and Satan in the wilderness and ending with that wonderful day in the future when "The devil...[will be] cast into the lake of fire and brimstone where the beast and false prophet are. And they will be tormented day and night forever and ever" (Rev. 20:10). Jesus' own ministry, including His death and resurrection, was carried out during this same time frame. That is why we read so much in the Gospels about Jesus doing spiritual warfare on all levels.

Michael Harper says, "Jesus Christ's coming was a head-on confrontation with satanic powers. His ministry included exorcisms or deliverances....More healings of Jesus are related to satanic influence than any other single factor, and some of these stories are amongst the most vivid and important in the New Testament."[1] Michael Green observes that "[Jesus] has more to say about Satan than anyone else in the Bible....The Gospels are full of his actual conflict with Satan, which reached its climax on the cross."[2] A famous New Testament scholar, George Eldon Ladd, summarizes the essence of Jesus' ministry by saying, "God's kingdom in Jesus' teaching has a twofold manifestation: at the end of the age to *destroy* Satan, and in Jesus' mission to *bind* Satan"[3] (emphasis mine).

When the apostle John later looked back at the ministry of Jesus, he characterized it in the same way. He said, "For this purpose the Son of God was manifested, that He might destroy the works of the devil" (1 John 3:8).

SHOULD WE IGNORE THE DEVIL?

Some pastors warn their people not to talk about the devil or think about the devil, but to keep their eyes only on the Lord. This would be good advice for some make-believe world. In the real world, Jesus talked about, thought about, taught about and personally confronted the devil and the demons under His command regularly. Right after his power encounter with Satan, Jesus "went about all Galilee, teaching in their synagogues, preaching the gospel of the kingdom, and healing all kinds of sickness and all kinds of disease among the people" (Matt. 4:23). The word got out. The sick began coming to Him for healing. Who were they? Those "afflicted with various diseases and torments, and *those who were demon-possessed,* epileptics, and paralytics; and He healed them" (v. 24, emphasis mine).

To ignore or underestimate a wicked and aggressive enemy is foolishness. Some world leaders thought the best thing would be to appease Adolf Hitler when he first began his expansive European conquests, and by doing so they helped kindle World War II. A serial killer nicknamed "Nightstalker" strangled many women in the Los Angeles area a few years ago. The Los Angeles Police Department immediately began to pour enormous amounts of time, energy and money, not in ignoring the Nightstalker, but in focusing on him, concentrating on him and studying his behavior patterns, until they finally brought him to justice.

Jesus faced a foe much more formidable than the Nightstalker. On at least three separate occasions, Jesus refers to Satan as "the ruler of this world" (John 12:31; 14:30; 16:11). This language must not be taken lightly. A Yale biblical scholar, Susan Garrett, in her outstanding book *The Demise of the Devil* focuses on the writings of Luke, and concludes: "The remarks about Satan in Luke's Gospel and in Acts are, if small in quantity, mammoth in significance...one can scarcely overestimate Satan's importance in the history of salvation as told by Luke. It is Satan's fierce opposition to the purposes of God that renders Jesus' battle to effect salvation so necessary and so arduous, and his victory so great."[4] Ed Murphy counts 150 references to conflict in the spirit world in the Gospels, and he comments, "There is no question that the gospel writers saw the spirit world as the very context in which they and Jesus lived and ministered."[5]

JESUS THE INVADER

It is not farfetched to understand Jesus' coming to earth as analogous to a military invasion. He came with the kingdom of

---

We now number our years from the time Jesus arrived and brought God's kingdom. Jesus came on the offensive. He stormed the beach!

God, and He preached the gospel of the kingdom. John the Baptist said the kingdom of God was coming (see Matt. 3:2). Jesus told His disciples to preach the kingdom of God (see 10:7). This became the most radical turning point in all of human history. We now number our years from the time Jesus arrived and brought God's kingdom. Jesus came on the offensive. He stormed the beach!

Who was on the defensive? Satan, the ruler of this world, who was being decisively attacked. Before Jesus came, Satan's rule had gone virtually unchallenged for who knows how many millennia. It is instructive to take note that when Satan offered to Jesus "the kingdoms of the world and their glory"

(4:8), Jesus did not dispute his ownership. If Satan had not been the owner, the temptation involving them would have been a farce. Satan had, and still has, awesome power.

None of this should in any way cause us to forget that the ultimate owner of the whole world, including planet Earth, is God. God created the world, and it is His. "The earth is the Lord's and all its fullness" (Ps. 24:1). Satan never has been, nor ever will be, the owner of planet Earth. His kingdom consists in the control he possesses over *people* who inhabit the earth, and he maintains that control by securing their allegiance through various means known as "the wiles of the devil" (Eph. 6:11). Likewise, the kingdom of God that Jesus brought is not a land that has territorial boundaries, but rather the reign of Jesus Christ over human beings. Wherever people declare their allegiance to Jesus Christ, the kingdom of God is in their midst. The battle between the kingdom of God and the kingdom of Satan is essentially a battle for people and for their allegiance.

Before Jesus came, virtually every person on the face of the earth had pledged allegiance to Satan. The exception was the relatively small group of descendants of Abraham called "the people of God," the Jewish people, but even they were not immune to serious problems with spiritual allegiance, especially before their captivity in Babylon.

The New Displaces the Old

When Jesus came, the situation changed permanently, and Satan was the first to realize its full significance. Jesus contrasted the Old Testament era with the new when He told His disciples that they were particularly privileged to see what they were seeing at the time. Jesus said, "I tell you that many prophets and kings [representing the Old Testament period] have desired to see what you see, and have not seen it" (Luke 10:24). To what was Jesus referring? He was referring to the experience His disciples had just enjoyed, causing them to report, "Lord, even the demons are subject to us in Your name" (v. 17).

We read no such report in the Old Testament. No such direct threat had been made to Satan's dominion before Jesus came. That was one of the reasons Jesus said that although there was no greater prophet than John the Baptist, who was symbolically the last representative of the pre-Jesus era, "he who is least in the kingdom of God is greater than he" (7:28). The difference is enormous.

No wonder Satan did, and continues to do, everything he possibly can to prevent the spread of the kingdom of God. He lusts for people's allegiance and their worship, but he is defeated and he is losing. Satan has incredible power, but it can never match the power of God. For two thousand years the kingdom of Satan has been pushed back and displaced by the kingdom of God, so that now, figuratively speaking, Satan's back is against the wall, the wall of the 10/40 Window. How is this happening? Beginning from the days of Jesus until now, every significant step forward for the Christian movement has been won through spiritual warfare. Jesus' first beachhead has become a continuing massive offensive and there is no turning back!

When Jesus died on the cross, Satan not only suffered his most crippling defeat, but from that time on his ultimate doom was sealed as well. Paul later writes about Jesus' crucifixion and says, "Having disarmed principalities and powers, He made a public spectacle of them, triumphing over them in it" (Col. 2:15). The metaphor Paul uses here is that of the Roman Legions bringing home prisoners of war and parading them naked through the streets of Rome and the public insulting them, cursing them and showering them with filth of all kinds.

The War Is Not Over

The war is not over. I like the way Ed Murphy puts it: "While our enemies are already defeated, they are not dead, not even sickly."[6] Even after Jesus' death and resurrection, the apostle Paul referred to Satan as "the god of this age" (2 Cor. 4:4). Peter sees him walking around "like a roaring lion, seeking whom he may devour" (1 Pet. 5:8). Like Paul and Peter, the best of spiritual warriors today avoid the mistake of naively underestimating the power of the devil. Satan is no wimp.

It is precisely because the devil still maintains the allegiance of large numbers of people, 3 billion at the last count, that Jesus sends His troops out to do spiritual warfare today just as He did when He was on earth. The very first time Jesus ever allowed His 12 disciples to go out to minister on their own, He did two important things relating to the spiritual warfare undergirding their evangelistic mission:

- "He gave them power over unclean spirits" (Matt. 10:1).
- He commanded them, "And as you go, preach, saying, 'The kingdom of heaven is at hand.' Heal the sick, cleanse the lepers, raise the dead, *cast out demons*" (vv. 7,8, emphasis mine).

Likewise, when Jesus later trained and sent out 70 disciples, they followed the normal pattern of ministry that accompanied the preaching of the kingdom of God, established first by Jesus and then by the 12. So much spiritual power had been released by their frontal attack on the invisible world that Jesus said, when they returned, "I saw Satan fall like lightning from heaven" (Luke 10:18).

This pattern for evangelistic ministry did not stop with the Cross or with the Resurrection. After the Resurrection, Jesus commissioned His disciples to make disciples of all peoples, to baptize them, and to "[teach] them to observe all things that I have commanded you" (Matt. 28:20). Obviously, one of the major things Jesus had been commanding His disciples to do was to cast out demons. And later, when He met Paul personally on the Damascus road, He sent him as a missionary to the nations, "to open their eyes, in order to turn them from darkness to light, and from the *power of Satan to God*" (Acts 26:18, emphasis mine). Because the devil gives up no one under his power without a fight, little doubt remained in Paul's mind that he was in for a career involving heavy-duty spiritual warfare.

If anyone thinks the task of world evangelization today is different from the days of Jesus and the apostles, I suggest that position be reconsidered. The kingdom of God is still penetrating the kingdom of Satan on every continent. The battle for the ultimate allegiance of men, women and children in cities and countries and people groups around the world is the same. Therefore, those among God's people today who are called to the front lines to take unbelievers from darkness to light will need the same spiritual equipment Jesus Himself had.

How could we humans possibly duplicate what Jesus the Son of God did?

WE DRINK FROM THE SAME WELL

Jesus said, "He who believes in Me, the works that I do he will do also; and greater works than these he will do, because I go to My Father" (John 14:12). The only way such a thing could happen would be for us to drink from the same well from which Jesus drank. The water in this well is the Holy Spirit. Jesus also said, "He who believes in Me,...out of his heart will flow rivers of living water" (7:38), which John explains in this way: "This He spoke concerning the Spirit, whom those believing in Him would receive" (v. 39).

Not everyone has recognized this, but when you think it through you will see that Jesus did none of His marvelous works because He was the second Person of the Trinity, but rather because He allowed the Holy Spirit, the third Person of the Trinity, to work through Him. Colin Brown, a theologian, calls this "Spirit Christology."[7] Brown says, "Jesus' miracles are given a prominent place, but they are not attributed to Jesus as the Second Person of the Trinity. They are not presented as manifestations of His personal divinity."[8]

This is such a crucial issue for power ministries, including strategic-level spiritual warfare today, that I want to make sure what Colin Brown and I have just said is very clear. Here is my theological hypothesis restated in a more precise way:

> *The Holy Spirit was the source of all of Jesus' power during His earthly ministry. Jesus exercised no power of or by Himself. We can do the same or greater things than Jesus did because we have access to the same power source.*

Jesus is the only being who ever did have, or ever will have, two natures in the same person, a divine nature and a human nature. And both of these natures are complete. Jesus isn't half God and half human. He is 100 percent God and 100 percent human. This, for orthodox believers, is a theological nonnegotiable.

Why Didn't Jesus Know?

How do the two natures relate? When Jesus' disciples once asked Him when the end would come, Jesus replied, "Of that day and hour no one knows, not even the angels in heaven, *nor the Son,* but only the Father" (Mark 13:32, emphasis mine). Obviously, at least one thing Jesus didn't know, but how could such a thing be if He was 100 percent God? God is omniscient; He knows everything.

Several explanations have been suggested by certain theologians. Some say it is a mystery and we will never know.

Others don't believe that Jesus was God in the first place, so they use this text to prove their point. A more frequent explanation is what I call the "two channel theory," which suggests that while He was on earth, some of the time Jesus ministered from His divine nature, but other times He switched to His human nature. This theory says that when He fed the five thousand, He was using His divine nature, but when He Himself got hungry, this was His human nature.

In my opinion, the "two channel theory" is a poor explanation. It breaks down quite decisively in Jesus' response to the disciples in Mark 13:32 about when the end would come. Proponents of the "two channel theory" would argue that when Jesus said *"nor the Son,"* that was His human nature "channel." But then, where did He get the information that *the angels* didn't know? Humans could not know something like that. In my opinion, to suppose that Jesus would switch channels, not only from one day to the next, but even in the middle of the same sentence, stretches the imagination a bit too much. There is a better answer.

As I have said, I believe that everything Jesus did on earth He did through His human nature. He always kept His divine nature and He always was 100 percent God. But Philippians 2 details what happened. It says that Jesus was always God, but that "[He] did not consider it robbery to be equal with God" (v. 6). This means that Jesus subordinated Himself to God. After His incarnation, Jesus was different from what He was before. How did He subordinate Himself? Obviously not by giving up His divinity, because He was always God. The way Jesus subordinated Himself was to take on something new, namely His humanity: "[He] made Himself of no reputation, taking the form of a bondservant, and coming in the likeness of men" (v. 7). From that point on, Jesus was different from either the Father or the Holy Spirit, both of whom have only one nature, not two as Jesus had.

Jesus also agreed to obey the Father completely during His time on earth. "He humbled Himself and became obedient to the point of death, even the death of the cross" (v. 8). Jesus' obedience was voluntary and it was temporary. It consisted of the greatest display of humility ever known—agreeing to totally suspend the use (not the possession) of His divine attributes so that the only nature Jesus was using on earth was His human nature.

The "Second Adam"
That is why Jesus is called the "second Adam" (see 1 Cor. 15:45-47). Both Jesus and Adam were special and unique creations, Adam from the dust of the ground and Jesus through a virgin birth. Both were under a covenant of obedience to the Father. Neither one had been contaminated by original sin. And both were tempted by the devil in the same way—invited to break their covenant of obedience. Adam's temptation was to eat the forbidden fruit, which he did. Jesus' temptation was to violate His agreement of obedience by using His divine nature. Let's look at that.

As I said earlier, Jesus defeated the devil through the world's highest-level power encounter, the temptation in the desert. The point that is so important for us to remember is that Jesus won this ferocious spiritual battle not because He was God, but through His human nature, a nature just like ours. Jesus could have used His divine nature and turned the bread into stones and He could have called angels to save Him if He jumped from the peak of the temple, but He didn't. He could have taken possession of Satan's kingdoms *without* worshiping Satan, but He didn't. If He had, He would have disobeyed the Father. The temptation ended, Jesus' covenant of obedience had remained intact, and the devil had been defeated.

Afterward, all of Jesus' ministry was done as a human being. He depended entirely on knowing the will of the Father: "The

Son can do nothing of Himself, but what He sees the Father do" (John 5:19). He depended entirely on the power of the Holy Spirit: "God anointed Jesus of Nazareth with the Holy Spirit and with power" (Acts 10:38). He said, "I cast out demons by the Spirit of God" (Matt. 12:28). He judged only because the Father had delegated that authority to Him (see John 5:22). The only thing Jesus did that no human being can properly do was to receive worship. Because Jesus was always God, He always could receive worship, which, of course, He did.

Doing the Works of Jesus

This is what I mean by drinking from the same well as Jesus—receiving the power of the Holy Spirit. We can do the same works as Jesus, as He said we would, if we, like Jesus, are entirely dependent on knowing the will of the Father and on the power of the Holy Spirit. Granted, we will never do the works as well as Jesus because He enjoyed several advantages we don't have. Jesus had no sin, either original sin or actual sin. Jesus had a completely unobstructed channel to the Father along with a combination of complete faith and complete obedience. The corollary is that although we may never reach the perfection of Jesus, the nearer we *do* approach it, the more powerful we can expect our ministry to be.

Can we withstand the devil in a high-level power encounter as Jesus did? Can we cast out demons as Jesus did? Can we live holy lives and display righteousness as Jesus did? Why not? Jesus said we could. Our human nature is not the variable. The variables are our characters, our obedience, our faith and our fullness of the power of the Holy Spirit.

It took the disciples awhile to understand the significance of the power of the Holy Spirit for carrying out their ministry on behalf of the kingdom of God. The disciples had been with Jesus for almost three years. Their attention, their obedience and their love had been focused on the second Person of the

Trinity. They were hoping that this would last forever, but then one day Jesus informed them He was going to leave. Quite naturally, they were upset. Peter protested so harshly that Jesus had to say to him, "Get behind Me, Satan!" (see Matt. 16:21-23).

The Holy Spirit Gives Us the Advantage
When things calmed down, Jesus gave the disciples a lengthy and detailed explanation of why He needed to leave. He said, "Nevertheless, I tell you the truth. It is to *your advantage* that I go away" (John 16:7, emphasis mine). This must have been

---

Everything Jesus did by way of power ministries He did by the Holy Spirit. Furthermore, He let the disciples know in very clear terms that they would in turn only be successful in ministry if they did the same. Good Christology leads to good pneumatology, and vice versa.

---

one of the strangest things the disciples had ever heard. How could anything be considered an *advantage* over personally being with the Son of God? Very simple. Jesus said, "If I do not go away, the Helper will not come to you" (v. 7). The Helper, of course, is the Holy Spirit. In a nutshell, Jesus was saying that we believers are better off with the third Person of the Trinity than we would be with the second Person of the Trinity here with us in the flesh.

From time to time, some of my critics have suggested I may be giving undue attention to the Holy Spirit. One of them thought my pneumatology had weakened my Christology. However, I always believe my pneumatology is correct to the degree it matches what Christ taught about the Holy Spirit. For a starter, everything Jesus did by way of power ministries He did by the Holy Spirit. Furthermore, He let the disciples know in very clear terms that they would in turn only be successful in ministry if they did the same. Good Christology leads to good pneumatology, and vice versa.

The disciples received the best of training. In three years Jesus taught them evangelism, healing, holiness, ethics, stewardship, deliverance, preaching, theology, morality, Old Testament, missions and everything else that would be included in a good curriculum. Not only had He taught them how to do ministry, but He had also modeled it for them and had personally supervised their field experience. By the time Jesus left, the disciples would be well prepared to pick up where He left off to advance the kingdom of God. Jesus then informed them that their training, by itself, was not enough.

Before they were to go out to minister, Jesus said, "Tarry in the city of Jerusalem until you are endued with power from on high" (Luke 24:49). They did as Jesus told them, and on the Day of Pentecost, they received the power of the Holy Spirit, exactly the same power through which Jesus had ministered all the days of His life.

If, as I have argued, spiritual warfare was at the heart of Jesus' ministry on behalf of the kingdom of God; the disciples would have anticipated nothing different. Satan's doom had been sealed, but the war was still on. And we have every reason to believe that such has been the case for the followers of Jesus through the ages.

IS THE POWER LIMITED?

How much power did Jesus give His disciples? I have already mentioned that because not one of us is the Son of God, we cannot expect the same unobstructed relationship with the

Father or the Holy Spirit without measure. *Practically,* we may not see divine power operating so regularly in our ministries, but *potentially,* the same degree of power Jesus possessed is there. Nothing less.

This is an important issue, because some critics of strategic-level spiritual warfare argue that Jesus set boundaries to the power He offered the disciples through the Holy Spirit. They suggest that we may not have authority over all the powers of darkness, just over the lower-level demons that may be demonizing human beings. Therefore we should stay away from strategic-level spiritual warfare, lest we overstep our legitimate authority.

As I reread the passages of the Gospels in which Jesus equips and sends out His disciples, I find no suggestions of limitations. It is true, as the critics point out, that the examples we have in the Gospels of the ministry of Jesus' disciples deal by and large with what is called ground-level spiritual warfare or casting demons out of people. Possible other examples of Jesus Himself dealing with higher-level spirits might include the Legion spirit (see Mark 5:9), and addressing the spirit who caused the storm on the Sea of Galilee (see 4:39), but the examples are not plentiful.

When we move on to study the evangelistic and church planting ministry of the apostles in the book of Acts, however, we then find several strategic-level examples. We find Peter dealing with Simon Magus in Acts 8, Paul dealing with Elymas or Bar-Jesus in Acts 13 and the Python spirit in Acts 16, and Diana of the Ephesians in Acts 19. Realizing that some will object to my classifying these as strategic-level spiritual warfare, I will deal with those objections in later chapters.

It is helpful to remind ourselves from time to time that the technical terms we have been using for the last few years—ground-level, occult-level and strategic (or cosmic)-level spiritual warfare—are somewhat artificial. Although they are helpful terms for teaching and comprehension, there are not three separate worlds, but only one invisible world of darkness. When Jesus sent His disciples into warfare against this spirit world, telling them to "cast out demons," He may or may not have meant to imply that they should only cast demons out of people, but leave the territorial spirits alone. Because we have silence about any possible limitations, that silence can be used as an argument from either side.

Jesus' one statement that does seem to imply we have no limitations to the authority in dealing with the powers of darkness comes in the context of the story where He sent out 70 of His followers to preach and minister the kingdom of God. As they went through the countryside and into the villages they, among other things, cast out many demons. Deliverance was so prominent that the only report of the trip the Scriptures subsequently record is, "Lord, even the demons are subject to us in Your name" (Luke 10:17).

Later, in His debriefing session with the disciples, Jesus makes two significant points, one relating to priorities and one relating to authority. Regarding *priorities*, Jesus said, "Do not rejoice in this, that the spirits are subject to you, but rather rejoice because your names are written in heaven" (v. 20). Spiritual warfare is not to be regarded as an end in itself, but a means to the end of seeing lost souls taken from darkness to light, from the power of Satan to God. Salvation is eternal, but spiritual warfare, at best, will give us only temporal results.

Did Jesus Really Mean "All"?

Regarding *authority,* Jesus said, "Behold, I give you the authority to trample on serpents and scorpions, *and over all the power of the enemy,* and nothing shall by any means hurt you" (Luke 10:19, emphasis mine). Some may point out that in biblical exegesis "all" does not invariably mean "all," and I concede this. The question then becomes, did Jesus mean "all" when He made this particular promise? I think He did. I agree with Francis Frangipane, who writes, "I believe the Scriptures are clear: Not only do Christians have the authority to war against these powers of darkness, but we have the responsibility to as well. If we do not pray against our spiritual enemies, they will, indeed, prey upon us."[9]

If Francis Frangipane and I are correct, we then can be assured that we have the power to deal with the demonic forces of darkness through all levels of their hierarchy. Confronting Satan himself at the very top might fall into another category. Some think Jude 9 may preclude such a thing, but this I will discuss when we come to the chapter dealing with the Epistles.

The Power of the Name

Perhaps the most outright indication that Jesus gives us power over all the manifestations of the enemy is the permission to use His name. Jesus said, "If you ask anything in My name, I will do it" (John 14:14). More specifically applying it to spiritual warfare: "In My name they will cast out demons" (Mark 16:17).

Much authority is vested in a name. For example, an American ambassador goes to Japan, not in his or her own name, but in the name of the president of the United States. Without the authority conferred through the president's permission to use his name, the ambassador would be nothing but another tourist. The name, however, cannot be used carelessly. If I went to Japan and announced that I was coming in the name of the president of the United States, I would not get past the immigration desk in the airport.

The seven sons of Sceva discovered the hard way that the name of Jesus was not another magical formula that could be used by anyone. They were impressed by the power Paul had in Ephesus through using Jesus' name, so they tried it. The demon said, "Jesus I know, and Paul I know; but who are you?" (Acts 19:15). Just to prove that the seven sons of Sceva were powerless, the evil spirit jumped on them, stripped them naked and sent them running out of the house.

The seven sons of Sceva had not been authorized to use Jesus' name, but we are. When we enter into battle, we do so in the name of the Son of God. Our authority is awesome if we use it with the wisdom God gives to guide us.

SUMMARY

Jesus brought the kingdom of God to earth to displace the long-standing kingdom of Satan. He ministered through a human nature like ours under the authority of God the Father. When He left, He transferred that authority to His disciples, and through His disciples to us. Jesus said, "All authority has been given to Me in heaven and on earth. Go therefore and make disciples of all the nations" (Matt. 28:18,19). Satan has from day one regarded that statement—the Great Commission—as a declaration of war.

For that reason, Jesus said the kingdom of God comes with violence, "and the violent take it by force" (11:12). One of the important ways we need to use this power if the kingdom of God is to advance over the earth is to overcome or bind the strongman. I will explain what that means in the next chapter.

■ REFLECTION QUESTIONS ■

1. Paul says that if we are ignorant of the devices of Satan, he will take advantage of us. Name two or three ways the devil could do that.
2. Discuss the differences in the way the people of God

dealt with the demonic in Old Testament times as opposed to New Testament times. Why was there a difference?

3. What does Ed Murphy mean by saying, "While our enemies are already defeated, they are not dead, not even sickly"? Is he giving too much credit to the devil?

4. If Jesus carried out His ministry on earth by the power of the Holy Spirit, does that mean He was not God? Why?

5. What do you think Jesus really meant when He said He would give His disciples authority "over all the power of the enemy"?

Notes

1. Michael Harper, *The Healings of Jesus* (Downers Grove, Ill.: InterVarsity Press, 1986), pp. 29-30.

2. Michael Green, *I Believe in Satan's Downfall* (Grand Rapids: William B. Eerdmans Publishing Company, 1981), pp. 26-27.

3. George Eldon Ladd, *A Theology of the New Testament* (Grand Rapids: William B. Eerdmans Publishing Company, 1983), pp. 66-67.

4. Susan R. Garrett, *The Demise of the Devil* (Minneapolis: Fortress Press, 1989), p. 37.

5. Ed Murphy, *The Handbook of Spiritual Warfare* (Nashville: Thomas Nelson Publishers, 1992), p. 290.

6. Ibid., p. 301.

7. Colin Brown, *That You May Believe* (Grand Rapids: William B. Eerdmans Publishing Company, 1985), p. 121.

8. Ibid., p. 97.

9. Francis Frangipane, "Our Authority in Christ," *Charisma* (July 1993): 40.

Binding the Strongman for Saving Souls

JESUS' LIFE FROM HIS BAPTISM TO HIS RESURRECTION WAS characterized by spiritual warfare. The kingdom of God He brought was resisted at every turn by Satan and his forces of darkness. When Jesus left the earth, He left His disciples with the same power source He used from beginning to end—the third Person of the Trinity, the Holy Spirit.

Jesus left His disciples to carry on the war. They would not be exempt from the same incessant struggle against the devil Jesus experienced. Jesus prayed to the Father, "I do not pray that You should take them out of the world, but that You should keep them from the evil one" (John 17:15).

As would be expected, Jesus had prepared His disciples for fighting and winning the war to which He had assigned them. Not only did He commission *them*, but I believe that, by implication, He also commissions *us* for the battle. In this chapter, I hope to clarify the ongoing responsibility Jesus has given to the Church at large to engage the enemy at all levels, including strategic-level spiritual warfare.

WHAT THE SPIRIT IS SAYING TO THE CHURCHES

Most committed Christians have a desire to hear "what the Spirit says to the churches." This well-known phrase is repeated seven times in the book of Revelation, in each of the seven epistles to the churches of Asia Minor found in Revelation 2 and 3. Let's tune in to what I believe is one of the most crucial things the Spirit is saying in our times.

Almost all the words coming directly from Jesus are found in the four Gospels, but not all. The most extensive passage containing Jesus' words outside of the Gospels are these two chapters in Revelation. The letters to the seven churches were written by "the First and the Last" (Rev. 1:17), "One like the Son of Man" (v. 13) and "the Alpha and the Omega" (v. 11). I stress this because these epistles give us an excellent starting place for understanding that Jesus actually *commissions* us to engage in strategic-level spiritual warfare. His words here are no less valid for those of us who desire to obey Him than those words we find in Matthew, Mark, Luke and John.

Besides the phrase, "He who has an ear, let him hear what the Spirit says to the churches," the only other actionlike expression in all seven epistles is the concept of *overcoming*. Take, for example, the letter to the church in Philadelphia, the only one of the seven churches, incidentally, to which Jesus had nothing negative to say. The church was doing several good things. The church had kept Jesus' word (see 3:8), had not denied His name (see v. 8) and had kept His command to persevere (see v. 10).

Jesus said the church in Philadelphia should do two things:

1. Hold fast. Jesus said, "Hold fast what you have" (v. 11). He was in all probability referring to those three good things they had been doing. "Holding fast" is an expression that starts in the present and looks back. What they had been doing right in the past should be continued. Tradition has its positive values that deserve to be maintained.

2. Overcome. "He who overcomes, I will make him a pillar in the temple of My God" (v. 12). Unlike holding fast to the good of the *past,* overcoming places the focus on the present toward the *future.* Believers should overcome now, and continue to overcome as time goes on. The significance of overcoming as a mandate for strategic-level spiritual warfare has been largely overlooked by biblical scholars, so I will take some time to explain how I believe it relates.

REWARDS FOR OVERCOMING

Not only does the word "overcome" appear in each of the seven epistles to the churches, but in every case a promise to those who take it seriously is attached as well. The following are the promises to the overcomers in the seven churches (italics mine):

- **Ephesus.** "To him who *overcomes* I will give to eat from the tree of life, which is in the midst of the Paradise of God" (2:7).
- **Smyrna.** "He who *overcomes* shall not be hurt by the second death" (v. 11).
- **Pergamos.** "To him who *overcomes* I will give some of the hidden manna to eat" (v. 17).
- **Thyatira.** "He who *overcomes,* and keeps My works until the end, to him I will give power over the nations" (v. 26).
- **Sardis.** "He who *overcomes* shall be clothed in white

garments, and I will not blot out his name from the Book of Life" (3:5).

- **Philadelphia.** "He who *overcomes,* I will make him a pillar in the temple of My God" (v. 12).
- **Laodicea.** "To him who *overcomes* I will grant to sit with Me on My throne" (v. 21).

Keep in mind that these instructions to *overcome* are made by Jesus after His death on the cross and after the resurrection. They therefore imply that church members in any age can and should play a crucial role in fulfilling the purposes of God in the world. Because of the weight Jesus apparently gives to *overcoming,* it is important for those of us who desire to be faithful to know as accurately as possible what Jesus means by the term.

Overcoming = *Nikao*

The Greek word for overcome is *nikao,* which means "to conquer." It is a warfare term commonly used by Greek people. It is not unusual, for example, for Greek parents to name a son "Nicholas" implying that the boy will be a winner. A popular brand of athletic shoes is called "Nike," designed to send the advertising message that those who wear Nike shoes will win the game.

In the New Testament, *nikao* often carries a more specific meaning. *The Dictionary of New Testament Theology,* edited by Colin Brown, says, "New Testament usage of the word group almost always presupposes the conflict between God or Christ and *opposing demonic powers*" (emphasis mine).[1] In the New Testament, therefore, overcoming is not just winning warfare in general, but also winning *spiritual warfare.*

Seven times in the book of Revelation, the risen Christ tells His people, by using the word *nikao,* that He wants them engaged in spiritual warfare. If they choose to obey Him, they can expect to receive substantial rewards from the Master.

Although the word *nikao* and its derivatives are used another 17 times in the New Testament outside of what we have just seen from Revelation 2 and 3, Jesus Himself is recorded as using it only twice more.

JESUS DEFEATS THE PRINCE OF THIS WORLD

Almost all Christians have taken comfort in Jesus' well-known words, "I have overcome [*nikao*] the world" (John 16:33). When He came to earth, Jesus invaded the kingdom of Satan whom He called the "ruler of this world" (see John 12:31; 14:30; 16:11). Jesus emerged the clear winner. He is the prototype of the *overcomer*. The cross of Christ sealed forever the fate of the devil and the hosts of hell. As I have stressed several times, we go into spiritual warfare with no question in our minds about who wins the war, and nothing could be more of a comfort and an assurance to those of us following in the footsteps of Jesus.

This, however, is not to be interpreted as meaning that the war has ended. Far from it. If the war had ended, somehow terminated by Jesus' victory on the cross, Jesus' repeated commands to us His followers to *overcome* would have little meaning. On the contrary, if we live our lives today as active and aggressive Christians we will find ourselves in constant warfare. Many years after Jesus died on the cross, Paul referred to Satan as "the god of this age" (2 Cor. 4:4), unusually strong terminology that should keep believers in any age from false complacency.

The only other time Jesus uses *nikao* in the New Testament is in Luke 11:21,22, when He speaks of *overcoming* the "strong man." This is a key text for understanding the concept that Jesus commissions us to do strategic-level spiritual warfare, so it will be worthwhile spending whatever time is necessary to explain the passage thoroughly and accurately.

OVERCOMING THE STRONGMAN

Luke 11 is a chapter about demons, beginning with verse 14 where Jesus casts a demon out of a mute man and the man speaks.

Carefully observing Jesus is a group of Pharisees. The Pharisees are not identified as such in Luke's account, but we learn who they are from the parallel passage in Matthew (see Matt. 12:24). These Pharisees, Jesus' enemies, were following Him around and trying to accumulate evidence on which to accuse and arrest Him. When they saw and heard the mute man speak for the first time in his life, there was no question in their minds, or in the minds of anyone else watching, that Jesus had ministered in extraordinary power. The question the Pharisees raised, a legitimate question incidentally, was: "Where did He get that power?"

The Pharisees' answer was a logical conclusion from their particular perspective. They knew they had witnessed supernatural power, but they did not believe that Jesus was the Son of God, so they automatically ruled out the possibility of that power being the power of God. The alternative hypothesis would be that the power came from the invisible world of *darkness*, so they attributed the healing to the power of Beelzebub.

Notice what the Pharisees did. The event began with ground-level spiritual warfare, namely Jesus casting a demon out of a person. By mentioning Beelzebub, however, the Pharisees escalated the scenario to strategic-level spiritual warfare.

Beelzebub and Satan

Beelzebub is well known as one of the highest ranking principalities in the invisible world of darkness. He is so powerful that some confuse him with Satan himself. Beelzebub is known as "the ruler of the demons" (Luke 11:15), but he rules these demons under the high command of Satan. Beelzebub is not Satan. It would be like characterizing a general in the army as the "ruler of soldiers," understanding that there is also a commander-in-chief to whom the general reports.

I am aware that this is somewhat of a delicate point because many biblical scholars could be cited who have assumed and even argued that Beelzebub is simply an alias for Satan. They frequently assume the same thing about other principalities specifically named in the New Testament such as Wormwood (Rev. 8:11) or Abaddon, also known as Apollyon (9:11). I personally do not think they have arrived at an accurate conclusion. I suspect that their hypotheses may have been strongly influenced by their paradigms, paradigms that, in many cases, have not encouraged them to engage in firsthand research into the world of darkness. Many who have not developed independent expertise in demonology simply rely on the opinions of other scholars who in turn may or may not have expressed their opinions apart from personal expertise in that rather specialized field.

As far as I can see, the Bible does not provide us with sufficiently clear evidence to prove either the point that Beelzebub *is* the same person as Satan or that he is *not.* Our conclusions either way are most likely based much more on certain assumptions we bring to the text rather than an exegesis of the text itself. I readily admit that, and I would hope that those who see it differently would admit it as well. Once we do agree on that point, however, we are then left to explain where our particular assumptions originated. If and when we do, the reasons for our differences may become much clearer.

In chapter 2, I deal in some depth with epistemology, probing the question of how we know what we know. In it I suggest that it may be possible to receive selected, but valid, information from the world of darkness itself. I am careful to stress strongly that discernment is needed while attempting to do this because evil spirits are by nature deceivers and they must be treated as hostile witnesses. Nevertheless, certain people such as shamans, witch doctors, practitioners of Eastern religions, New Age gurus or professors of the occult on university faculties are examples of the kind of people who may have much more extensive knowledge of the spirit world than most Christians have. Some of the information they furnish is accurate. Many of them are not only intelligent, but they are also sincere people of integrity. Particularly former occult practitioners who have been converted to Jesus Christ and filled with the Holy Spirit can reveal valuable things about the spirit world that may not have been recorded by the biblical writers.

Although I argued this point in chapter 2 as strongly as I could, I am well aware that some readers will remain unconvinced. That is their prerogative, and I respect it; but back to whether Beelzebub is to be equated with Satan. The reason I have concluded he is a principality under the command of Satan is that the consensus of written materials I have examined and of personal interviews I have conducted with experts about the occult lead me to that judgment. I have seen those who know this smile somewhat patronizingly at my apparent naiveté when I suggest that Beelzebub may be Satan. They generally know very well who the notorious Beelzebub is, and to ask whether he is Satan seems absurd to many who operate professionally in the spirit world.

Critics who think I have used an inadequate source of information to arrive at my conclusion will need to argue against it by contending that their alternative source of information, showing that Beelzebub is indeed an alias for Satan, is a superior one to mine. Neither of us, I repeat, has an air-tight *biblical* case for our position.

Defeating Demons with the Finger of God

I believe defeating demons with the finger of God is an important point because it helps us understand the precise context in which Jesus makes His remarks in Luke 11:20-22. Responding to the Pharisees, Jesus affirms that He did not cast out demons with the power of Beelzebub but rather with the "finger of God." What is the "finger of God"? To answer that question we go to the parallel passage in Matthew 12 where Jesus said, "I cast out demons by the Spirit of God" (v. 28). The "finger of God" is therefore a synonym for the Holy Spirit.

Jesus said to the Pharisees, "But if I cast out demons with the finger of God, surely the kingdom of God has come upon you" (Luke 11:20). This prepares the way for the statement about the strongman, a statement crucial to my argument in this chapter that Jesus commissions us to do strategic-level spiritual warfare.

THE POWER OF THE STRONGMAN

Jesus adds, "When a strong man, fully armed, guards his own palace, his goods are in peace" (Luke 11:21). Notice some important points about this statement:

- *The "strong man" is a reference to Beelzebub,* a high-ranking demonic principality. The inference, however, is that it could be *any* principality serving under the rulership of Satan. In my mind this is a description of a classic territorial spirit. It is one of the key teachings of Jesus related directly to world evangelization, and therefore is more interesting to me professionally than it might be to some others.
- *This principality possesses "goods."* What are the most precious goods to a territorial spirit? Obviously people,

and more specifically unsaved souls. A primary desire of any ruler of demons is, through any means possible, to keep people in spiritual captivity. When the Bible speaks of people "whose minds the god of this age has blinded, who do not believe" (2 Cor. 4:4), it must be understood that Satan does not and cannot personally blind the minds of millions of people, but that he delegates it to various members of his hierarchy of evil. It is the first assignment of every demonic strongman to keep as many people as possible in spiritual darkness so that they ultimately go to hell.

- *The principality has some kind of armament.* If nothing happens to this armament and he remains "fully armed," then he is home free because "his goods are in peace." The unsaved people under his control will not be saved. Satan will rejoice.

This is an awesome point. When I think of the people in my city and in my nation and in unreached people groups who have been in spiritual darkness for generations and in some cases for millennia, I become upset. Territorial spirits or "strong men" have succeeded throughout history in sending enormous populations of people to hell. In our generation, they currently have the upper hand with about 3 billion men, women and children. They shouldn't be getting away with this! It certainly is not God's Plan A for these lost people. The spirits are able to keep people in captivity because their armament has until now remained intact, at least according to what Jesus says.

Who Is Stronger than the Strongman?
Can something be done about this horrendous situation? Definitely it can. Jesus goes on to say, "But when a stronger than he comes upon him and overcomes him, he takes from him all his armor in which he trusted, and divides his spoils" (Luke

11:22). When this is understood in the context I have just developed, I don't know of any more important statement of Jesus relating to the actual nuts and bolts of evangelism. Let's look at it:

- The word "overcome" is *nikao*. This is the command-like verb that appears seven times in the book of Revelation, accompanied each time with an extravagant promise. Those who love Jesus and want to obey Him will desire to be, among other things, *overcomers*.
- What will *overcome* the strongman? Someone "stronger than he." Who is stronger than a high-ranking demonic principality? Certainly no human being is stronger. Martin Luther had it right when he wrote in his song "A Mighty Fortress Is Our God" the line referring to Satan: "On earth is not his equal."

Some rather hastily may say, "The stronger one is Jesus." But this is not accurate. Jesus certainly is stronger, but He was

---

Jesus assured His disciples that the same power He used while on earth would be fully available to them. And it was up to them to move out and do the work of evangelism.

---

not referring to Himself in this teaching. He was referring to the "finger of God"—the third Person of the Trinity, the Holy Spirit. As I detailed in the last chapter, Jesus Himself cast out demons, not as the second Person of the Trinity, but through the power of the Holy Spirit in Him.

Only the Holy Spirit can overcome the territorial spirits, destroy their armor and release the captives under their wicked control. Where is the Holy Spirit today? He is in us who have been born again and have asked God to fill us with the Holy Spirit. Jesus' last words ever spoken directly to His disciples were, "But you shall receive power when the Holy Spirit has come upon you; and you shall be witnesses to Me" (Acts 1:8). Here we find spiritual power tied in directly with evangelism. Jesus assured His disciples that the same power He used while on earth would be fully available to them. And it was up to them to move out and do the work of evangelism.

One high-priority use of this Holy Spirit power by those who wish to serve Jesus in evangelism is to overcome whatever strongman may be holding a particular neighborhood or city or people group in spiritual captivity. Nothing I know of could be more important for winning the lost. If we are not satisfied with the fruit of our current evangelistic activities, whatever they may be, strategic-level spiritual warfare might at least be worthy of some experimentation. Possibly a strongman needs to be bound by the power of the Holy Spirit given to us.

The word *nikao,* or "overcome," is used in Luke 11, but another word is used in the parallel passage in Matthew 12: the Greek verb *deo,* "to bind." There Jesus is quoted as saying, "How can one enter a strong man's house and plunder his goods, unless he first *binds* the strong man?" (v. 29, emphasis mine). This means that the two words can be used interchangeably. In Christian circles the phrase "binding the strongman" is considerably more common than "overcoming the strongman," but they mean the same thing. I chose to use "binding" in the title of this chapter because *deo* is used by Jesus in another significant passage relating directly to strategic-level spiritual warfare. Let's look at it.

Binding and Loosing

Jesus picks up on the word *deo,* or "binding," in the context of what some biblical scholars have regarded as arguably the most significant event in Jesus' life between His baptism and His crucifixion. In Matthew 16:19 Jesus says, "Whatever you *bind* on earth will *be bound* in heaven, and whatever you loose on earth will be loosed in heaven" (emphasis mine).

This concept of "binding and loosing" is the climax of a series of three rapid-fire revelations featured in Matthew 16:

1. The Messiah has come (vv. 13-17). In Caesarea Philippi, Jesus asked His disciples who people were saying He was. They mentioned names such as John the Baptist and Elijah. Then Jesus said, "Who do you say that I am?" Peter, speaking for the group, said, "You are the Christ [the Messiah], the Son of the living God" (v. 16). This was the first time, after about a year and a half with Jesus, the disciples recognized for sure that Jesus was the long-awaited Jewish Messiah.

2. The Church has come (v. 18). Only after they had known who Jesus really *was* could He reveal to the disciples precisely *why* He came to earth. For the very first time, Jesus mentions the Church: "On this rock I will build My church." The one tangible thing Jesus desired to leave on earth as a result of His ministry was the Church. He loved the Church so much that He called it His bride!

At the same time, Jesus recognized that the growth of the Church in the world would not go unopposed. Multiplying churches would involve spiritual warfare from beginning to end. In the same breath with which Jesus said He would build His Church He added, "and the gates of Hades shall not prevail against it." Satan would rise up and unleash all the demons of hell in an attempt to prevent world evangelization and church growth. The devil would try to quench the spread of the gospel, but he would not ultimately succeed.

3. The kingdom has come (v. 19). This was not a new revelation for the disciples, for Jesus had been preaching the kingdom from day one, and the disciples had themselves been preaching the kingdom. Now Jesus, for the first time, connects the kingdom with the Church and directly with the spiritual warfare involved in church growth. The gates of hell would constantly produce obstacles to the spread of the gospel, but these gates would not be able to withstand. How could they be opened?

Jesus said to His disciples, "I will give you the keys of the kingdom of heaven" (v. 19). This means that the disciples themselves would be the primary agents to move the kingdom of God through these formidable gates of the enemy. It is not something God would choose to do sovereignly, although He could if He wished, but rather a task that would directly involve the initiative of the disciples. The resources for the task would be provided by God, but the *use* of the resources would be up to the discretion of the disciples.

What, then, are the keys that would have the power to unlock and penetrate the gates of hell? They are *binding and loosing*. "Whatever you bind on earth will be bound in heaven, and whatever you loose on earth will be loosed in heaven" (v. 19). Binding and loosing are directly related to the advance of God's kingdom through the outreach of Jesus' disciples, whether they be first-century disciples or twentieth-century disciples.

We must not underestimate the magnitude of the authority Jesus delegates and entrusts to His disciples through binding and loosing. Jesus refers to it again in Matthew 18, this time not in the context of world evangelization, but in the context of church discipline. Jesus delegates to church leaders authority in judging and punishing Christians who sin and refuse to repent of their sin (see v. 18). Here we have one instance of binding and loosing connected to evangelism and another, two chapters later, connected to Christian nurturing. The use of such power apparently was intended to be broad across the spectrum of the ministry of the Church.

Synchronizing Earth with Heaven

Our *New King James* translation, "Whatever you bind on earth will be bound in heaven," fails to convey an extremely significant nuance of the original Greek. The more literal translation would be: "Whatever you bind on earth *will have been bound* in heaven and whatever you loose *will have been loosed* in heaven." This means that an essential synchronization exists between activities on earth and activities in heaven. And it establishes the crucial sequence: heaven *first*, then earth.

This reminds us once again of the absolute necessity of hearing from God in the ministry of spiritual warfare. In chapter 2, I discussed the concept of *rhema*, or a direct word of God to us. At this point the personal prayer life of one who would attempt to bind the strongman is essential. Through prayer we draw into intimacy with the Father so that we can most clearly hear His voice to us. Through our personal prayer lives, and also through association with other members of the Body of Christ who have gifts of intercession and prophecy and discernment of spirits, we can know what has or has not been bound in heaven. It is foolish, as well as dangerous, to confront the enemy by binding and loosing outside the will of God or outside His timing.

I have observed many efforts of binding and loosing, which, although done with high purposes and out of a good heart, have not produced satisfactory results either short term or long term. Many of these ineffective initiatives have been based on the mistaken premise that *we* first choose what we want to bind, and *then* heaven will follow suit. That is not the way it works.

Even when it is the will of God that a certain territorial spirit be bound, efforts to do so might not succeed for yet other reasons. The power of the Holy Spirit is not some magic charm activated by a certain formula or by screaming in a loud voice or through a crowd that has been raised to a high emotional pitch. For one thing, those who desire to lead effective spiritual warfare must themselves be holy before the Lord, have no unconfessed sin and be free of carnal motives. For another, we must be realistic enough and humble enough to admit that certain spiritual powers could be too mighty for us to handle at a certain time and in a certain place. I strongly suspect that such was the case when Paul went to Athens as I explain in my book *Blazing the Way* (Regal Books).

Let's Keep Our Focus

Before I leave this subject, I want to make sure we are keeping our focus, particularly about three important points.

> **Let's remember that binding the strongman never saved a soul. Lost souls are saved only through preaching the gospel of the cross of Christ and His resurrection, followed by repentance and allegiance to Jesus Christ as Lord and Savior.**

First, let's avoid becoming overly fascinated by the demonic. Spiritual warfare on any level is not to be regarded as an end in itself. The end is the fulfillment of the will of God in people, in families, in churches, in communities, in nations and in entire people groups. Evil spirits should be seen simply as obstacles that must be removed. On the strategic level, binding territorial spirits is a means toward winning the lost.

Second, let's remember that binding the strongman never saved a soul. Lost souls are saved only through preaching the gospel of the cross of Christ and His resurrection, followed by repentance and allegiance to Jesus Christ as Lord and Savior. Binding the strongman helps prepare the way for this because if the armor of the dominating principality remains intact, "his goods are in peace" and his spiritual captives have great difficulty *hearing* the gospel we may be trying to communicate (see 2 Cor. 4:3,4). When the strongman is *overcome (nikao)* or *bound (deo)*, only then are the captives released and for the first time they can hear the gospel and then make their personal choices whether they will accept Jesus Christ or not.

I want to stress this, because some of my critics have accused me of suggesting that spiritual warfare is proposed as a new way of doing evangelism. I can see how they might come to that conclusion because I have not always taken the time to explain the point I am making here. If they were right, I would be the first one to confess I am out of focus.

My contention is simply that spiritual warfare should be incorporated as a *part*, and an important part at that, of our evangelistic *process*. In no way does it substitute for the hard work of identifying with lost people, learning the language, contextualizing the message, preaching the gospel, planting churches, nurturing believers, translating the Bible, ministering to social needs and selecting and training leaders. What I am saying is that everything I have just discussed will be greatly facilitated and immeasurably more successful if the power of the enemy to prevent them is first neutralized to whatever extent possible through strategic-level spiritual warfare.

The Strongman Can Return

Third, let's remember that what is *gained* through spiritual warfare must be *maintained* through spiritual warfare. In all the study I have done of the realm of darkness, I have never found what to me is a satisfactory answer to exactly what happens to demons when we cast them out. We don't kill them. They leave, but where they actually go remains a mystery to me. The power of territorial spirits can be neutralized, but obviously not forever.

Right after Jesus teaches about overcoming the strongman in Luke 11, He goes on to say that when spirits are cast out of people they go through dry places, but they have a continuing desire to return to wherever they have been. Jesus is speaking here of demons cast out of people, but the same could apply, I think, to demons on any level, including territorial spirits. They can actually return if they find the place "swept and put in order" (v. 25). I take this to mean that the person or the place the evil spirit has vacated has not subsequently been filled with the presence of God as it should be, not only permitting the spirit to return, but also to bring with it "seven other spirits more wicked than himself" (v. 26).

A vivid case study of this is Europe, which now calls itself "post Christian." I love to drive through the Swiss Alps, where around almost every curve appears a neat village in a picturesque valley. The most prominent piece of architecture in a village is almost invariably the Christian church, which is centrally located, with its steeple and its cross lifted high above all other buildings. At one time God was truly glorified by virtually the entire population of the village. His kingdom was present, and whatever demonic principalities might have dominated that region for millennia before the coming of Christianity had been pushed back and had their armors severely damaged. This is no longer the case. Only a tiny handful of people in those villages are born again today. The great majority of the people there die and go to hell, sad to say. The enemy gets much more glory than God, although the church buildings are still there and maintained by public funds.

One of the reasons evil spirits succeed in returning is that the strongholds on which they had based their legal rights to control that area and its people have not been thoroughly removed.[2] We know a great deal more about this than we did previously, largely through our understanding that a crucial part of much strategic-level spiritual warfare should be identificational repentance. Through accurate and sensitive spiritual mapping we can identify strongholds rooted in unremitted sins of past generations and we now understand the ways and means of dealing with those sins of the past in our own generation. Our principal guide at the moment for doing this is John Dawson's important book *Healing America's Wounds* (Regal Books).

SUMMARY

Nothing is closer to the heart of Jesus than winning the lost. The last command He gave to His disciples was the Great Commission to preach the gospel to every creature and make disciples in every nation or people group (see Matt. 28:19,20). The Great Commission will continue to be Jesus' highest priority until it is completed. In moving out to reach the lost, Jesus has instructed us to *overcome* or to *bind the strongman*. Part of the Great Commission is Jesus' specific commission to His disciples and to us today to engage proactively in strategic-level spiritual warfare.

▬ REFLECTION QUESTIONS ▬

1. Why does this chapter say that the biblical word "overcome" really means "do spiritual warfare"?
2. Discuss whether you think Beelzebub is the same as

Satan or a different spiritual principality. Give your reasons.

3. If "binding and loosing" are keys to advancing the kingdom of God, should missionaries today practice it? How?

4. What is your understanding of the literal translation of the Greek, "Whatever you bind on earth will have been bound in heaven"?

5. Once a strongman is bound or demons are expelled, what can be done to keep them from returning?

Notes

1. W. Gunther, *"Nikao," The New International Dictionary of New Testament Theology*, Vol. 1, ed. Colin Brown (Grand Rapids: Zondervan Publishing House, 1975), p. 650.

2. Courtroom scenes in Scripture dealing with Satan and demons suggest that Satan must seek legal rights to do what he does on earth (Job 1—2; Ps. 82; Rev. 12:10).

How Peter Dealt with Principalities

I F JESUS COMMISSIONED HIS DISCIPLES TO DO STRATEGIC-level spiritual warfare, what happened after He left? Did the disciples actually do it?

WHAT DID THE APOSTLES DO?

What the apostles did is a question foremost in the minds of many who are cautious about, or skeptical of, strategic-level spiritual warfare. In chapter 3, I quoted a person called "Critic A" as objecting to strategic-level spiritual warfare by stating: "How can strategic-level spiritual warfare be God's clearly biblical method when the apostles themselves are not seen exercising that pre-rogative?"

My approach in that chapter was to argue that in the hypothetical case the apostles might *not* have done strategic-level spiritual warfare, that in itself would not necessarily preclude the Holy Spirit moving us out in strategic-level spiritual warfare today. I mentioned there that the Holy Spirit has subsequently led us to do many other things we have no record of the apostles doing either, such as referring to God as "the Trinity," celebrating Christmas and Easter, freeing the slaves, casting demons out of Christians and designating Sunday as our primary day of worship, just to name a few. As I said, I do not agree that the so-called "apostles' example principle of hermeneutics" is a useful principle, because virtually no one has ever been consistent in its application.

I use the phrase "hypothetical case" because furthermore, I do not agree with those who might think we have no records of the apostles doing strategic-level spiritual warfare. I will share the examples I believe I have found, particularly in the ministries of Peter and Paul, in this chapter and the next two. Naturally, the examples will come primarily from the book of Acts, the chief historical record we have of the ministry of the apostles.

THE BOOK OF ACTS

The book of Acts is particularly interesting to me. If there is a New Testament book on which I could say I have specialized the most, it would be Acts. I have taught the book of Acts for 15 years. In doing so, I have studied many commentaries and other literature related to Acts in much detail, but as time went on I became more and more frustrated. I was continually finding and teaching important things in Acts that the most popular commentators had scarcely mentioned, particularly in the areas of power ministries and missiology. The material was provided for us by Luke, the author of Acts, but the mental filters of the commentators apparently had been blocking out some of the material.

For years I was hoping that a new commentary would be

published that would adequately cover these crucial areas, but I found none. So I considered writing one of my own. I did a library search and found that no fewer than 1,398 commentaries about Acts had already been published, so I felt I had to have pretty good reasons to justify writing commentary number 1,399. I finally justified it on the basis that virtually every commentator affirms that Acts 1:8 provides for us the major themes that run through the whole book: "But you shall receive power when the Holy Spirit has come upon you; and you shall be witnesses to Me in Jerusalem, and in all Judea and Samaria, and to the end of the earth." The two emphases here are *power ministries* and *cross-cultural missions* or *missiology*. None of the commentators I have yet read, however, had acquired professional expertise in both of those areas.

EXAMPLES OF STRATEGIC-LEVEL WARFARE

By the providence of God, for some time I have been teaching several graduate-level courses at Fuller Theological Seminary related to both power ministries and missiology. So I launched out and wrote the Acts commentary in three volumes: *Spreading the Fire, Lighting the World* and *Blazing the Way* (Regal Books). As I did, I looked for, and I believe I found five examples of the ministry of the apostles that can be interpreted as strategic-level spiritual warfare. They include (1) Peter versus Simon Magus, (2) Peter versus Herod, (3) Paul versus Bar-Jesus (or Elymas), (4) Paul versus the Python Spirit and (5) Paul versus Diana (or Artemis) of the Ephesians.

I do not hesitate to admit at the outset that each of these events could conceivably be interpreted as something other than strategic-level spiritual warfare. Most commentaries do. The possibility that Peter and Paul might have been engaging such beings as "territorial spirits" had never entered the minds of most commentators. Thus, I brought a set of questions to the text that apparently was not on their agendas, and I believe I have found reasonably good answers. I will present my evidence as cogently as I can, but I hope with great respect for those who might beg to disagree. Although I may not always succeed, I want to balance strong convictions with deep humility. Heaven forbid, but let's admit it: I may even be wrong!

Some critics have argued that if one or all five of these incidents really turned out to be strategic-level spiritual warfare, the examples would still be too few to build a strong case for doing it today. I don't believe this line of thinking holds much water. If it did, they could also argue that we shouldn't teach the virgin birth of Christ because we don't have one example of the apostles teaching this important doctrine. We also have only one example in the book of Acts of Paul preaching justification by faith, but I will expand on that in the next chapter.

THE PATTERN OF POWER

It is possible today to make a random visit to the first 10 churches one might find by driving through the streets of a given city, and to discover that in none of them could the church leadership cite one miracle, one case of supernatural healing or one demon cast out through the ministry of the church in the past five years. That is because the ordinary pattern of our American Christian lifestyle today is relatively powerless. At the same time, each of these churches could probably report 52 or perhaps 104 meetings during the past year in which the featured event was a sermon. Our churches tend to stress the *word* much more than the *deed.*

This carries over into the way many of us interpret the Bible. For example, when Jesus sent out His disciples on their own for the first time, the initial thing He did was to call the 12 and give "them power over unclean spirits, to cast them out, and to heal all kinds of sickness and all kinds of disease" (Matt. 10:1).

Then He told them to "preach, saying, 'The kingdom of heaven is at hand'" (v. 7). That was the *word.* Jesus, in the same breath, also commanded them to "heal the sick, cleanse the

---

The apostles took Jesus literally, and it never entered their minds to separate deeds from words, or power ministries from gospel preaching. They were two parts making up one and the same evangelistic method.

---

lepers, raise the dead, cast out demons" (v. 8). That was the accompanying *deed.* Our tendency today, however, is to read that as if it were ancient history and not to be a bit concerned if nothing along these lines ever seems to happen in our churches. Preaching a sermon is enough!

This was not the case with the apostles in the book of Acts. They took Jesus literally, and it never entered their minds to separate deeds from words, or power ministries from gospel preaching. They were two parts making up one and the same evangelistic method. Especially when the apostles preached to the Gentiles, the pattern was first demonstrating the power of God, and then preaching the word, leading people to Christ and multiplying churches. The *deeds* were what prepared people for and what later confirmed the *word.* In Iconium, for example, "the Lord...was bearing witness to the word of His grace, *granting signs and wonders* to be done by [Paul and Barnabas's] hands" (Acts 14:3, emphasis mine). When the apostles later appeared before the Jerusalem Council, "All the multitude kept silent and listened to Barnabas and Paul declaring how many *miracles and wonders* God had worked through them among the Gentiles" (15:12, emphasis mine). This was normal for church-planting evangelists in the first century and, as we saw in chapter 4, for several centuries to follow.

My point is that ministering with supernatural power was so much a part of the *assumed* pattern of evangelism in those days that Luke would have little reason to make a special issue of it, as I have been forced by my critics to do in this book. I think I am justified, then, in assuming that the apostles would in all likelihood have actually done much more strategic-level spiritual warfare than we are specifically told by Luke. I think they really believed that Jesus had given them authority "over *all* the power of the enemy" (Luke 10:19), and that they regularly dealt with demons on all levels, not limiting themselves simply to the ground level as some attempt to argue.

Now let's look more closely at Peter.

PETER WAS FILLED WITH THE HOLY SPIRIT

As we saw in the last chapter, the only one stronger than the strongman is the Holy Spirit. Without the Holy Spirit we are powerless in the invisible world. Peter knew this, and he had the necessary power—He was filled with the Holy Spirit.

Peter was one of those who had obeyed Jesus when He said to His disciples, "Tarry in the city of Jerusalem until you are endued with power from on high" (Luke 24:49). He, along with the others in the Upper Room, "continued with one accord in prayer and supplication" (Acts 1:14). After praying for 10 days, the Holy Spirit came as promised, and on the Day of Pentecost "they were all filled with the Holy Spirit" (2:4).

Apparently, this filling of the Holy Spirit was not a once-in-a-lifetime event that would then qualify Peter as a "Spirit-filled" believer for the rest of his life. The filling of the Spirit is something that must frequently be repeated throughout the life of a committed believer, some say as often as every day. In Peter's case, it was only a few days after Pentecost when Luke again writes that "they were all filled with the Holy Spirit" (4:31), empowering Peter and others to preach more boldly.

If Jesus, the second Person of the Trinity, needed the power of the Holy Spirit to confront the powers and cast out demons, so much more do we need the same power. I recommend that anyone who does not know how to be filled with the Holy Spirit should avoid attempting strategic-level spiritual warfare.

Actually, being filled with the Holy Spirit is not complicated. Just ask God to do it, and He will. Jesus said, "If a son asks for bread from any father among you, will he give him a stone?...How much more will your heavenly Father give the Holy Spirit to those who ask Him!" (Luke 11:11,13). I am not talking about some unforgettable emotional experience, going forward in a meeting, seeing some bright light or falling on the floor, although all of these are often used by God for bringing believers in touch with the Holy Spirit. Apart from all that, just asking God to do it is enough, because He wants to do it and He will.

Obviously, Peter was filled with the Holy Spirit when he healed the lame man at the Temple gate, when he prophesied to Ananias and Sapphira and when people were healed instantly when only his shadow passed over them. We can be confident that He was equally filled with the Holy Spirit when he and John were sent by the other apostles in Jerusalem to check out the ministry of Philip, the evangelist, in Samaria.

THE BATTLE IN SAMARIA

Philip has gone down in history as the first authentic cross-cultural missionary. Paul and Barnabas are sometimes thought of in this role, but they came along about 14 years later. Jesus and the apostles had limited their preaching in the beginning to Jews—first Hebrew Jews and then Hellenistic Jews. Philip was the first to move out of the Jewish culture and evangelize a non-Jewish people group—the Samaritans.

Philip did what any first-century evangelist would have done—he ministered both in *word* and in *deed*. He "preached Christ to them" (Acts 8:5). "And the multitudes with one accord heeded the things spoken by Philip" (v. 6). Why did they listen to and believe what the evangelist was preaching? Was it that Philip was especially eloquent? Was it his magnetic personality? Did he have impeccable logic? All of these things might have been true of Philip, but none of them is what Luke chooses to stress when he tells the story. Luke informs us that they accepted Philip's message because they were "hearing and seeing the miracles which he did" (v. 6). Philip believed in and was practicing what my friend John Wimber would call, to use the title of one of his best-selling books, *Power Evangelism* (Harper-Collins).

I am particularly interested at the first outward manifestation of power evangelism Luke relates as a part of Philip's extraordinarily successful evangelistic ministry: "For unclean spirits, crying with a loud voice, came out of many who were possessed" (v. 7). Luke later mentions that paralyzed and lame people were also healed, but the headline here is spiritual warfare. Philip was a practicing "overcomer." On behalf of God, he was causing great havoc in the demonic world.

It seems a bit strange when Luke says that the Samaritans were *hearing* the miracles Philip did, until we come to that part about demons screaming in loud voices as they were coming out of people. I can understand this because I have witnessed acts of mass deliverance in Argentina in which I, along with everyone else present, have heard loud and unmistakable shouts of many demons at the same time in the meetings of the evangelist, Carlos Annacondia. I can imagine that Philip's meetings in Samaria would have been similar.

I have friends who dislike those kinds of meetings. I met

one well-known citywide evangelist who told me he habitually makes an agreement with the demonic powers in the cities in which he ministers: "You leave me alone, and I'll leave you alone!" He puts a high value on decorum and orderliness. Such was not the case with Philip. I can well imagine that His meetings were noisy, boisterous and probably somewhat messy.

Philip, however, reaped tremendous fruit: "But when they believed Philip as he preached the things concerning the kingdom of God and the name of Jesus Christ, both men and women were baptized" (v. 12).

Help Comes from Jerusalem

Whether Philip thought he needed help from the apostles in Jerusalem we are not told. The church leaders in Jerusalem thought so, however, because for the first time they were faced with a crucial missiological question that would subsequently plague them for a generation: Could non-Jews, such as Samaritans, be legitimately baptized without first becoming Jews and agreeing to keep the law of Moses?

By now, Jerusalem was full of "Messianic Jews," but could there also be any such thing as "Messianic Samaritans"? Peter and John went to Samaria from Jerusalem to investigate, and in their judgment it would be acceptable to baptize Samaritans. Along with this missiological issue, though, they also had to deal with an issue involving spiritual warfare.

As we have seen, ground-level spiritual warfare was very much a part of Philip's initial evangelistic methodology. Many converts in Samaria had been personally and dramatically delivered from demons. Spiritual captives had been freed, probably a large number of them from what we read. In the church I belong to here in the United States, I rarely, if ever, hear the testimony of a person who has been saved through getting rid of evil spirits. On the other hand, I have listened to pastors from India and Nepal, just as two examples, who have assured me that virtually every single member of their churches and other churches round about have been outwardly and knowingly delivered from demons as a part of their conversion experiences. Although it may be the exception in the United States, it is the rule in India and Nepal. It was more than likely the rule in Samaria also.

Some will observe that Philip's doing ground-level spiritual warfare did not necessarily mean he was involved either in occult-level or strategic-level spiritual warfare. This could be true, but I personally think we see them both here, particularly after the arrival of Peter and John—especially Peter who seems to be the main player.

PETER VERSUS SIMON THE SORCERER

Luke devotes about half of his entire account of the evangelization of the Samaritans to the power encounter with Simon the Sorcerer, who is sometimes called Simon Magus. It can be understood, therefore, as the primary event that opened the Samaritans to the gospel. This is not to imply that Philip's "preaching Christ to them" or healing "many who were paralyzed and lame" were unimportant. Both were very important. It is to imply, however, that somehow the power of the strongman who had been holding the Samaritans in spiritual captivity had been considerably weakened.

In my opinion, such is not necessarily the case when the spiritual harvest consists of a few converts here and there and perhaps a struggling church or two. For years my wife, Doris, and I were engaged in that kind of relatively fruitless missionary work in Bolivia. Paul's evangelistic ministry in Athens furnishes another excellent example. In neither case was the territorial spirit or strongman assigned by the evil one to those people groups greatly disturbed. His armor, for the most part, apparently had remained intact, and therefore his goods (the lost souls) were intact, despite Paul's well-meaning efforts.

Such, however, was not the case in Samaria. Philip was experiencing what missiologists refer to as a "people movement," and not a few, but "multitudes with one accord" were coming to Christ. Paul said that when the gospel is *not* going forth as hoped, it is because "the god of this age has blinded [the minds of those] who do not believe" (2 Cor. 4:4). Apparently in Samaria, this spiritual blinder had been removed just far enough so that "the gospel of the glory of Christ, who is the image of God, should shine on them" (v. 4).

It seems, then, that something had been happening in Samaria in the higher realms of the invisible world of darkness. The enemy was in disarray. Much of this was undoubtedly caused by ministries to people involving healing and salvation and deliverance, all of which are embarrassments to Satan. On the other hand, the ground-level activity could have succeeded to such an extent only if the strongman had been bound. The enemy's goods certainly were "not remaining in peace," to use Jesus' words. We need to remind ourselves that the world of darkness is not three separate compartments, but an interrelated whole.

The appearance of Simon the Sorcerer may give us a clue about who might have been the strongman over Samaria. The magician might have been empowered directly by the so-called "territorial spirit" over the area.

THE REALITY OF TERRITORIAL SPIRITS

Although evil spirits commonly are assigned by their higher-ups to demonize certain people, other dark angels have been given a broader jurisdiction. For want of a better term, we have been calling them "territorial spirits" in recent years. The existence, identity and activities of territorial spirits are particularly well known by those who live in or travel frequently to the Third World.

Some, however, deny their existence. In a standard missiological journal, which I choose not to cite by name, a recent article appeared in which the author argues as strongly as he can against the "ontological" reality of territorial spirits. He thinks that, though some people in the Third World may *perceive* such things exist, they do not really (*ontologically*) exist, because he cannot find such a teaching in the Bible. I was fascinated to see that in the same issue of the same journal another author analyzes the fastest-growing churches in Africa—those churches seeing the largest number of converts year after year. One of the reasons he gives for their dynamic evangelistic ministry is that the church leaders affirm, without any question at all, that the spiritual powers that manifest through traditional religions are real, not simply perceived. Those African church leaders would be surprised to hear that some in the Western world think the existence of territorial spirits is a subject for debate. To them, it would be like debating whether water flows downhill.

In his excellent book *City of God; City of Satan,* Robert Linthicum, an urbanologist, provides for us a vivid description of how a territorial spirit named Kali keeps the city of Calcutta, India, in spiritual captivity. He tells how he observed young men, day after day, during the annual festival to this Hindu goddess, pledging their very souls to her in hope of receiving material goods to break their vicious cycle of poverty.

"Who is Kali who gathers souls of young men?" asks Linthicum. "She is the goddess of darkness, evil and destruction in the Hindu pantheon. This is the goddess to whom the entire city is dedicated."[1]

Territorial Spirits in the Scriptures

The Bible teaches that the things we today call "territorial spirits" do exist. A key passage is found in Daniel 10 where the "prince of Persia" and the "prince of Greece" are mentioned specifically (see v. 20). These are, quite evidently, seen as "ontological" realities, powerful enough in the invisible world to have delayed Michael, an angel sent by God Himself to deliver an answer to prayer to Daniel, for no less than 21 days. C. F. Keil and Franz Delitzch, Old Testament scholars, conclude that the "prince of Persia" is indeed the demon of the Persian kingdom. They refer to him as "the supernatural spiritual power standing behind the national gods, which we may properly call *the guardian spirit of the kingdom*" (emphasis mine).[2]

Following the reading of the Septuagint and the Qumran versions (which are hidden in some of our English versions), Deuteronomy 32:8 says, "When the Most High divided the inheritance to the nations, when He separated the sons of Adam, He set the boundaries of the peoples *according to the number of the angels of God*" (emphasis mine). F. F. Bruce, the famous biblical scholar, comments, "This reading implies that the administration of various nations has been parceled out among a corresponding number of angelic powers."[3]

Lest we forget that not all angels are good angels, F. F. Bruce goes on to show that Deuteronomy 32:8 directly relates to the "prince of Persia" and the "prince of Greece," which we mentioned from Daniel 10. He then associates these two passages with the New Testament by saying, "In a number of places some at least of these angelic governors are portrayed as hostile principalities and powers—the 'world rulers of this darkness' of Ephesians 6:12."[4]

Don Williams, a Vineyard pastor and also a recognized biblical scholar, has studied the worldview of the Sumerian people in Ur of the Chaldees, from which Abraham was called by God. In recognizing that Yahweh, the true God, was not just another territorial spirit, but the God and Creator of the whole universe, Abraham had made a radical break with those around him. The ontological reality of territorial spirits was very much a central part of the worldview of the Sumerians. In Ur of the Chaldees, a territorial spirit named "Enlil" headed up the divine hierarchy, ruling the Sumerians in consultation with a divine council of demon spirits.

Williams says, "Each city was the property of its god, and its citizens were its slaves."[5] Abraham would not have denied the existence of the spirits in Sumeria. He was distinguished by being the first to understand that the mightiest of them was still inferior to Yahweh, who had originally created them all.

It is difficult to understand much of what is written in the historical and prophetic books of the Old Testament without affirming the reality of these principalities and powers to whom God had assigned the "boundaries of the peoples" according to Deuteronomy 32:8. Many of them are called by names such as Succoth Benoth (see 2 Kings 17:30), Adrammelech (see v. 31), Baal (see Num. 22:41), Merodach (see Jer. 50:2), Queen of Heaven (see 44:17-25) and many others. When God says through Jeremiah "Has a nation changed its gods, which are not gods?" (2:11), He means that the nations are worshiping *creatures* instead of the *Creator.* This should not be taken to imply that they are worshiping figments of their imaginations. No. They are worshiping real, live rulers of darkness who have personalities and have names, much to their own misfortune in this life and in the life to come. God says He is jealous of His own people, Israel, committing *adultery* with the spirits, and He warns them, "Your lovers will despise you; they will seek your life" (4:30). This seems to be more than just *perception*; it seems to be *ontological reality.*

SIMON: "THE GREAT POWER OF GOD"

Simon Magus was not himself a territorial spirit. He was a human being whom Philip met in Samaria, but Simon was not an average human being. He was one of the recognized leaders of Samaria, having gained great prestige through visible displays of supernatural power. It is important to realize that Simon's magical power was the real thing. He was not some magician entertaining audiences through slight of hand. He was publicly and successfully performing miracles, healings, extrasensory perception, curses and all the rest that normally accompanies high-level occult practices then and now.

Neither was Simon just an average sorcerer. Many sorcerers existed in the ancient world, and undoubtedly Samaria had its share. Simon Magus was outstanding because he had gained power, not over a certain clientele he had accumulated through the years as do most witch doctors, but over the entire population of Samaria. The Samaritans had all but deified Simon by saying, "This man is the great power of God" (Acts 8:10). Who had deified him? "The people of Samaria,...from the least to the greatest" (vv. 9,10), meaning just about everyone living there.

Considering everything I have just said about territorial spirits, I am now going to make an assumption on which I base my interpretation of this scenario, although I know some may disagree with my assumption. My assumption is that a territorial principality of some kind had been assigned by the evil one to keep Samaria in spiritual captivity. We do not know what its name was, but generically we could say that it was the "prince of Samaria." This territorial spirit had chosen Simon Magus as the chief object in the visible world through which he would carry out his deeds of wickedness, deception and destruction. That would explain, among other things, why Simon would be recognized as having more power than the average sorcerer in Samaria.

Endowed with the Power of Satan

Few biblical scholars have studied the incident involving Simon Magus in more depth and detail than Susan Garrett, a Louisville Seminary professor. She argues that the stories Luke chooses to narrate in Acts, like this one in Samaria, "are not merely skir-mishes between prophets or wonder-workers, but confronta-tions between Satan and the Spirit of God."[6] Garrett contends that by describing Simon as engaging in "classically satanic pat-terns of behavior, Luke informs his reader that the depicted events involve more than meets the eye."[7] She does not use the terms I use, but as I do, she believes the incident is a high-er-level power encounter than is normally thought. Susan Gar-rett adds, "Simon is no mere con artist or cheap charlatan, but someone far more sinister, *endowed with the power of Satan* and disguising himself as the "great power of God"[8] (emphasis mine). It seems to me that this could easily be seen as strategic-level spiritual warfare.

Although the story takes some puzzling turns, it appears that Simon had made a profession of faith under Philip's ministry because he "was amazed, seeing the miracles and signs which were done" (Acts 8:13). We have no way of knowing for sure whether Simon was truly born again at that time, although he was baptized. In any case, the real power encounter came after Peter arrived, and Simon wanted to buy the apostles' power to impart the Holy Spirit with money—probably a good deal of money.

Peter, facing this community leader who had commanded the allegiance of all Samaritans from the least to the greatest, used language not customary in diplomatic circles. Having no pretense of subtlety, Peter rejected his offer: "Your money per-ish with you" (v. 20). Then he dealt directly with Simon himself: "Your heart is not right in the sight of God" (v. 21). Escalating the confrontation, Peter used even stronger language: "You are poisoned by bitterness and bound by iniquity" (v. 23).

Repeating what I have said several times, I could not claim this is *proof* that Peter did strategic-level spiritual warfare. On the other hand, I think we have some good biblical *evidence* that he might well have done it in Samaria. Simon certainly exercised *territorial* influence. The ministry of the disciples affected the whole territory of Samaria in a magnitude that at least suggests it might have been nothing less than a territorial spirit Peter had encountered through Simon. This warfare was related directly to evangelism because the ensuing harvest was great, and multitudes were baptized.

Here is the way Susan Garrett summarizes it: "Satan does still have some power, but he is handily subjugated when confronted with the vastly greater divine authority that Christians wield. Peter's righteous rebuke reduces Simon from a famous magician, impiously acclaimed by all the people of Samaria as 'the great power of God,' to a meek man who fears his own destruction and so asks the servant of the Lord to intercede for him."[9]

PETER VERSUS HEROD

Let's look at another probable case of strategic-level spiritual warfare.

Luke begins Acts 12 by saying that King Herod put two leaders of the Jerusalem church on his hit list. He determined to execute both James and Peter. He killed James, but although he tried hard to do it, he couldn't kill Peter. Why? I read this incident as another example of strategic-level spiritual warfare.

The apostle Paul said, "We do not look at the things which are seen, but at the things which are not seen. For the things which are seen are temporary, but the things which are not seen are eternal" (2 Cor. 4:18). There is a visible world and an invisible world. Both, for those who have eyes to see, are equally real. Paul suggests, however, that when it is possible, it is more important to understand what is happening in the invisible world than what is happening in the visible world. I see a battle in the invisible world here in Jerusalem. I see a *power encounter* behind the *political encounter.*

Herod was the king, and therefore had supreme jurisdiction over a certain political territory. What would happen to Herod was not just individual, but territorial. Dark angels had been assigned by Satan to prevent the light of the gospel from spreading any more than necessary in Jerusalem at that time. My assumption is that one or more of those territorial principalities would have chosen to work through the king. Their job would be, as Jesus said, "to steal, and to kill, and to destroy" (John 10:10), so Herod's orders for execution would fit perfectly. These were red-alert activities in the invisible world of darkness.

When Herod, willingly cued by the forces of wickedness with whom he had become familiar, chose Peter as his target, he more than met his match. Peter had no political power, but he had enormous spiritual power. Why Herod succeeded with James we do not know, but Luke's record does show something in the case of Peter that it does not mention with James: "Constant prayer was offered to God for [Peter] by the church" (Acts 12:5).

This prayer, which we later discover took place in the house of Mary, the mother of Mark (see v. 12), is not recorded by Luke as rhetoric or tokenism, in my opinion. It lies at the very heart of this power encounter. The major spiritual weapon in power encounters involving territorial spirits is prayer, and here we have a story of prayer at its mightiest. The battle was not really between Herod and Peter; it was between Herod and Peter's intercessors.

Personal Intercessors

It is interesting to me that, although the battle was won by prayer, nothing is said of Peter doing any praying. When he was in jail, all Luke tells us is that Peter was sleeping! This reminds me of Joshua winning the Battle of Rephidim through the power of prayer, but not his prayer; in that case it was the intercession of Moses on his behalf (see Exod. 17:8-14). This highlights the extremely crucial issue of personal intercession for Christian leaders, which I develop in great detail in my book *Prayer Shield* (Regal Books). In that book, I tell how the prayers of committed and gifted intercessors can indeed win wars and save lives. One of the stories is how it literally saved my own life back in 1983, so I believe I am very much in touch with what was happening to Peter.

A Christian pastor or other leader can be intensely involved in spiritual warfare and be called upon to do little of the actual fighting himself or herself if a powerful prayer shield of faithful intercessors is in place. The apostle Paul hints of this when he mentions two of his personal intercessors in the book of Philippians—Euodia and Syntyche. In our English versions, we usually don't see Paul commending these two women as having "labored with me in the gospel" (see Phil. 4:2,3). A better translation of the Greek would indicate that Paul was saying "they did spiritual warfare on my behalf."[10]

We have another example of personal intercessors in the struggle to prevent Herod from executing Peter. It would seem from this and other evidence that Mary, the mother of Mark, could well have been Peter's chief intercessor. When Peter's life was threatened, she did what my closest intercessors would certainly do—organize intense and constant prayer on my behalf. While Herod and Peter were acting this out in the visible world, the real battle was occurring in the invisible world between Mary's prayer team and the territorial spirits attempting to use Herod for the purposes of the evil one. Peter was sleeping while Mary was praying! Herod was trying to figure out what had happened, but he never could. He lost the battle; and he lost twice because he soon "was eaten by worms and died"! (Acts 12:23).

If this was not an instance of strategic-level spiritual warfare, it was something very close to it. The result? "The word of God grew and multiplied" (v. 24).

The Devil Is a Roaring Lion

These kind of experiences, and undoubtedly many more that Luke did not record, constituted Peter as a veteran of strategic-level spiritual warfare. He had not forgotten it when he wrote 1 Peter years later. He says there: "Be sober, be vigilant; because your adversary the devil walks about like a roaring lion, seeking whom he may devour" (5:8).

I think Peter chose those words carefully. I think Peter really did not mean the devil is a "toothless lion," as some might wish.

> The premise that the Christian life should be a comfortable life, protected from suffering, is not the way Peter saw it in his Epistles. Peter was a warrior, and therefore Peter took his hits. His major comfort was that Jesus also suffered.

What we agree on, however, is that no believer has to be victimized by the devil "because He who is in you is greater than he who is in the world" (1 John 4:4). Although Jesus has given us authority over all the powers of the enemy, if we ignore it, fail to use it, use it foolishly, act from the wrong motives or lack protection from intercessors, we may not prevail.

WARFARE INVOLVES CASUALTIES

Throughout history, every war that has occurred has involved casualties. This is true about spiritual warfare as well, and the rule is that the higher the level, the more casualties. In chapter 2, I mentioned that some pastors have so much compassion for the well-being of their church members that they would never encourage them to step out in strategic-level spiritual warfare. They believe their churches should be hospitals rather than barracks, and maybe they should. God does not call all people in the Body of Christ to be and do the same things, nor does He want local churches to all be the same.

The premise that the Christian life should be a comfortable life, protected from suffering, is not the way Peter saw it in his Epistles. More is said about suffering in 1 Peter than in any other book in the New Testament. Peter was a warrior, and therefore Peter took his hits. His major comfort was that Jesus also suffered. Peter said, "When you do good and *suffer*, if you take it patiently, this is commendable before God" (1 Pet. 2:20, emphasis mine).

Why would suffering be commendable? "For to this you were called, because Christ also *suffered* for us, leaving us an example, that you should follow His steps" (v. 21, emphasis mine). Peter said we should "rejoice to the extent that you partake of Christ's *sufferings*" (4:13, emphasis mine). And "If anyone *suffers* as a Christian, let him not be ashamed, but let him glorify God in this matter" (v. 16, emphasis mine).

History tells us that Peter continued in front-line warfare right to the end, and he paid the ultimate price of martyrdom.[11] Many comfortable Christians are unaware that martyrdom is happening in the world today. As I mentioned previously, David Barrett's estimate for the 1990s is somewhere around 150,000 martyrs for Christ each year or more than 400 a day!

According to research done by Christian Solidarity International, more Christians have been murdered for their faith in the twentieth century than all other centuries combined.

The battle may be intense, but the victory is ours if we are faithful to Christ. News Network International reports that recently in Sudan an observer told how, on a trip there, he heard eyewitnesses and documented accounts of murdered church leaders, children sold into slavery, the elderly slaughtered and dumped into mass graves and dozens of churches burned down. The Sudan Christians were suffering, but not defeated. According to his report, 32,000 people had been baptized in one area within two weeks of the martyrdom of a local pastor!

Peter would say, "But may the God of all grace, who called us to His eternal glory by Christ Jesus, *after you have suffered a while*, perfect, establish, strengthen, and settle you" (5:10, emphasis mine).

REFLECTION QUESTIONS

1. The ministry of the apostles in the book of Acts was characterized by outward demonstrations of the mighty power of God. Is this true of your church? If not, why not?

2. What do you think of being filled with the Holy Spirit? Is it once-for-all or does it keep happening? How can you tell if someone is Spirit-filled?

3. This chapter discusses the reality of "territorial spirits." Do you believe there is such a thing? Could one be influencing your community?

4. What would cause someone like Susan Garrett to argue that Peter's encounter with Simon Magus was equivalent to an encounter with Satan himself?

5. In all probability, the prayers of Peter's personal intercessors saved his life. Could you name individuals who today are known to have a ministry of personal intercession for certain leaders?

Notes

1. Robert C. Linthicum, *City of God; City of Satan* (Grand Rapids: Zondervan Publishing House, 1991), pp. 64-65.
2. C. F. Keil, *Biblical Commentary on the Book of Daniel* (Grand Rapids: William B. Eerdmans Publishing Co., 1949), p. 416.
3. F. F. Bruce, *The Epistle to the Hebrews* (Grand Rapids: William B. Eerdmans Publishing Co., 1964), p. 33.
4. Ibid.
5. Don Williams, *Signs, Wonders and the Kingdom of God* (Ann Arbor: Vine Books, Servant Publications, 1989), p. 35.
6. Susan Garrett, *The Demise of the Devil* (Minneapolis: Fortress Press, 1989), p. 75.
7. Ibid.
8. Ibid.
9. Ibid., p. 74.
10. For details of the exegesis of this passage in Philippians 4:2,3, see my book *Prayer Shield* (Ventura, Calif.: Regal Books, 1992), pp. 36-37.
11. According to Origen, in the reign of Nero, about A.D. 64, Peter was crucified head downward at his request because he did not consider himself worthy enough to be crucified in the same position as his Master.

Paul Confronts the Powers

THE CONVERSION EXPERIENCE OF THE APOSTLE PAUL HAS gone down as one of the most dramatic ever recorded. Paul was the most notorious enemy of the Christian faith at the time. He was known in Jerusalem as one constantly "breathing threats and murder against the disciples of the Lord" (Acts 9:1). He was on his way to destroy the nucleus of this new faith in the city of Damascus. At the time he left Jerusalem for Damascus, however, he had no idea at all of what was then taking place in the invisible world. God had just decided to surprise this fanatic terrorist with a supernatural appearance of the very One he was persecuting—Jesus Christ. His name was still Saul of Tarsus.

CONVERSION THROUGH DIVINE INTERVENTION

Paul was among the relatively few people who could

trace conversion to a divine intervention. The normal way of conversion was through a preacher such as Philip. Paul himself later writes: "How shall they believe in Him of whom they have not heard? And how shall they hear without a preacher?" (Rom. 10:14). There are exceptions, however, even today.

Those of us who try to keep track of what God is doing in the world agree with each other that never before have we seen or even heard of so many conversions through divine intervention as have been reported in the last few years, particularly among Muslims. In some instances Jesus appears as He did to Saul, in others it is an angel, in others it is an aura of light and a voice. Sometimes it is a dream, sometimes a daytime vision. Many are accompanied by physical healing or other miracles. Bibles have supernaturally appeared in mosques or Muslim homes. I recently learned of an Indonesian Muslim woman who was physically transported from her home to a church by supernatural power. She accepted Christ the same day!

On the road to Damascus, Saul saw the light, heard the voice and actually saw Jesus in person as he tells us in 1 Corinthians 9:1: "Have I not seen Jesus Christ our Lord?" In Acts 9 we read that Paul fell to the ground or, to use current terminology, he was "slain in the Spirit." His traveling companions saw him fall, they saw the light, they knew a voice was speaking, although they could not hear the words, but they did not see Jesus as Saul did. Saul got up from the ground blind, and had to be led by the hand to Damascus. In Damascus a believer named Ananias prophesied over Saul and he received his sight.

This story is well known, but I have summarized it here to remind us of the extraordinary spiritual magnitude of the event. There is nothing else like it in the New Testament. What occurred during that event deserves more than casual attention. I believe that at the time of his conversion, Jesus commissioned Paul to build a ministry of strategic-level spiritual warfare into his future activities. Let me explain.

PAUL'S DIVINE COMMISSION TO SERIOUS WARFARE

Let's look closely at part of what Jesus Himself said to Paul on the day he was converted:

> I will deliver you from the Jewish people, as well as from the Gentiles, to whom I now send you, to open their eyes, and to turn them from darkness to light, and from the power of Satan to God, that they may receive forgiveness of sins and an inheritance among those who are sanctified by faith in Me (Acts 26:17,18).

This was the commission to which Paul energetically dedicated the rest of his life. He later refers to it as his "heavenly vision" (v. 19). In it he had been told that he would be sent to the "Gentiles," which could also be translated "nations," or "people groups." In a word, Paul had been called to world evangelization. His role would be that of a cross-cultural missionary. His primary task would be evangelism and church planting. This is what God expected Paul to do in the visible world.

In the divine commission, Jesus also used language referring to the *invisible world.* He said that when Paul would arrive at a given nation or people group he would find them in darkness and under the power of Satan. Wherever Satan is in control, people are in spiritual darkness. Satan's desire is that they suffer as much as possible in this life and that they spend the life to come in hell. Jesus sent Paul, as He sends many of us today, to bring Jesus Christ, who said, "I am the light of the world. He who follows Me shall not walk in darkness, but have the light of life" (John 8:12).

The process of bringing the light of Jesus Christ to people

groups bound in spiritual darkness involves, according to Paul's commission, taking that nation "from the power of Satan to God" (Acts 26:18). This seems to be unusually strong language, used in the context of a high-profile divine-human encounter. If, as I have argued previously, it is true that Satan assigns certain principalities and powers to keep specific peoples in spiritual darkness, a clear implication of Paul's commission would be that turning people groups from darkness to light would involve aggressively confronting such powers.

Such a confrontation would be no simple thing. I believe I am right in asserting that Satan lets no one under his power go without a fight. The contemporary words we use for such a fight are "spiritual warfare." Jesus, in all likelihood, was telling Paul to be an "overcomer," one of those who, according to the letters to the seven churches in Revelation 2 and 3, would in turn receive great rewards. He was telling Paul that to free the enemy's spiritual captives he would have to overcome, or bind, the strongman, as He had said to His disciples in Luke 11. In my opinion, we have substantial evidence that on the Damascus road Paul was commissioned by the Lord to do strategic-level spiritual warfare.

THREE EXAMPLES

Did Paul go out and do it?

I have mentioned that in my study of Acts I believe I have found five incidents that, if certain assumptions are valid, could be understood as describing strategic-level spiritual warfare. I analyzed two of these incidents involving Peter in the last chapter. In the other three, Paul is the main actor: (1) Paul versus Bar Jesus (or Elymas), (2) Paul versus the Python Spirit and (3) Paul versus Diana (or Artemis) of the Ephesians. I will explain the first two in this chapter, and the third in the next chapter.

Were There More?

Before I explain these incidents, I want to say that I think Paul did strategic-level spiritual warfare much more than on these three occasions. I base this on the fact that in the book of Acts Luke records only a small and select portion of the ministry of the apostles. Believing as I do in biblical inspiration, I recognize that Luke's selection process was supervised by the Holy Spirit and what we have in Acts is what God mainly wants us to know about the apostles' work during the time period the book covers. This is not to say we have no other information about the apostles, but it is to say that extrabiblical historical records are not to be considered as divinely inspired. For example, many are confident that Peter was martyred for his faith and that Thomas went to India, although we do not find that information in Scripture.

I believe that Luke expects us to assume that wherever he says Paul preached the gospel, he preached justification by faith.

The places we find Paul doing strategic-level spiritual warfare are in Western Cyprus, Philippi and Ephesus. This is not to say that he didn't also do it in Antioch of Pisidia, Iconium, Lystra, Thessalonica or Corinth, just to name a few other possibilities. As a good historian, Luke is not overly repetitious. He makes sure he establishes certain patterns, then allows the reader to assume the pattern would have probably continued.

An outstanding example is Paul's message of justification by faith apart from the law of Moses, which he expounds so eloquently in Romans and Galatians. In the book of Acts, Luke records Paul preaching justification by faith only once—in Antioch of Pisidia (see 13:38,39). I am confident Paul also preached justification by faith in Lystra, Berea, Iconium, Ephesus, Derbe, Antioch of Syria and many other places, but I do not find this in Scripture. I believe that Luke expects us to *assume* that wherever he says Paul preached the gospel, he preached justification by faith.

As far as Paul dealing directly with demonic spirits, Luke chooses to give us only two accounts—one in Philippi and one in Ephesus. That is one more account than is given about preaching justification by faith, but still it is not many. Paul later writes about it in his Epistles, just as he writes about justification by faith. He says, "For we do not wrestle against flesh and blood, but against principalities, against powers, against the rulers of the darkness of this age, against spiritual hosts of wickedness in the heavenly places" (Eph. 6:12). Paul knew how to do this wrestling through experience, more, I believe, than only the two or three direct confrontations with the demonic we find referenced in the book of Acts.

Paul Versus Bar-Jesus the Sorcerer

On virtually anyone's list, Paul is the greatest cross-cultural missionary of all time. Many consider him second only to Jesus Christ as far as influencing the entire Christian movement is concerned. Therefore, those of us professionally committed to contemporary world evangelization pay more than passing attention to the way Paul went about doing his missionary work.

After the events surrounding his conversion and the ministry among the house churches of Antioch of Syria, the first anecdote Luke records in Paul's evangelistic and church-planting career occurs on the Island of Cyprus (see Acts 13:6-12). I believe it would not be stretching the point to expect that Luke might have chosen this particular anecdote to set the tone for all of Paul's subsequent ministry. It could be seen as a prophetic introduction to everything Paul would subsequently do in taking people from the power of Satan to God. If so, spiritual warfare and power encounters would be prominent features of his ongoing modus operandi.

In the city of Paphos in Western Cyprus lived the political authority over the Island—the Roman proconsul, Sergius Paulus. As I said about King Herod in the last chapter, I believe when the chief figure in an episode such as this happens to be the highest political authority of the particular place, the scenario lends itself to possible interpretation as strategic-level spiritual warfare.

This is especially true in Paphos, because we learn that the proconsul had established a relationship with an occult practitioner named Bar-Jesus or Elymas. This kind of liaison is not altogether strange. A recent study showed that a substantial majority of Latin American presidents maintain such relationships. Hitler's allegiance to the world of darkness is well documented, as is that of Saddam Hussein. Closer to home, Mrs. Ronald Reagan retained an astrologer to help plan the schedule of the President of the United States. Similar examples abound. Through his sorcerer, Sergius Paulus would have maintained some sort of formalized contact with the invisible world of darkness. Worse yet, the proconsul seemed to be interested in the gospel, but Bar-Jesus "withstood [the missionaries], seeking to turn the proconsul away from the faith" (v. 8).

The Holy Spirit Versus the Devil

The public stage is therefore set for an intense episode of spiritual warfare. On what level? Although we are dealing with a person, Bar-Jesus (ground level), and although that person is an occult practitioner (occult level), I believe the magnitude of the event places it, in the invisible world, on the strategic level.

John Stott sees the intensity: "[Luke] brings before his readers a dramatic power encounter, in which the Holy Spirit overthrew the evil one, the apostle confounded the sorcerer, and the gospel triumphed over the occult."[1] Susan Garrett agrees: "The confrontation between Bar-Jesus and Paul is also a confrontation between the Holy Spirit and the devil."[2] If she is right, that is as high as it gets!

We do not know the identity of the territorial spirit who was apparently using Bar-Jesus as his instrument to keep the Cypriot people group in captivity. Those experienced in strategic-level spiritual warfare agree that such information is not essential, although it can help, as I will explain later in the chapter. What is clear at least to me, however, is that we are not dealing here with your rank-and-file demon who might be assigned to make someone ill or cause an accident. Susan Garrett's studies seem to confirm this, for she says, "Bar-Jesus is closely linked with the figure of Satan."[3]

If Sergius Paulus would be converted, it could influence the whole region. Paul knew this, but so did Bar-Jesus. Bar-Jesus had a lot at stake: (1) His job was at stake. If Sergius Paulus became a Christian, a court sorcerer would no longer be needed. (2) His well-being as well as his life could have been at stake. No one would have known better than he of the hideous punishments that await those who disappoint their superiors in the demonic realm.

Paul and Bar-Jesus, the two combatants in the visible world, were both "filled." Bar-Jesus was "full of all deceit and all fraud" (Acts 13:10). Paul was "filled with the Holy Spirit" (v. 9), as was Peter when he took on Simon Magus in Samaria. Paul's declaration that Bar-Jesus was a "son of the devil" (v. 10), is a further indication that we are not dealing with a run-of-the-mill witch doctor here, but with a representative of some of the highest powers of evil. As Susan Garrett says, "The human combatants Paul and Bar-Jesus in turn represent superhuman figures."[4] Bar-

Jesus appears to be a clear example of a human being used as a front for what Jesus would call a strongman. If nothing happens to Bar-Jesus, "his goods are in peace" (Luke 11:21), and the souls in Cyprus will not be saved.

Paul did not doubt his spiritual authority. I like the way John Dawson puts it: "While God's Word tells believers to treat [principalities and powers] with respect, it also commands us to take captivity captive, to bind the strong man, to plunder his goods, and to tear down the rule and authority of the evil one."[5] This is exactly what Paul did. Acting on what must have been a *rhema* word to him from God, Paul rebuked him in no uncertain terms and declared: "Indeed, the hand of the Lord is upon you, and you shall be blind, not seeing the sun for a time" (Acts 13:11).

Bar-Jesus went blind, Sergius Paulus was saved and, although Luke does not give us this detail, I assume the gospel spread throughout Paphos and beyond.

Was this strategic-level spiritual warfare? Although some may still disagree, I think so. The spiritual authority upon which Paul drew was far above the ordinary. To confront the enemy on such a public stage and with so much at stake, Paul must have been taking Jesus' words literally: "Behold, I give you the authority to trample on serpents and scorpions, and *over all the power of the enemy*" (Luke 10:19, emphasis mine). Susan Garrett agrees by commenting that he could only have done this because "*Paul must be invested with authority that is greater than Satan's own* [emphasis hers]. In depicting Paul's successful unmasking and punishment of Bar-Jesus, Luke is saying that Paul could do the work to which he had been called because he possessed authority over all the power of the Enemy (cf. Luke 10:19)."[6]

WHAT HAPPENED TO MARK?

Young John Mark had accompanied Paul and Barnabas when

they went out to evangelize Cyprus, but afterward he chose not to continue with them. "And John, departing from them, returned to Jerusalem" (Acts 13:13). Later on, when Paul and Barnabas were ready to set out for their second term, they entered into a heated argument about whether they should take Mark along again. Barnabas, Mark's cousin, wanted him to go, but Paul would not agree because "[he] had departed from them in Pamphylia" (15:38). The upshot of this was that Paul and Barnabas parted ways, but my question is: Why was it that Mark went back?

Luke doesn't give us the details, but commentators consider various hypotheses. My hypothesis is related to this incident of high-level, public power encounter. It could well be that Luke's description of this, vivid as it is, was at the same time somewhat subdued. I know of many similar confrontations today that are much messier than Luke acknowledges. In any case, Mark might not have liked what he saw. He might have thought he hadn't signed up for this kind of ministry. Witnessing one strategic-level confrontation could have been enough for him. Assuming that other similar events would follow, he decided to go home instead.

I know many people who are like Mark, if indeed my hypothesis is correct. When I took leadership of the Spiritual Warfare Network in 1990, I found, to my sorrow, that several of my friends deserted me, some more radically than others. I'd love to be close to some of them once again, but it has not been possible until now. Five influential families left my 120 Fellowship adult Sunday School class, never to return. I know very well the pain Paul must have felt when he first lost Mark, and then Barnabas. Not everyone likes the idea of warfare.

At the same time, Mark was a wonderful person and an outstanding Christian leader. He was born into the home of a powerful intercessor—his mother, Mary. He must have known a lot about prayer, and maybe he was there when his mother's prayer team saved Peter's life. He became the author of one of the four Gospels no less. Later on, Mark's close relationship to Paul was restored, and Paul writes to Timothy, "Get Mark and bring him with you, for he is useful to me for ministry" (2 Tim. 4:11).

I described the "law of warfare" at the end of chapter 1, and I affirmed there what I want to repeat here: *not everyone is called to the front lines of spiritual warfare.* I highly respect the John Marks in my life, and regret any of my attitudes or actions that might have alienated them. Having said that, I cannot turn back. I, like Paul, must be faithful to my "heavenly vision."

EVICTING THE PYTHON SPIRIT

When Paul gets to Philippi, this time with Silas, Timothy and Luke, he finds himself in another strategic-level confrontation with the powers. This time, however, there are some differences. For example, this time we *do* know the name of the territorial spirit—Python. There are also some similarities. For example, in Philippi, as in Cyprus, the demonic principality had chosen to manifest through a human being—this time through a slave girl.

Some have a hard time separating power encounters such as these from ordinary ground-level spiritual warfare, because a human agent is involved. They believe the only way true strategic-level warfare is done is to confront a spirit that is not manifesting through a person. I think this is incorrect. The variable is not whether or not a person is involved, the variable is the rank of the spirit we are confronting at the time. If it is a territorial spirit, which Paul calls a principality or power, it doesn't matter whether that spirit manifests in an oak tree as in the case of Thor, or in a sorcerer named Bar-Jesus as in Cyprus.

Binding such a spirit from the invisible world, however it might choose to manifest in the visible world is at least what I understand to be strategic-level spiritual warfare.

In Philippi, the fortune-teller—a slave girl—was demonized by a Python Spirit. I have made this a proper name because I think that is what the Greek text actually reflects. In my English version it says "a spirit of divination" (Acts 16:16), but the Greek is *pneuma pythona*. Simon Kistemaker, a biblical scholar, tells us that the best way to translate the term into English would be "a spirit, namely a Python."[7] In those days the Python spirit was well known in Greece and Macedonia. The original home of the spirit was the Greek city of Delphi in which a famous temple of Apollo was located. The so-called "oracle of Delphi" was a human priestess through whom Apollo communicated periodically with human beings. The proper name of the priestess was "the Pythia" because she was empowered by the Python spirit.

Paul Pulls the Trigger!

This spirit, much higher-ranking than an ordinary demon, was the one Paul encountered in Philippi. David Finnell suggests that this confrontation "was probably over Paul's intrusion into this territory which was under the control and authority of the prince of Greece...This was more than a battle over a single demon. The power of Satan in this city was evident."[8] After putting up with some harassment through the fortune-teller for several days, Paul finally pulled the trigger. "Paul, greatly annoyed, turned and said to the spirit, 'I command you in the name of Jesus Christ to come out of her.' And he came out that very hour" (Acts 16:18).

Was Python a territorial spirit? Was this strategic-level spiritual warfare? I am led to believe that the strongman over the city of Philippi was bound at that time. This was not an isolated incident that might have affected a few people or a family or two. This was an event that shook an entire city. Paul and Silas were beaten and jailed after a riot, a supernatural earthquake freed the prisoners, the jailer and his household were converted, Paul shook up the government authorities by claiming Roman citizenship, and a solid, thriving church was planted.

Python had harassed Paul for several days before Paul finally confronted him and cast him out of the slave girl. Some have wondered if this is a principle—don't cast out demons when you first encounter them. There is a principle here, but that is not it. The principle is this: *In strategic-level spiritual warfare proceed only on God's timing.* This principle is valid for all areas of Christian life and ministry, but it is more crucial than otherwise when dealing with forces of darkness on the higher levels. I have seen more casualties in spiritual warfare because of violations of this principle than anything else, the possible exception being in the area of personal holiness. Because Paul was filled with the Holy Spirit and was in intimate contact with the Father, he knew when *not* to confront Python eyeball-to-eyeball and when to confront it.

Before we move on, this incident in Philippi highlights two important issues that have raised questions in the minds of many who have reservations about strategic-level spiritual warfare: (1) Should we address demonic spirits directly? and (2) Should we seek to learn the names of the spirits?

ADDRESSING THE SPIRITS

All Christians know we are encouraged to speak directly to God, thus making contact with the invisible world. Not all are sure, however, that we should address spirits directly, especially on the strategic level. Some have an aversion to it because they have seen attempts at strategic-level warfare in which well-meaning brothers and sisters have spent considerable periods of time engaged in high-volume, but somewhat fruitless, rebuke of principalities. "Spirit of greed over this city, we come against you in Jesus' name!" "We rebuke you, spirit of lust and immorality, and tell you to go—now!" "We bind you, Satan, and declare that you have no more authority over this nation!" Such language is often used with great enthusiasm, followed with shouts of victory, but all too frequently the next day nothing has changed.

How are we to react to this kind of behavior? To be honest, I have a lot of tolerance for this kind of activity, although I do not engage in it myself. At times I will get caught up in it, but those times are few and far between. Because of my work with the prayer movement, I am in personal contact with many who habitually address the realm of darkness in this manner, and I know the hearts of those who practice it. Their hearts are as pure before God as any, their desire to see the captives freed and souls saved is more intense than most, but their sincere understanding of how to go about aggressive spiritual warfare is a bit different from mine. I also disagree, incidentally, with those who insist on baptizing infants, those who think that speaking in tongues is the initial physical evidence of being baptized in the Holy Spirit and those who conduct a worship service by following a previously published liturgy, but I have an equally wide tolerance for their beliefs as well.

Some of my friends have shorter fuses. One strongly disagreed when Francis Frangipane wrote: "I believe the Scriptures are clear: Not only do Christians have the authority to war against these powers of darkness, but we have the responsibility to as well. If we do not *pray* against our spiritual enemies, they will, indeed, *prey* upon us!" [emphasis mine].[9] Prayer, to my friend, is supposed to be talking to God in the Kingdom of light, not addressing beings in the kingdom of darkness. Let's take a closer look.

The Wider Meaning of Prayer
In common language, "prayer" actually has the wider meaning. My dictionary says that prayer is "a devout petition to God or an object of worship." Satanists pray to Satan. Native American shamans pray to the Great Spirit. Catholics pray to Mary

---

Christians should not attempt to pray to any being in the invisible world except to God. All our "devout petitions" should be directed to Him and to Him alone.

---

and some of the saints. Hindus pray to any number of gods on their god shelf. None of these is praying to *God*, but it is all "prayer," nevertheless.

In my opinion, Christians should not attempt to pray *to* any being in the invisible world except to God. All our "devout petitions" should be directed to Him and to Him alone. That is why Francis Frangipane carefully said we pray *against* our spiritual enemies. When we pray against evil spirits, much of our prayer is to God to deal directly with them or to give us the power and authority to engage them on His behalf in the name of Jesus. Then when we do address the evil spirits, it is not with petitions, but with authoritative *commands* and *rebukes*.

That is what Paul did with the Python Spirit. He said, perhaps in a loud voice that many others would have heard, "I command you in the name of Jesus Christ to come out of her" (Acts 16:18).

Tom White of Frontline Ministries agrees. He says that when we resist evil, we should not see it as "prayer" per se. Rather "It is encounter, engagement, and enforcement of the divine will....It is appropriate to remind the devil who he is and where he can go."[10] Tom White goes further. He publishes a statement of the kind of thing he believes we could say when we engage the enemy in spiritual warfare:

> *I remind you, Satan, that Jesus came to destroy your works. I expose your work in this church. I deny you further access and serve you notice that divine light is penetrating your darkness. The healing of relationships here is closing the door on your influence. You are defeated. Jesus is Victor!*[11] [emphasis his].

NAMING THE SPIRITS

Evil spirits have two kinds of names: functional names and proper names. In the episode we just examined in Philippi, both names are used in describing the spirit in the slave girl. As we saw, the Greek uses a *proper* name—Python. Those who translated the version I use *(The New King James Version)* chose to translate it as a *functional* name—spirit of divination. Both are accurate.

In practice, our spiritual mapping, which I will discuss in more detail in chapter 10, frequently reveals the names of the spirits with which we are dealing, but not always. Effective spiritual warfare does not *require* knowing the names of the spirits, but experience has shown that when we are able to identify them specifically by name, we seem to have more authority over them, and therefore we can be more effective.

Those who minister frequently in individual demonic deliverance on the ground level have the same experiences. Naming the spirits and addressing them directly with commands and rebukes is common, although not universal. Neil Anderson of Freedom in Christ Ministries uses a "truth encounter" approach as opposed to direct confrontation with demons, and many captives are set free through helping people understand and act upon who they really are in Christ.

We have examples of Jesus both naming and addressing demons. In one instance He learned the name of the demon by asking the demon itself. Jesus said to a demonized man, "What is your name?" And the demon, not the man, answered and said, "My name is Legion; for we are many." (Mark 5:9). Jesus said, quite directly, "Come out of the man, unclean spirit!" (v. 8). Doing the same today, whether on the ground level or on the strategic level, is helpful whenever it is possible.

SUMMARY

In this chapter we have examined two instances of the apostle Paul engaging in what can be interpreted as strategic-level spiritual warfare. He was doing that by way of fulfilling the commission Jesus had given him on the Damascus road the same day as his conversion—namely to go to the nations and turn them from darkness to light and from the power of Satan to God. In the next chapter we will see one instance where Paul failed and another where he was highly successful.

■ REFLECTION QUESTIONS ■

1. What is your opinion of the possibility of someone being saved through divine intervention? Have you heard of any such recent case?
2. It isn't often that we associate evangelism with spiritual warfare. Why does Paul's experience on the Damascus road cause us to make the association?
3. Some believe that people such as witches or fortune-

tellers are just oddballs, but that they can't really cause any harm. Do you agree?

4. As the case of John Mark suggests, not all are called to the ministry of strategic-level spiritual warfare. What do you consider your calling might be?

5. We are used to praying to God, whom we do not see. What do you think about addressing invisible demonic spirits?

Notes

1. John Stott, *The Spirit, the Church and the World: The Message of Acts* (Downers Grove: InterVarsity Press, 1990), p. 220.
2. Susan R. Garrett, *The Demise of the Devil* (Minneapolis: Fortress Press, 1989), p. 80.
3. Ibid.
4. Ibid.
5. John Dawson, *Taking Our Cities for God* (Lake Mary, Fla.: Creation House, 1989), p. 137.
6. Garrett, *The Demise of the Devil*, p. 84.
7. Simon J. Kistemaker, *Exposition of the Acts of the Apostles* (Grand Rapids: Baker Book House, 1990), p. 594.
8. David L. Finnell, "Territorial Powers and Church Planting: A Search for Biblical Truth," *Church Planter's Link* (Fourth Quarter and First Quarter 1995): 20.
9. Francis Frangipane, "Our Authority in Christ," *Charisma* (July 1993): 40.
10. Tom White, *Breaking Strongholds: How Spiritual Warfare Sets Captives Free* (Ann Arbor: Vine Books, 1993), p. 156.
11. Ibid.

Plundering the Goods of Diana of the Ephesians

CHAPTER NINE

O N THE ASSUMPTION THAT THE APOSTLE PAUL DID NOT
have a divine nature, as did Jesus, I am going to suggest that not everything he did in his career was
equally successful. I am supposing that Paul, as a
human being, made his share of mistakes and suffered
the resultant setbacks.

The main subject of this chapter is Paul's greatest
missionary and evangelistic success, namely his ministry
in Ephesus and the surrounding Asia Minor. Before I
get to that, however, I also want to look into his greatest evangelistic failure, namely Athens. Both of these, in
my opinion, are related to strategic-level spiritual warfare.

ATHENS: AN IMPREGNABLE ENEMY STRONGHOLD

After Paul left Philippi where he battled the Python Spirit, he and his missionary team had outstanding success in planting churches in Thessalonica and Berea. Then Paul, apparently contrary to their original plans, had to flee from Berea and he ended up in Athens, leaving Silas and Timothy behind.

Making the best of the situation, Paul energetically attempted to evangelize Athens, but with notably scant success. Luke seems to be scraping the bottom of the barrel when he finishes the story in Acts 17 by saying, "However, some men joined him and believed, among them Dionysius the Areopagite, a woman named Damaris, and others with them" (v. 34). Afterward we never hear another thing about Dionysius or Damaris, nor is a Christian church in Athens ever mentioned in Scripture.

How could this be? What were the variables? If it is true, as I have previously argued, that the real battle for world evangelization is a spiritual battle, it would seem that our search for an answer should begin in the invisible world. My hypothesis is that the territorial spirits assigned to the city of Athens were so powerful and so deeply entrenched that Paul was not able to overcome them. The strongholds that had furnished them the right to rule the city for centuries were awesome, at the time virtually impenetrable.

After Philippi, Thessalonica and Berea, Athens must have been an extremely depressing experience for Paul. I imagine that Paul, any day, would rather be driven out of a city by angry mobs, as he was from Berea, than to be mocked, laughed at and effectively neutralized by a group of sophisticated intellectuals as he was in Athens. I am positive that no matter how he left a city, he would be happier to have left behind a growing church than none at all.

A City Given Over to Idols

The only place in the Bible where we find the phrase "given over to idols" (from the Greek *kateidolos*) is where Luke describes Athens in Acts 17:16. Athens was the idol capital of the ancient world, possibly comparable to Kyoto, Japan, today. The literature of that day describes Athens as a forest of idols in which it is easier to find a god than a human being. Certain streets had so many idols that pedestrian traffic was difficult. One observer estimated that Athens contained more idols than the rest of Greece combined!

Because idols themselves are only made of wood or stone or metal, some are not concerned about their presence. These idols, however, were not just any piece of wood, stone or metal. They had been carefully and intentionally crafted by human beings as forms in the visible world through which the forces of the invisible world of darkness were invited to control the lives of people, families and the city as a whole, locking the people in spiritual darkness. That's why we read that Paul's "spirit was provoked within him" (v. 16). He knew that behind the thick cloud of evil over the city were conscious decisions that had been made, in the past and in the present, by human beings in rebellion against God. The population of Athens had voluntarily pledged allegiance to any number of principalities, powers and rulers of the darkness of this age, many of which could be identified by name.

The city itself had taken its name from its patron deity, the goddess Athena, the "virgin goddess of wisdom, fine and skilled arts."[1] Functionally, Athena could be seen as the "spirit of art" and also the "spirit of wisdom." No wonder brilliant philosophers gravitated to Athens, and no wonder they served these miserable creatures rather than serving the Creator. Socrates, for example, prayed to Pan, a spirit that had the legs and face of a goat: "O beloved Pan...grant to me that I may be made beautiful in my soul within, and that all external possessions be in harmony with my inner man."[2] The famous Plato spoke glowingly of pagan priests in Athens who "know how to give the gods gifts from men in the form of sacrifices which are acceptable to them, and to ask on our behalf blessings in return from them."[3]

Plato had a high regard for demons, and had no doubt in his mind of the "ontological reality" of territorial spirits. He taught that "[a] demon [is] a destiny spirit somewhat like a guardian angel as a companion of man, *or of cities,* as well as individuals"[4] [emphasis mine]. In Athens, Paul would have met any number of people like Plato who would advocate that each person should have what some call today a "spirit guide," and that cities should pay homage and give their allegiance to their patron territorial spirits.

Day by day the people of Athens were living their beliefs in the worship of idols, petitions to specific demonic spirits, sacrifices of all kinds and eight major, plus many other minor, public festivals to honor the highest ranking of the territorial spirits of the city. George Otis Jr. warns us about such festivals: "These celebrations are decidedly not the benign, quaint and colorful cultural spectacles they are often made out to be. They are conscious transactions with the spirit world. They are opportunities for contemporary generations to reaffirm the choices and pacts made by their forefathers and ancestors. They are occasions to dust off ancient welcome mats and extend the devil's right to rule over specific peoples and places today."[5]

Little wonder Paul had more than his share of problems trying to move the people of Athens from darkness to light and from the power of Satan to God, as was his heart's desire. Then a funny thing happened to Paul in Athens. He deviated from his tried-and-true evangelistic strategy of building the nucleus of the new church primarily with converted Gentile God-fearers who had been attending the synagogues, and then reaching out to win Gentiles at large through them. Instead, Paul himself decided to go out to the marketplace and the Areopagus and face the Gentile philosophers who had called him a "babbler"

(Acts 17:18). Why Paul accepted their challenge to do this is not clear, but it is not beyond reason to suspect that some sort of powerful and perverse spiritual influence might have been at work. The result? He presented a sermon widely regarded as among his most brilliant discourses, but at the same time among his most ineffective.

What was the end result of Paul's experience in Athens? In *The Message*, Eugene Peterson translates Acts 17:32, "Some laughed at him and walked off making jokes."[6] For Paul it was not a good day.

EPHESUS: AN ABUNDANT HARVEST

In Ephesus, by contrast, Paul not only had a good day, but many of them. There he took a different approach. Things changed considerably when Paul left Athens for his next stop: Corinth.

As Paul reflected on his time in Athens, it became clearer to him that brilliant and true words, unaccompanied by the deeds that demonstrate openly the power of God, can be of little avail.

From Human Wisdom to the Power of God

As Paul reflected on his time in Athens, it became clearer to him that brilliant and true words, unaccompanied by the deeds that demonstrate openly the power of God, can be of little avail. After arriving in Corinth, he was ready to say, "And my speech and my preaching were not with persuasive words of human wisdom, but in *demonstration* of the Spirit and of power, that your faith should not be in the wisdom of men but *in the power of God*" (1 Cor. 2:4,5, emphasis mine).

Richard Rackham, a commentator, concurs. He says, "At Athens St. Paul tried the wisdom of the world and found it wanting....His disappointment at the failure of the former method to touch the frivolous Athenians no doubt kindled the fire with which he denounces the wisdom of the world in his first epistle to the Corinthians."[7]

In Athens the word overshadowed the deed, but in Corinth the deeds of supernatural power supported and confirmed the word. In Athens Paul saw little fruit, but his evangelistic ministry in Corinth produced a great harvest of souls.

Paul had made an attempt to go to Ephesus years before he actually arrived there. Luke tells us that he and his missionary team did not go there at that time because "they were forbidden by the Holy Spirit to preach the word in Asia" (Acts 16:6). I believe a major reason they were not permitted to go to Ephesus was that they were not yet ready. Paul's defeat in Athens and his reassessment of priorities in Corinth was a major and necessary learning experience prior to Ephesus. So was his high-level power encounter with the Python Spirit in Philippi.

Paul and his team spent almost three years in Ephesus, much longer than usual, because the harvest was abundant. House churches, which was where Christians met for worship in those days, multiplied throughout the city and into its suburbs such as Metropolis, Hypaipa, Diashieron, Neikaia, Koloe and Palaiapolis. Paul trained church planters in a school owned by a man named Tyrannus, sending them out to evangelize other cities in Asia Minor such as Philadelphia, Sardis, Thyatira, Laodicea, Pergamos and Smyrna. In summary, Luke says things such as, "So the word of the Lord grew mightily and prevailed" (19:20), and "all who dwelt in Asia heard the word of the Lord Jesus, both Jews and Greeks" (v. 10). As well, Paul's enemies were admitting "that not only at Ephesus, but throughout almost all Asia, this Paul has persuaded and turned away people [from worshiping Diana]" (v. 26).

Never before or after did Paul have an experience that matched the success of this ministry in Ephesus. This is what missionary work was all about. Paul had laid such a good foundation that vigorous church growth continued for a long time after he left. F. F. Bruce says, "The province [of Asia Minor] was intensely evangelized and remained one of the leading centers of Christianity for many centuries."[8]

Strongholds of Darkness

Perhaps the strongholds of darkness in Ephesus were not as formidable as they were in Athens—nothing we know of would equal Athens—but they were not far from it. The major key to opening Ephesus and Asia Minor to the gospel was not brilliant preaching or persuasive words of human wisdom, but spiritual warfare on all levels, including strategic-level spiritual warfare. Paul's experience in Ephesus caused him to write back to the believers there, saying, "For we do not wrestle against flesh and blood, but against principalities, against powers, against the rulers of the darkness of this age, against spiritual hosts of wickedness in the heavenly places" (Eph. 6:12). Clinton Arnold, a Biola University scholar and a specialist on Ephesians, says that the Epistle to the Ephesians contains "a substantially higher concentration of power terminology than in any other epistle attributed to Paul."[9] Powerful action in "the heavenly places," or in the invisible world, prepared the way for the spread of the Word of God in the visible world.

Paul wrote 1 Corinthians while he was in Ephesus. Something he said there could be interpreted as referring to his strategic-level spiritual warfare in Ephesus. Paul said to the Corinthians, "If, in the manner of men, I have fought with beasts at Ephesus" (15:32). What does he mean by "beasts"? Were they literal beasts as in the coliseum in Rome? F. F. Bruce thinks we should take Paul's language figuratively, not literally,[10] and I would agree. Some commentators suggest that he might be referring to human opponents. That could be, but I think it is more likely that Paul was referring to fighting in "the heavenly places" because he clearly said that the battle is not against flesh and blood. If so, the "beasts" could well be territorial spirits or strongmen whom Paul had bound, thus clearing the spiritual environment for extraordinary church growth.

What, exactly, were the spiritual forces facing Paul in Ephesus? It was a large city, the fourth largest in the Roman Empire. According to Bruce Metzger, Ephesus was the magic capital of the whole ancient world. He says, "Of all ancient Graeco-Roman cities, Ephesus...was by far the most hospitable to magicians, sorcerers, and charlatans of all sorts."[11] As such, it is not surprising that Ephesus was a major producer of fetishes, which were key tools of the forces of darkness in almost all animistic societies. The silversmiths of Ephesus had developed a lucrative business in the manufacture and sale of fetishes. The so-called "Ephesian writings" were known throughout the Roman Empire. F. F. Bruce comments, "The phrase 'Ephesian writings' was commonly used in antiquity for documents containing spells and formulae...to be placed in small cylinders or lockets worn around the neck or elsewhere about the person."[12]

Diana Was Supreme

Supernatural powers of darkness were rampant in Ephesus when Paul arrived. He did not have to be an expert in spiritual mapping to discover that the highest-ranking spirit of all was Diana, sometimes called Artemis, of the Ephesians. Diana was extraordinarily well known not only in Asia Minor, but throughout the whole Roman Empire as well. Clinton Arnold says that Diana "was worshipped more widely by individuals than any other deity known to Pausanius."[13] The silversmiths who sold fetishes made in Diana's image used extravagantly blasphemous language when referring to her: "the great goddess," "her magnificence," "all Asia and the world worship [her]" (Acts 19:27). Their shout was, "Great is Diana of the Ephesians!" (v. 28). In other literature she was exalted as "greatest," "holiest," "most manifest," "Lady," "Savior" and "Queen of the Cosmos."[14]

In the mind of anyone familiar with the operations of the kingdom of Satan, there could be little doubt that not only was Diana of the Ephesians a territorial spirit over the City of Ephesus and Asia Minor, but that her evil power exceeded that of most as well. Her influence had extended well beyond those boundaries. F. F. Bruce quotes a source indicating that she was worshiped in at least 33 places within the Roman Empire.[15] Diana was actually ruling her territory before the Greeks arrived. They gave her the name "Artemis," but that is not a Greek name. Her image is not a typical work of elegant Greek art, but a grotesque, many-breasted pagan idol of Asia. Clinton Arnold has discovered that Diana was "the only divinity to depict visibly her divine superiority with the signs of the zodiac."[16]

Although scholars of the ancient world whom I have consulted do not use the term "territorial spirits," their descriptions of Diana fit my working definition perfectly. Take, for example, Paul Trebilco of New Zealand, who finds that "While Ephesus was the home of many cults, the *most significant and powerful deity* was Artemis of the Ephesians"[17] [emphasis mine]. If she were a true territorial spirit, she would control much of the life of the city. Such was the case, according to Trebilco: "It was the cult of the Ephesian Artemis which, *more than anything else,* made Ephesus a centre of religious life during our period. But the influence of the cult of Artemis extended beyond the religious sphere to the civic, economic, and cultural life of the city"[18] [emphasis mine]. He goes on to add: "Any factor which sidelined Artemis would affect not only the religious, but also virtually all facets of life of the city."[19] In other words, if Paul went to Ephesus to preach the kingdom of God, his most formidable opponent in the invisible world would be Diana.

Paul, well experienced by now in evangelism, church planting and spiritual warfare on all levels, is ready to take on the fortress of Diana. He must have been stunned when he first saw Diana's temple, one of the most beautiful pieces of architecture in history. It was later classified as one of the Seven Wonders of the Ancient World. Its 93,500 square feet was four times the size of the Parthenon in Athens. Each of its 127, 60-foot-high columns had been donated by a different king, another indication of Diana's widespread influence. Its position in the visible world was evident to all, and its awesome standing as a power center in the invisible world was recognized by any who had eyes to see that dimension of reality.

In Ephesus, Paul went on the offensive against the forces of darkness. Some warn against attempting this, saying that Christians should only *defend* themselves against attacks of the enemy, not step out seeking to engage demonic spirits in battle. Others, however, such as Tom White, advocate a more aggressive approach. White says, "Certain 'high places' in our land are unholy, dark corners in our cities that keep doors open to demonic hosts. Many times I have led prayer walks to such high places—shrines, New Age bookstores, pornography shops, university campuses, town halls, courthouses and headquarters of occult organizations. I have often experienced the strange tension between following a prompting that is pleasing to God and feeling the resistance of hell in leading such an offensive charge."[20] Tom White could well have been describing the feelings of the apostle Paul as he entered the city of Ephesus.

LEVELS OF SPIRITUAL WARFARE IN EPHESUS

As far as we know from Luke's account in Acts, in Ephesus, Paul overtly engaged in spiritual warfare on the ground level and on the occult level, but not on the strategic level. He was falsely accused of provoking strategic-level encounters when the rioting silversmiths and others falsely testified that he had gone into the temple of Diana and insulted the spirit herself. The judgment of the political authority hearing the case was that Paul and his team "are neither robbers of temples nor blasphemers of your goddess" (Acts 19:37). We can surmise, then, that Paul did not have a head-on encounter with Diana in Ephesus, as he did with Python in Philippi.

If this is the case, some will ask why I include it in my list of five instances of strategic-level spiritual warfare in the book of Acts. First, I have said that "fighting the beasts in Ephesus" could well have referred to strategic-level spiritual warfare, but that is only one way of interpreting it. I also have two other reasons for including it: (1) Often significant damage is done on the strategic level to territorial spirits through power ministries on the ground and occult levels. This is the way I like to interpret Paul's ministry in Ephesus. (2) After Paul left, the apostle John came to Ephesus and he *did* enter into the temple of Diana and engage her head-on. Let me explain both.

Ground-Level Warfare

Luke's account in Acts 19 of doing ground-level spiritual warfare, that is, casting demons out of people, contains two parts: how to do it and how *not* to do it. He uses Paul as the example of how to do it, and he uses the seven sons of Sceva as examples of how not to do it.

Luke says that *unusual* miracles occurred in Ephesus through the hands of Paul. I have mentioned this previously, explaining how some people, even today, find it necessary to distinguish between usual and unusual miracles because the power of God is so strong in their churches or in their ministries. I know that this is not a problem for all. Unfortunately, in some churches any miracle at all would be considered "unusual"!

One of the unusual events in Ephesus was that demons were expelled by carrying handkerchiefs or articles of clothing that Paul had physically touched and laying them on the demonized person (see Acts 19:11,12). Other than the story of the Python spirit in Philippi, this is the only other instance Luke gives us of Paul doing deliverance. I have already commented that this should by no means be taken to imply that deliverance was only a minor feature in Paul's career or that he didn't cast out demons regularly. It is noteworthy that Luke would attach one of his rare mentions of it to the use of objects, such as handkerchiefs.

Some of my friends are extremely, I would say overly, concerned that when we begin to do power ministries of various kinds we can become susceptible to allowing "magic" to infiltrate our modus operandi. I do not deny the possibility that such a thing could happen or that it perhaps has happened in some instances. Now that I have logged more than a decade of researching, teaching, writing about and practicing power ministries, I must testify that such cases seem to be few and far between. As I understand it, magic is the ability acquired by a human being to manipulate supernatural powers of darkness to do the person's bidding. I have had a difficult time trying to understand why some Christian leaders, because of the use of anointing oil or the "name of Jesus" or the exercise of faith that God will heal the sick, associate divine healing with magic or in some cases the New Age.

We see here that Paul used healing cloths to a positive effect. In casting out demons with handkerchiefs, Paul wasn't doing magic, he was instead launching a frontal attack on the spiritual forces empowering the magic capital of the Roman Empire. The supernatural power operating through Paul was not the power of the demonic world on which magicians have drawn throughout history, but it was the power of the true God who had commissioned His emissaries to "Heal the sick, cleanse the lepers, raise the dead, cast out demons" (Matt. 10:8).

Occult-Level Spiritual Warfare

In Ephesus, perhaps more than most places, spiritual warfare at any level would necessarily have something to do with magicians. Occult-level spiritual warfare, by definition, involves such practitioners. Some of the most notable conversions in Ephesus occurred among magicians. The account has the characteristics of a people movement, especially considering the communal decision to burn magical books and other paraphernalia publicly. The magnitude of the bonfire is often overlooked because the phrase "fifty thousand pieces of silver" (Acts 19:19) does not register with most of us. The maximum value we might instinctively put on it would be $50,000 on the assumption they were silver dollars. Once we recognize that in those days a piece of silver was a day's wage and do some calculations, suddenly the value of the articles burned rises to around $4 million!

What prepared the way for such a massive prophetic act and public declaration of the lordship of Jesus Christ? Many things, but probably the major factor was the encounter with the seven sons of Sceva.

These Jewish exorcists practiced real magic and, like most magicians, they were always looking for more power. As they observed Paul, they noticed that he used what they interpreted to be a magic formula—"in the name of Jesus." The results were something they had never seen before, so they were interested. They tested the formula by approaching some demonized people, addressing the evil spirits and saying, "We exorcise you by the Jesus whom Paul preaches" (v. 13). Big mistake!

The sons of Sceva used the name of Jesus, but without previously having received authorization from Jesus to use it. The first ones who recognized their stupidity were the spirits themselves. One of them mocked them and said, "Jesus I know and Paul I know; but who are you?" (v. 15). A demonized man then jumped on the seven sons of Sceva, ripped off their clothes and chased them out of the house naked!

According to Susan Garrett, when word of this got around the network of magicians in Ephesus, many of them decided to turn to the Lord. She asks what the relationship between the sons of Sceva incident and the conversion of the magicians could have been, and concludes, "the obvious answer is that in Luke's understanding, the Ephesians perceived the defeat of the seven sons to be a defeat of magic in general."[21] Clinton Arnold adds, "There can be no question that spirit beings were perceived as the functionaries behind the magic."[22]

Interconnecting the Spirit World

Better than any other passage of Scripture, Acts 19 shows us clearly how the world of darkness is interconnected, overriding the somewhat artificial lines some of us have drawn separating ground-level, occult-level and strategic-level spiritual warfare. Casting out demons with handkerchiefs strongly influenced the people movement among Ephesian magicians, as did the foolish arrogance of the seven exorcists in Sceva's household. Both of these had their influence on the power of Diana of the Ephesians. Without overtly confronting Diana herself, Paul and the missionaries had weakened her authority so much that the silversmiths and others rioted. They, along with the general population of Ephesus, were alarmed that Diana's temple could be despised and her magnificence was being destroyed (see v. 27). Diana had been so powerful that many people thought the very fabric of their lives might be ripped apart if she were harmed.

The result was that the kingdom of God came to Ephesus

and the surrounding area of Asia Minor in a more widespread and more notable way than any other place in which Paul had ministered. The strongman, in this case strong woman, had been bound, the spiritual blinders were removed from the multitudes, souls were saved, churches multiplied and Ephesus became a long-term center of gravity for the whole Christian movement.

THE DEFEAT OF MAXIMON

So as not to relegate such a spiritual victory as Paul had in Ephesus to some faded pages of yesteryear, let me relate a similar event I personally have witnessed. I have in my hand a copy of the Guatemalan equivalent to *Time* or *Newsweek: Cronica Semanal* (June 24-30, 1994). The cover story carries the headline, "The Defeat of Maximon: Protestant Fundamentalism Alters the Culture of the Altiplano and Turns the Native Religions into Tourist Attractions." Maximon was a territorial spirit similar to Diana, and he also was defeated essentially through ground-level spiritual warfare.

The small city of Almolonga is a three-hour drive over beautiful mountains west of Guatemala City. The population of 12,000, almost all Quiche Indians, are descendants of the vast Mayan Empire. Almolonga is known as the garden city of Central America, growing and marketing fresh vegetables from Mexico to Panama.

A central characteristic of the city, which is built on the hills overlooking a rich valley, is 20 evangelical churches. They are the most prominent features of the urban landscape. All of them are alive and well and relatively large. At least 80 percent of the people of Almolonga are born-again Christians.

It was not always like this. Prior to the late 1970s, Almolonga was little different from neighboring cities such as Olintepeque and Zunil. It was characterized by misery, poverty, immorality, corruption, violence, dissension and disease. Men would typically receive their pay on Friday, spend it on drunken orgies and return home to distressed wives and children on Monday. According to one observer, "Drunks were laid out in the streets like cordwood." Many never awoke from their stupors.

The gospel came to Almolonga in 1951. Three churches were planted, but made virtually no headway. Their spiritual power was minimal, and the community remained under the control of the god of this age. Then a pagan named Mariano Riscajche was saved in 1974, hearing a voice from God, as did Paul, on the day of his conversion, saying, "I have chosen you to serve Me." Soon afterward a sick and demonized man asked Mariano to pray for him and he was miraculously healed and delivered.

Deliverance from Demons

The word got out, more sick came and many were also healed. Churches began to grow. The opposition to evangelicals then intensified and unbelieving merchants would not sell food to the Christians. The spiritual battle was on full force. In 1975 Mariano received a new filling of the Holy Spirit, began large-scale deliverance and soon had freed more than 400 people who had been held captive by demons in Almolonga. The spiritual atmosphere of Almolonga began to change radically.

Almost immediately the physical and social atmosphere of the community began to change also. Barrooms closed down. Restaurants and stores and businesses now carry biblical names such as "Bethany" and "Jerusalem" and "Shalom." Almolonga has become a city of entrepreneurs who purchase Mercedes trucks, paying cash, to deliver their vegetables on international routes. Families are together and happy. Schools are thriving. Mariano Riscajche has recently completed an elegant sanctuary accommodating 2,000 right next to the central plaza of the city.

Doris and I traveled to Almolonga in 1992 with our friends Harold and Cecelia Caballeros of the El Shaddai Church in Guatemala City. We had heard that the territorial spirit over the whole area was a notorious demon named Maximon. We wanted to see Almolonga, where his power had been broken, and also neighboring Zunil where a shrine housed the revolting idol that represented the principality.

Maximon did not want us to invade his territory. The private airplane we had chartered crashed on landing when the landing gear did not come down as the pilot thought it had. We thought we were goners, but God protected us from serious harm. An intercessor who was on the ground waiting for us to land reported he had been told by the Holy Spirit that Maximon was about to attack us, and he had been praying fervently for our protection. The plane was split open and mangled, so we had to take a bus back to Guatemala City.

The shrine of Maximon had to be the threshold of hell itself. Five warlocks and one witch were hard at work when we paid our brief visit, invoking the activities of dark angels. It was the most revolting spiritual activity I ever want to see, and I do not care to record any more of the hideous details. Have these beings really come to steal, to kill and to destroy? In Zunil, disease, hunger, drunkenness, accidents, poverty, immorality and violence are part and parcel of daily life. Recent natural disasters have torn the town apart, but Almolonga, only 3 kilometers away, has remained unscathed. Maximon was in his glory in Zunil.

Maximon was on the retreat, however, and still is. The report of the *Cronica Semanal* cover story tells of a city such as Zunil, formerly under Maximon's perverse power, and it says, "The cult of Maximon and its followers has been reduced to a mere handful of individuals, and, due to his downfall, the men of the city no longer drink liquor because of their evangelical faith and therefore the annual festival to the idol...is now financed only by money collected from sightseeing tours of Japanese, Germans and Americans."[23]

The territorial spirit that had Almolonga bound in spiritual captivity for centuries was well known by name. His power over Almolonga and other places had been neutralized through the power ministries of Mariano Riscajche and other servants of the Most High God. As in Ephesus, the supreme spirit of the area had lost its authority through vigorous activity on the ground-level, casting out large numbers of demons from people. As a result, the physical, social, material and spiritual blessings of the kingdom of God were able totally to transform the city. This helps us understand why we must never forget that Satan's kingdom is one, and that successful spiritual warfare on any level will influence all levels to one extent or another.

SCENE II: JOHN VERSUS DIANA

When Paul left Ephesus, Diana of the Ephesians had been thoroughly embarrassed, and her power had been severely weakened. Now the book of Acts closes and history begins. Ramsay MacMullen, a Yale University historian, fills us in on some of the things that later happened in Ephesus. I featured MacMullen in chapter 4, telling how he concludes that the major factor, above all others, that led to the Christianization of the Roman Empire was dealing directly with the demonic. He speaks of the tremendous evangelistic power that is accompanied with what I call strategic-level spiritual warfare or what he calls "head-on confrontation with supernatural beings inferior to God."[24]

Sometime after Paul left Ephesus, the apostle John went there to live and to minister. We saw that during Paul's ministry there, he did not enter the temple of Diana, nor did he engage the territorial spirit in overt strategic-level spiritual warfare. John did both of these things, however, according to Ramsay Mac-Mullen. MacMullen says that John was winning unbelievers to the faith through power ministries such as miraculous healings. But more important than the healings was his personal encounter with Diana.

One day John walked into the huge, ornate temple—one of the wonders of the ancient world—and "in the very temple of [Diana herself], he prayed, 'O God...at whose name every idol takes flight and every demon and every unclean power: now let the demon that is here [in this temple] take flight in thy name.'"[25] A more direct power encounter could hardly be imagined.

The real confrontation took place in the invisible world. As frequently happens, though, the immediate effects were seen in

---

In strategic-level spiritual warfare, proceed only on God's timing.

---

the visible world. Dramatic physical manifestations occurred. First, the altar of Diana split into many pieces! Second, half the temple of Diana fell crashing to the ground! Visible spiritual effects also were occurring. According to the record, "the assembled Ephesians cried out, '[There is but] one God, [the God] of John!...We are converted, now that we have seen thy marvelous works!'"[26]

An obvious question arises. Why was it that Paul did not go into the temple of Diana, but John did. The answer is simple, because it rests on a principle I have mentioned several times: *In strategic-level spiritual warfare, proceed only on God's timing.* Both Paul and John had the discernment and the experience to know this principle well. I would surmise that if Paul had violated the principle and gone into Diana's temple to take her on, he, rather than her altar, might have ended up split in pieces. It is dangerous to trifle with territorial spirits.

Could This Be True?

What Ramsay MacMullen quotes, of course, is not the Bible, so we cannot equate its veracity with the book of Ephesians. Just because it is not Scripture, however, would not mean that it is necessarily false. Part of the historian's job is to help us separate what is in all probability valid from what is in all probability false.

Realizing that this event involving the apostle John might be called into question by some who read it, MacMullen quickly goes on to say, "I don't think the explanatory force of this scene should be discounted on the grounds that it cannot really have happened, that it is fiction, that no one was meant to believe it." He is anticipating that the paradigms of some historians and perhaps some biblical scholars might block them from accepting it. "I suppose instead," MacMullen continues, "that it was quite widely believed in the second and third centuries with which we are concerned at the moment; and I assume that its substance, mostly in oral form, led through belief to conversion. Why not? *Such wonderful stories were most reliably reported*"[27] [emphasis mine].

Subsequent historical records indicate that, building on the momentum of centuries, Diana managed to maintain some influence for at least 50 years after John's head-on power encounter. She didn't last much longer than that though. Clinton Arnold reports that the "influx and expansion of Christianity eventually wrought the demise of the cult of the Ephesian Artemis."[28]

SUMMARY

The invasion of the territory of Diana and her defeat constitute the fifth and final episode of strategic-level spiritual warfare I believe we find in the New Testament. In Athens Paul learned that human wisdom is not enough to penetrate a city "given over to idols." He corrected it by moving in demonstrations of supernatural power in Corinth, and especially in Ephesus. Ephesus provides for us the most vivid example in the Bible that "we do not wrestle against flesh and blood, but against principalities, against powers, against the rulers of the darkness of this age, against spiritual hosts of wickedness in the heavenly places" (Eph. 6:12). Defeating the powers on the strategic level will clear the way for the vigorous spread of the gospel, whether in the first century or in modern times.

■ REFLECTION QUESTIONS ■

1. Can you think of any areas today that might be like Athens—under so much spiritual darkness that it is almost impossible to preach the gospel effectively?

2. The temple of Diana was one of the principal "power points" in Ephesus. What are some similar "power points" in your community?

3. What are the major differences that distinguish Christian prayer and spiritual warfare from non-Christian magic?

4. In Ephesus the converted magicians staged a public book burning. Do you think Christians ought to do similar things today? Would you participate?

5. History, not the Bible, tells us that John had a power encounter with Diana of the Ephesians. Should we really believe such historical accounts?

Notes

1. Everett Ferguson, *Backgrounds of Early Christianity* (Grand Rapids: William B. Eerdmans Publishing Company, 1987; revised edition, 1993), p. 143.
2. Ibid., p. 136.
3. Ibid., p. 141.
4. Ibid., p. 185.
5. George Otis Jr., "An Overview of Spiritual Mapping," *Breaking Strongholds in Your City*, ed. C. Peter Wagner (Ventura, Calif.: Regal Books, 1993), p. 42.
6. Eugene H. Peterson, *The Message: The New Testament in Contemporary English* (Colorado Springs: NavPress, 1993), p. 329.
7. Richard Belward Rackham, *The Acts of the Apostles: An Exposition* (London, England: Methuen & Company Ltd., 1901), p. 320.
8. F. F. Bruce, *The Book of Acts* (Grand Rapids: William B. Eerdmans Publishing Company, 1954; revised edition, 1988), p. 366.
9. Clinton E. Arnold, *Ephesians: Power and Magic* (Grand Rapids: Baker Book House, 1992), p. 1.
10. See F. F. Bruce, *Paul: Apostle of the Heart Set Free* (Grand Rapids: William B. Eerdmans Publishing Company, 1977), p. 295.
11. Bruce M. Metzger, "St. Paul and the Magicians," *Princeton Seminary Bulletin* 38 (June 1944): 27.
12. Bruce, *Paul: Apostle of the Heart Set Free*, p. 291.
13. Arnold, *Ephesians*, p. 20.
14. Paul Trebilco, "Asia," *The Book of Acts in Its Graeco-Roman Setting*, ed. David W. J. Gill and Conrad Gempf (Grand Rapids: William B. Eerdmans Publishing Company, 1944), p. 317-318.
15. Bruce, *The Book of Acts*, p. 375.
16. Arnold, *Ephesians*, p. 21.
17. Trebilco, "Asia," p. 316.
18. Ibid.
19. Ibid., p. 329.
20. Tom White, *Breaking Strongholds: How Spiritual Warfare Sets Captives Free* (Ann Arbor: Vine Books, 1993), p. 172. In this approach, White teaches and practices a style of intercessory prayer warfare that is visible and verbal. The primary emphases are the worship and exaltation of God's name and character, and a faith-filled appeal to the Lord to expose and weaken strongholds of darkness with His superior and sovereign authority.
21. Susan Garrett, *The Demise of the Devil* (Minneapolis: Fortress Press, 1989), p. 95.
22. Arnold, *Ephesians*, p. 18.
23. Mario Roberto Morales, "La Quiebra de Maximon," *Cronica Semanal* (June 20-24, 1994): 17.
24. Ramsay MacMullen, *Christianizing the Roman Empire (A.D. 100-400)* (New Haven, Conn.: Yale University Press, 1984), p. 112.
25. Ibid., p. 26.
26. Ibid.
27. Ibid.
28. Arnold, *Ephesians*, p. 28.

Warfare in the Epistles

J ESUS SET THE TONE FOR SPIRITUAL WARFARE. HE PRAC-
ticed it on all levels, the highest being His power
encounter with Satan himself in the desert. Then by
providing His followers with the "keys of the Kingdom,"
which is the God-given authority to bind and loose, He
gave them and us the spiritual equipment we need to
"bind the strong man" and to help free lost souls being
held captive by territorial spirits and other forces of
darkness.

The book of Acts contains several accounts of its
two main characters—Peter and Paul—obeying the
Master's commission and incorporating strategic-level
spiritual warfare into their evangelistic ministries. History tells us that the apostle John also engaged in head-on
confrontation with the powers, especially when he
moved to Ephesus and challenged Diana of the Ephesians.

We find substantial biblical teaching about strategic-level spiritual warfare in the Gospels and in the book of Acts. As might be expected, the Epistles also contain important instructions for us as we move out in our cities and around the world with the gospel of Jesus Christ.

WHAT ABOUT THE BOOK OF REVELATION?

When we come to the final book of the Bible—the book of Revelation—written by none other than the apostle John, we find that the principal themes of the book involve spiritual warfare. Such statements as "And war broke out in heaven: Michael and his angels fought with the dragon; and the dragon and his angels fought. For the devil has come down to you, having great wrath, because he knows that he has a short time. And the dragon...went to make war with...[those who] have the testimony of Jesus Christ" (12:7,12,17) are typical of the book of Revelation.

I have chosen not to attempt a chapter in this book detailing the aspects of spiritual warfare throughout Revelation for two reasons. First, the book of Revelation lends itself to a wide spectrum of differing interpretations, and mine will be seen by many as just another one of them. Second, those who have raised critical questions about the biblical validity of strategic-level spiritual warfare have not seen fit to focus on the content of the book of Revelation to any great extent. If I did undertake commenting on Revelation, it might better take the form of another book, rather than an additional chapter in this one.

At the same time, it will be well to recall that in an earlier chapter I did stress the words of Jesus that we find in Revelation 2 and 3—the epistles to the seven churches of Asia Minor. There we find Jesus telling His followers seven times to "overcome," using the Greek verb *nikao*. In another context Jesus explains to the disciples that *overcoming* is what we are expected to do when principalities such as Beelzebub become obstructions to the advance of the kingdom of God.

THE EPISTLES OF JOHN AND PETER

The three apostles who have gone on record as engaging in the highest-level power encounters with the rulers of darkness are Paul, Peter and John.

John not only wrote the book of Revelation, perhaps the most overt spiritual warfare book in the Bible, but he also wrote three Epistles. In them he has much to say about confronting our adversary, the devil. Lest we be complacent, John warns us that "the whole world lies under the sway of the wicked one" (1 John 5:19). When we go out in the world, we go with nothing less than the power of Christ. John wrote, "For this purpose the Son of God was manifested, that He might destroy the works of the devil" (3:8). We can also do it. John also picks up on the key word of Jesus, *"overcome,"* when he congratulates some young men because "you have *overcome* the wicked one" (2:14, emphasis mine).

Peter warns his readers in no uncertain terms about the spiritual warfare they can expect to encounter in their Christian walk: "Be sober, be vigilant; because your adversary the devil walks about like a roaring lion, seeking whom he may devour" (1 Pet. 5:8). Rather than ignoring the devil, Peter tells us to "resist him" (v. 9). This is not a defensive term. Suppose a real lion invades the town in which we live. We would not just close and lock the doors of our homes so the lion could not enter, but we would also take immediate steps to see that the lion itself is removed from our town. "Resisting" the lion means to go after it, pursuing it until the threat is removed. The best defense is a good offense.

These references to the devil in 1 John and 1 Peter seem to refer to spiritual warfare on something higher than ground level. They could and undoubtedly do embrace the assumption that "resisting the devil" includes casting out demons. Casting out demons was a high-profile activity of Christians in the Early Church, which Ramsay MacMullen tells us lasted for at least 400 years. I believe these references reflect the words of Jesus that He gives His followers authority "over *all* the power of the enemy" (Luke 10:19, emphasis mine).

WHAT IS JUDE SAYING?

When we mention taking an offensive stand against the devil or removing the roaring lion from our towns, some of those who do not approve of initiating such warfare cite Jude 9 to support their positions. Here is what Jude says: "Yet Michael the archangel, in contending with the devil, when he disputed about the body of Moses, dared not bring against him a reviling accusation, but said, 'The Lord rebuke you!'" (Jude 9). Some take Jude's words to be a biblical indication that we should steer away from strategic-level spiritual warfare.

Although it is obvious why some might jump to such a conclusion, more careful study indicates that this is not at all what Jude had in mind when he wrote this verse. I have several reasons for saying this.

1. Jude is not writing an Epistle about how to do spiritual warfare. He is writing about how to expose people who have spirits of rebellion and who insist on resisting authority. Wayne Grudem, a biblical scholar who has gone into this in some detail, agrees. He says, "The lesson of the verse is simply, 'Don't try to go beyond the authority God has given you!' When Jude 9 is viewed in this way, the only question that arises for a Christian is, 'What authority has God given us over demonic forces?' And the rest of the New Testament speaks clearly to that in several places."[1]

In other parts of the Bible, as we have seen, we are told to resist not only high-ranking evil spirits such as Beelzebub, but we are also told to resist the devil himself as we just saw from 1 Peter 5:9. James also mentions resisting the devil, as we shall soon see. Wayne Grudem adds: "During Jesus' earthly ministry, when He sent the 12 disciples ahead of Him to preach the kingdom of God, He 'gave them power *over all demons*' (Luke 9:1, italics added)."[2] We *do* have biblical authority to resist the forces of Satan wherever they may be found.

2. Even if Jude 9 were relating to strategic-level spiritual warfare, which it is not, the instructions there still would not apply to addressing demonic beings under Satan, but only to Satan himself. Few people I know who do strategic-level spiritual warfare today address Satan in anything other than a rhetorical form. From time to time I receive reports from those who believe they have encountered Satan in person, but cross-examination most frequently leads to the more probable conclusion that they may really have encountered high-ranking spirits such as perhaps the Python spirit in Philippi or Diana of the Ephesians, but not Lucifer. By saying that, I am not categorically denying the possibility that someone might have confronted Satan because I would have no way to prove it. I am saying that even stretching the meaning of Jude 9, it would only apply to such a rare situation as that, and not to strategic-level spiritual warfare in general.

3. As I have stressed in previous chapters, Jesus' death on the cross permanently and decisively changed human history. It also radically affected the situation in the invisible world, sealing the doom of the demonic principalities and powers. That is why Jesus makes it a point to say that the least in the kingdom of heaven (*after* the Cross) is greater than John the Baptist, representing all those who lived *before* the cross (see Matt. 11:11). As soon as Jesus said that, He went on to say that "the kingdom of heaven suffers violence, and the violent take it by force"

(v. 12). This seems to be a clear reference to aggressive spiritual warfare.

Jude 9 makes a reference to "the body of Moses," which sets the passage in the context of the Old Testament, or in the period before Jesus came and changed things radically. In the Old Testament, believers were not given the same authority over the powers of evil that Jesus has given to us. Nowhere in the Old Testament do we find incidents of demons being cast out as we see in the ministry of Jesus and the apostles or as Ramsay MacMullen finds through the pages of Christian history. The difference was that Jesus brought the kingdom of God in a unique way and sealed the doom of Satan with His blood on the cross. In verse 9, Jude is referring to an illustration from the past, not projecting what our future parameters of ministry in the extension of the kingdom of God might look like.

I could say more about Jude 9, but I think I have made it sufficiently clear that we do not find there any *prohibition* for Christians to do the kind of strategic-level spiritual warfare I am describing in this book, provided that such warfare is carefully done according to the guidelines we find in other parts of Scripture.

JAMES: RESIST THE DEVIL AND HE WILL FLEE

A key passage for understanding strategic-level spiritual warfare is found in the Epistle of James:

> Therefore submit to God. Resist the devil and he will flee from you. Draw near to God and He will draw near to you. Cleanse your hands, you sinners; and purify your hearts, you double-minded (4:7,8).

James describes two relationships in these verses by using seven verbs: five active verbs and two passive verbs. The first relationship is *upward* toward God and the second is *outward* toward the devil. Both are important, both demand that we take initiative and both bring forth predictable responses to our initiatives. They should be done simultaneously, but the second cannot happen apart from the first.

The *upward* relationship to God is achieved through our doing four things, described by four of the active verbs: submit, draw near, cleanse and purify. We *submit* to God by accepting Jesus Christ as our Lord and Savior, entering the family of God and relating to God as our Father. We *draw near* to God through spending time with the Father in prayer and by getting to know Him well. Only then can we hear His voice accurately and respond correctly to His assignments and to His timing for spiritual warfare.

We are also to *cleanse* our hands and *purify* our hearts. This relates both to what we *do* and to what we *think,* implying a life of holiness. Without holiness we may think we have put on the full armor of God to go into warfare against the forces of darkness, but we will soon find we have "holes in our armor," as I have heard Cindy Jacobs say many times. Holiness is being so full of God that there is no room for anything else. It is an indispensable precondition for entering into effective strategic-level spiritual warfare.

Once we take the initiative to submit, draw near, cleanse and purify, then the first passive verb comes into play: *God will draw near to you.* I use the word "passive," not in the grammatical sense, but in the sense that the initiative to act passes from us to God. He will respond by establishing the intimate relationship with Himself that we desire and that we need if we are going to take authority over the angels of darkness.

The *outward* movement involves appropriating the authority given by God and initiating the other active verb: *resist* the devil. This is the scary part, the part many choose to leave out. The *upward* movement is the bedroom and the *outward* movement is the battlefield. Facing a roaring lion, particularly one who has great wrath because it knows its end is near, is not an appealing thought. But if we do it, we need not fear, because the second passive verb will immediately come into play and the devil *will flee* from you. Jesus set the tone for us with his power encounter in the wilderness. He did not wait for Satan to come to Him, but rather, by the guidance of the Holy Spirit, He took the initiative and invaded the territory of Satan.

WARFARE IN PAUL'S LETTERS

What we know of the apostle Paul we learn from two sources: Luke's account in the book of Acts about how Paul evange-

---

We know that both evangelism and spiritual warfare were high-priority items for Paul mainly through what we learn from the book of Acts, which is explicitly written in the context of evangelism, and not Christian nurture.

---

lized and planted churches and also from Paul's letters, or Epistles, which he later wrote back to those churches and to some of his fellow workers. It seems to me that both of these sources are of utmost importance. I clearly recall that in the early years of our debates about strategic-level spiritual warfare, a respected biblical scholar wrote a detailed paper about Paul's views of spiritual warfare without once mentioning the material in the book of Acts. This was inconceivable to me, for I would not want to profess to understand what Paul wrote to the churches without first examining what ministry he previously had performed in those churches.

If theology emerges from ministry, as I argued in chapter 2, we must read Paul's letters in their ministry context. Of Paul's 13 Epistles in the New Testament, only 5 deal with spiritual warfare in enough explicit detail to mention here. Some may conclude from this that spiritual warfare was not high on Paul's agenda because he thought it was worth mentioning only about 35 percent of the time. This is not good reasoning. If it were, we might conclude that witnessing to our neighbors about Jesus Christ and personal soul winning were not on Paul's agenda at all, because he doesn't explicitly encourage the recipients of *any* of his letters written to the churches to do so.

This is explained by recognizing that Paul's letters to the churches were written in the context of Christian nurture, not evangelism. We know that both evangelism and spiritual warfare were high-priority items for Paul mainly through what we learn from the book of Acts, which is explicitly written in the context of evangelism, and not Christian nurture. This is why Acts and the Epistles need to be studied together if we want to get the whole picture, and not just a part of it.

As we have seen in previous chapters, Luke features Paul's experiences with strategic-level spiritual warfare in three places: Paphos in West Cyprus, Philippi and Ephesus. Nothing implies that Paul did *not* do strategic-level spiritual warfare elsewhere, for Luke's style of historiography is selective as shown by how he chose to describe Paul's message of justification by faith not three times, but only once—in Antioch of Pisidia.

The greatest evangelistic success Paul had in any place he ministered came in Ephesus. The preceding chapter describes that in considerable detail. It is understandable, then, that the four Epistles in which Paul does deal with strategic-level spiritual warfare were all written in the context of his ministry in Ephesus. Paul wrote *2 Corinthians* while he still was ministering in Ephesus. He wrote *Colossians* to one of the churches that his church-planting teams established as he trained his workers in the city of Ephesus and sent them out to evangelize the surrounding area of Asia Minor. He wrote *Ephesians* to the believers in Ephesus itself, and he wrote *1 and 2 Timothy* while Timothy was ministering in Ephesus and Asia Minor.[3]

SECOND CORINTHIANS: THE POWER OF THE GOD OF THIS AGE

While Paul was in Ephesus, casting out demons with handkerchiefs, witnessing magicians publicly burning their books and facing the wrath of silversmiths who saw the kingdom of Diana of the Ephesians crumbling, he wrote a letter to the believers in Corinth—2 Corinthians. Three notable passages are found in 2 Corinthians: (1) Chapter 4 relates to the god of this age, (2) Chapter 2 tells about Satan's devices and (3) Chapter 10 advocates tearing down strongholds.

Several times throughout this book I have mentioned 2 Corinthians 4:3,4:

> But even if our gospel is veiled, it is veiled to those who are perishing, whose minds the god of this age has blinded, who do not believe, lest the light of the gospel of the glory of Christ, who is the image of God, should shine on them.

Paul, as many of us are, was frustrated because not enough lost souls were being saved through his evangelistic ministry. This provoked him to pen the most explicit passage we have in the Scriptures concerning Satan's direct role in keeping the lost from hearing the gospel and being saved. The direct implication of this is that effective evangelism is primarily a battle against the god of this age—the devil.

It does not take a professional theologian to realize that Satan is not God, and therefore Satan does not possess any of the attributes of God. Satan is a creature, not the Creator. One of God's attributes is omnipresence, the quality of being everywhere at the same time. Because Satan is not omnipresent, he can be at only one place at one time. His influence, however, is widespread. The most reasonable way to explain Satan's almost universal influence is to postulate that he keeps people's minds blinded to the gospel through a whole hierarchy of demonic spirits who ultimately do his bidding.

Our battle for evangelism, then, is rarely, if ever, a direct confrontation with the god of this age, but rather against those principalities and powers assigned to certain networks of human beings by the evil one. This is what we are calling these days "strategic-level spiritual warfare."

Understanding the Devices of Satan

If this is true, then it becomes important to know just how the god of this age goes about keeping people blind to the gospel and on the road to hell. Paul refers to this in 2 Corinthians 2:11:

> Lest Satan should take advantage of us; for we are not ignorant of his devices.

As any military person will affirm, one of the most dangerous things in warfare is to go into battle without carefully evaluating the power and the strategy of the enemy. To change the order of Paul's words, he seems to be saying that if for any reason we *are* ignorant of Satan's devices, he would be expected to take advantage of us.

The immediate context in which Paul writes this is urging the Corinthians to forgive each other. One of the best known of Satan's devices, as all those who engage in a regular ministry of demonic deliverance will testify, is to maintain a spirit of unforgiveness. Much ministry experience has verified that this is one of the major obstacles to personal deliverance and also to corporate or social deliverance on the strategic level. I'll explain this when I come to 2 Corinthians 10.

Spiritual Mapping

A term coined by George Otis Jr. to describe the process of discovering the devices of Satan is "spiritual mapping." Because this plays such an important role in responsible strategic-level spiritual warfare, critics of one often tend to criticize the other also. I believe a good bit of this criticism is rooted in (1) failure to distinguish the difference between the two activities and (2) lack of understanding the nature of spiritual mapping.

One of America's foremost spiritual mappers, Pastor Bob Beckett of the Dwelling Place Church of Hemet, California, describes spiritual mapping as well as anyone. He says that in the Persian Gulf War, Saddam Hussein would shoot off his Scud missiles, and then turn on CNN television to find out where they hit. At the same time, the Allies would fire "smart bombs," which could be seen entering the exact smoke stacks or doors or window at which they were aimed. What made the difference? Before the war started, the Allies sent in carefully trained elite reconnaissance forces who infiltrated behind enemy lines and plotted the coordinates of the most strategic enemy targets. When the coordinates were entered into the computers of the smart bombs, they knew exactly where to go to do the most damage to the enemy.

I have often heard Bob Beckett say, "We do too much Scud missile praying for our communities." What we need is smart bomb praying." I couldn't agree more. What an X ray is to a surgeon, spiritual mapping is to an intercessor. One of the reasons we have seen relatively little success in praying for our communities is that many have not learned how to get their communities to talk back to them. Spiritual mapping shows us how. I have a hard time trying to understand why anyone would oppose, in principle, overt and systematic attempts to discover the devices of Satan.

Some say that spiritual mapping tends to glorify Satan. Others have expanded on this and warned that if we try to discover Satan's devices or learn the names of the spirits who are leading either individual or social oppression we empower the demonic spirits and make them more dangerous. This, to me, is like supposing that medical research glorifies the disease or empowers the viruses that cause it. In my lifetime, I have seen smallpox research virtually *eliminate* the dreadful disease of smallpox, not glorify it. We do medical research to destroy the disease, and we do spiritual mapping to neutralize the activities of the enemy and his forces of darkness.

Much more could be said about spiritual mapping, but another volume in the "Prayer Warrior Series," *Breaking Strongholds in Your City* (Regal Books), goes into all the further detail necessary.

Pulling Down Strongholds

One of the more curious aspects of my pilgrimage into the field of spiritual warfare during the past few years has been the discovery that those who had been talking about it and doing it long before I even thought much about it did not agree among themselves about the nature of strongholds. They agreed that strongholds provide the forces of darkness as a legal basis for doing their evil deeds both in individual people on the ground level and in cities or nations on the strategic level. Almost all of them, however, had their own opinions about the nature or identity of these strongholds. The rapidly emerging discipline of spiritual mapping is providing for us the method of discovering the identity of strongholds, but we have not been sure enough of what we are looking for exactly.

A consensus that 2 Corinthians 10:3-5 is the central biblical passage about strongholds also exists. What remains for us, then, is understanding as precisely as possible what the apostle Paul meant when he penned the following lines:

> For though we walk in the flesh, we do not war according to the flesh. For the weapons of our warfare are not carnal but mighty in God for pulling down strongholds, casting down *arguments* and every *high thing* that exalts itself against the knowledge of God, bringing every thought into captivity to the obedience of Christ.

I have italicized the words *arguments* and *high thing* to bring to our attention the two major forms that strongholds take, according to this passage. Understanding these should clear up a good bit of the fog that has surrounded this discussion, and it will also help us to comprehend one of the references Paul makes to strategic-level spiritual warfare.

The word for *arguments* in the Greek is *logizomai*. This reflects a human origin, human thoughts and attitudes and actions. What human beings choose to do can erect strongholds and the enemy takes advantage of them. These can be moral choices, unforgiveness as was previously discussed, corporate oppression, lust for power and control, murder, racism, evil thoughts or whatever else appears on the standard lists of sins in the Bible. Unless these are taken care of or "pulled down," the enemy will retain his legal right to keep people in captivity.

The Cosmic Powers

The word for *high things* in the Greek is *hypsoma*. Because this is crucial to my point, I will cite *The New International Dictionary of New Testament Theology* for the definition: "The New Testament use of *hypsoma* probably reflects astrological ideas, and hence denotes cosmic powers,...powers directed against God, seeking to intervene between God and [humans]."[4] Although *arguments* originate in and among human beings, *high things* originate in the invisible world and attack human beings, trying to keep them from God, and blinding their minds, as Paul says in 2 Corinthians 4. Both are strongholds and both need to be pulled down with spiritual, not carnal, weapons.

When spiritual mapping includes *logizomai* that need to be dealt with, our attention is directed to people. On the strategic level, repentance and reconciliation in the form of what John Dawson calls "identificational repentance" is one of the most powerful spiritual weapons that has surfaced in recent years. Dawson's textbook on the subject, *Healing America's Wounds* (Regal Books), is in my opinion one of just a handful of the most significant books published in the mid-1990s. When white Americans adequately repent of the slave trade, healing of racism will begin. When Japanese repent of bombing Pearl Harbor, the grip of the Sun Goddess will loosen. When Christians repent of the Crusades, doors will be opened for the evangelization of Muslims and Jews. These are only a few examples of pulling down strongholds in the form of *arguments* or *logizomai* on the current Spiritual Warfare Network agenda.

Spiritual mapping can and will often include *hypsoma* that also must be dealt with if the kingdom of God is to be spread. These are demonic beings, principalities and powers, which in many cases have been intentionally invited to take control of whole cities or people groups or nations. For example, the Emperor of Japan has officially invited the Sun Goddess to rule Japan through the famous *daijosai* ceremony. The spirit of death, called San La Muerte, had been invited to take charge of Resistencia, Argentina, by past generations. Both of these are *hypsoma* that should be pulled down. The power of San La Muerte was effectively broken in Resistencia through strategic-level spiritual warfare and churches were multiplied throughout the city.[5] The power of the Sun Goddess has remained virtually intact, although pulling down this stronghold is high on the agenda of the Japanese Spiritual Warfare Network.

If what I have said about high things, or *hypsoma*, is correct, we have here in 2 Corinthians 10 one of the most direct indications in the New Testament that we are to do strategic-level spiritual warfare.

COLOSSIANS: THE POWER OF THE CROSS

The Epistle of Paul's that contains proportionately the most power language is Ephesians. In second place is Colossians. Although Paul had never been to the church in Colossae, he had supervised the process of planting it from his base in Ephesus. As far as spiritual warfare is concerned, both the church in Colossae and the one in Ephesus were within the boundaries of the principal territorial jurisdiction of Diana of the Ephesians. In other words, both were established during the period when, according to Acts 19, Paul was engaged in his most intense episode of spiritual warfare.

In Colossians 2:15 we have one of the most encouraging Scriptures, one that assures us that the final victory in this war is ours:

Having disarmed principalities and powers, He made a public spectacle of them, triumphing over them in it.

The last word, "it," is a reference to the Cross. The previous verse, 14, ends with the phrase, "[Jesus] having nailed it to the cross." The cross of Jesus and the blood He shed there sealed the doom of the forces of darkness.

Another significant reference to the blood of Christ appears in Colossians 1:13,14:

> He has delivered us from the power of darkness and
> conveyed us into the kingdom of the Son of His love,
> in whom we have redemption through His blood.

Furthermore, Paul reminds us in Colossians that the powers
of darkness are mere creatures. God has created "thrones or
dominions or principalities or powers. All things were created
through Him and for Him" (v. 16). Paul adds that Christ "is the
head of all principality and power" (2:10).

Although this is a great assurance of triumph, at the same
time it raises a question in the minds of some of my critics.

**We must understand that our sovereign
God has for His own reasons so designed
this world that much of what is truly His will
He makes contingent on the attitudes and
actions of human beings. He allows
humans to make decisions that can influence history.**

They ask me why, if Jesus has paid the ultimate price and
defeated the principalities and powers on the cross, do I suggest that something is left for us to do? It seems to them that by
saying we should do spiritual warfare I am downgrading the
power of the blood.

Who Rules the City?
This is an important issue. It is possible to read into these
words of Paul in Colossians some things I do not believe he
ever intended. One of my critics took this so far that he raised

the question: Who really rules over my city? His answer was that Jesus rules, and he argued that the problems of poverty, violence, disease, hatred and immorality may increase year after year, but the powers cannot win, because Jesus rules.

Let's examine this. There is a true sense in affirming that Jesus is rightfully the Lord of our city because He is King of kings and Lord of lords. In our Marches for Jesus, we declare this to the principalities and powers. In an equally true sense, however, many of the citizens of my city are spiritual captives of the evil one who comes to steal, to kill and to destroy. How do we reconcile the two?

We must understand that our sovereign God has for His own reasons so designed this world that much of what is truly His will He makes contingent on the attitudes and actions of human beings. He allows humans to make decisions that can influence history. For example, we rarely question the fact that the blood Jesus shed on the cross was sufficient to pay the price for the sins of every person. This blood, however, is not applied automatically. That is why Jesus also sends His people out to proclaim the gospel and to win souls. If we do not evangelize, souls will not be saved, even though Jesus shed His blood to save them. Human inaction does not *nullify* the atonement, but human inaction can make the atonement *ineffective* for lost people.

Likewise, Jesus defeated the god of this age on the cross. He made a spectacle of the demonic principalities in the invisible world, just as the Romans would make a spectacle of their prisoners of war in the streets of Rome. Nevertheless, Satan and his demonic forces persist in blinding the minds of millions who end their lives on earth and go out to a Christless eternity. Jesus gave us the authority to "bind the strong man" and to neutralize the power of territorial spirits to blind people's minds. If we choose not to do this, the principalities can therefore keep possession of their human trophies and keep whole people groups in spiritual captivity. The choice is ours, not God's.

God has given us a digestive system, but He still expects us to take the initiative to eat to stay alive. He has also given us weapons of spiritual warfare, empowered through the blood of the Cross, but He expects us to use them properly, or they will not fulfill their intended purpose. Although Jesus secured the ultimate victory over the principalities, we have much to do in the meantime.

EPHESIANS:
WRESTLING WITH PRINCIPALITIES AND POWERS

The letter Paul wrote directly to the church at Ephesus contains the most extensive passage about spiritual warfare in the New Testament. Readers of Acts 19 could hardly doubt that prominent among the many things Paul would have had in mind as he wrote Ephesians would have been Diana of the Ephesians, the territorial spirit whose power had been severely damaged through Paul's on-site ministry there. Few believers in Ephesus who read his letter would have missed the veiled reference to Diana and her cohorts in this passage in Ephesians 6:12:

> For we do not wrestle against flesh and blood, but against principalities, against powers, against the rulers of the darkness of this age, against spiritual hosts of wickedness in the heavenly places.

Preceding this verse, Paul had just written:

> Put on the whole armor of God, that you may be able to stand against the wiles of the devil (v. 11).

As could well be understood, Ephesians 6 provides a formidable challenge for those who wish to argue that the New Testament gives us no indication God's people are to engage in strategic-level spiritual warfare. Just a simple reading of these verses and of the rest of the chapter leaves exactly the opposite impression. Paul is saying that all Christians are to take up the armor because all are in the battle.

As is typical of Paul's literary style, he mixes metaphors here. He likens us first to wrestlers, then to warriors.

Wrestling was a prominent sport in Greco-Roman culture. This sport of all sports demands the greatest degree of bodily contact. The goal of the wrestler was not to protect himself, although that was an important means to the end. The wrestler's goal was to conquer the opponent in physical engagement. Good defense was essential to win, but only good offense ultimately won the match.

Who is our opponent in this spiritual wrestling match? The language Paul uses in verse 12 is not ordinary language. "Principalities" and "powers" and "rulers" are terms clearly meant to denote much more than the average demon. Ground-level demons, I think, would be included among the "spiritual hosts of wickedness." Although biblical scholars have not been able to sort out a definitive hierarchical structure implied by the use of these terms, they do agree by and large that wrestling against them would include what we are calling strategic-level spiritual warfare, in addition to ground-level deliverance. Apparently, we're not regarded as spectators; we're actual *participants* in the cosmic wrestling match.

Paul's other analogy is that of the Roman Legion. The warriors then had, as we have now, both defensive and offensive military equipment. Some who think we should not proactively confront the powers have attempted to justify their viewpoints by indicating that most of the armor of God listed in Ephesians 6 is defensive, not offensive. They contend that only if the principalities and powers decide to come after us should we do battle to defend ourselves. We should never take the initiative to move into their territory and challenge them.

This was not the way the soldiers of the Roman Legions would have thought of their duty. They did not build high walls around Rome to defend themselves in case their enemies decided to attack them. On the contrary, they constantly moved out past the frontiers and into enemy lands, having the objective of taking more territory from the enemy. This was Paul's practice as well as his teaching. Jesus sends us with the gospel of the kingdom into enemy land to take spiritual territory from him and for the kingdom of God. Paul never forgot his "heavenly vision"—to bring people "from darkness to light, and from the power of Satan to God" (Acts 26:18). Going on the offensive and invading Satan's kingdom was his modus operandi, and I believe he expects it to be ours as well.

In another place in Ephesians, Paul says:

> To the intent that now the manifold wisdom of God might be made known by the church to the principalities and powers in the heavenly places (3:10).

In some way it is the duty of the Church to communicate God's wisdom to the beings inhabiting the invisible world. That is done both by deed and by word. The purity of the Church, which is the bride of Christ, the fruit of the Spirit in the lives of believers, the power of God manifested in healing and salvation and many more elements of Christian life and behavior, send a message. So do Marches for Jesus, prayerwalks, prophetic acts and strategic-level spiritual warfare involving the kind of head-on confrontation with the principalities and powers that Ramsay MacMullen describes happening throughout the first centuries of Christianity.

In an attempt to avoid distasteful triumphalism, some shy

away from such language. ("Triumphalism" is a term sometimes used by non-Western Christians to describe the arrogant self-confidence and lack of humility some Western Christian leaders exhibit.) In doing so, they are distancing themselves from the apostle Paul who had the faith to believe that Christ and His followers will get the victory. Paul said, "Now thanks be to God who always leads us in *triumph* in Christ, and through us diffuses the fragrance of His knowledge in every place" (2 Cor. 2:14, emphasis added). Paul believed that the gospel would spread, and that the realm of darkness would be defeated at every level.

TIMOTHY: FIGHT THE GOOD FIGHT

Paul had left Ephesus, and his apprentice, Timothy, was ministering there. Paul had done his share of spiritual warfare. He wrote to Timothy saying, "I have fought the good fight, I have finished the race, I have kept the faith" (2 Tim. 4:7). He was a veteran of many battles, some of which he won, some of which he lost. Now he was passing the baton to Timothy.

Among other instructions, Paul tells Timothy to continue in the spiritual warfare to which Paul had introduced him. Timothy had seen the power encounter with the Python spirit in Philippi. Timothy had watched the magicians burn their books in Ephesus, and he had seen the mighty Diana lose so much power that her silversmiths rioted. Here are some of the instructions Paul left with Timothy:

> This charge I commit to you, son Timothy, according to the prophecies previously made concerning you, that by them you may wage the good warfare (1 Tim. 1:18). Fight the good fight (6:12).

> You therefore must endure hardship as a good soldier of Jesus Christ (2 Tim. 2:3).

No one engaged in warfare entangles himself with the affairs of this life, that he may please him who enlisted him as a soldier (v. 4).

According to the biblical law of warfare, not everybody is to go to the front lines. Some must stay home with the goods. Timothy was not one of those called to stay home, but he was commissioned for war. The Body of Christ today is like this. Some will go to the battlefield, some will stay home in the bedroom. Whatever God's plan may be for each of us, we must be faithful.

David said, "As his part is who goes down to the battle, so shall his part be who stays by the supplies; they shall share alike" (1 Sam. 30:24). If this was true in the kingdom of Israel, so much more must it be in the kingdom of God. If we plan to complete the task of world evangelization so that in our generation there will be "A church for every people and the gospel for every person," every one of us is needed. If I am more like Paul and Timothy, ready for the battlefield, I also want to honor those who stay home and take care of the supplies.

In this book I have tried my best to show substantial justification for regarding strategic-level spiritual warfare as the will of God. I have also tried to recognize that not everyone is, or should be, like many of my friends and I who believe they are called to participate in warfare at the highest levels. If only we can love each other, if only we can respect each other's callings without rancor or criticism and if only we can establish and sustain a relationship of interdependence in the Body of Christ, we will have gone a long way to satisfy a deep desire of Jesus' own heart. Jesus prayed to the Father: "That they all may be one,...that the world may believe that You sent Me" (John 17:21).

■ REFLECTION QUESTIONS ■

1. What does Jude mean when he says that Michael would not bring a direct accusation against Satan?
2. Is "resisting the devil" just protecting ourselves from the devil's attacks or does it mean we should take initiation against him?
3. How do you think "spiritual mapping"—trying to expose the devices of Satan—could be applied to your community?
4. There are two kinds of strongholds: "arguments" and "high things." Discuss the differences between the two and give examples from the world around us today.
5. If Jesus' blood on the cross defeated Satan, why is it that we are told in the Scriptures to continue to do spiritual warfare?

Notes

1. Wayne Grudem, "Miracles Today," *The Kingdom and the Power,* ed. Gary Greig and Kevin Springer (Ventura, Calif.: Regal Books, 1993), p. 75.
2. Ibid., pp. 75-76.
3. If anyone would like more information about Paul's ministry in Ephesus and elsewhere, I would urge them to secure the three volumes of my Acts commentary: *Spreading the Fire, Lighting the World* and *Blazing the Way,* all published by Regal Books. Some readers of this book may think I assume too much about the interpretation of Acts, but I have tried to avoid duplicating here the information covered in those more than 700 pages of commentary.
4. J. Blunck, "Height," *The New International Dictionary of New Testament Theology,* Vol. 2, ed. Colin Brown (Grand Rapids: Zondervan Publishing House, 1975), p. 200.
5. For further information about Resistencia, see another book in this "Prayer Warrior Series," *Warfare Prayer* (Regal Books).

The Philosophy of Prayer for World Evangelization Adopted by the A.D. 2000 United Prayer Track

BY C. PETER WAGNER
UNITED PRAYER TRACK COORDINATOR

A PERSONAL INTRODUCTION

From its inception in 1989, the A.D. 2000 and Beyond Movement resolved to assign a high priority to the mobilization of united prayer for world evangelization. As the various tracks or resource networks were taking shape in the early 1990s, I was humbled by the invitation from Luis Bush to coordinate the United Prayer Track. After seeking the advice of experienced prayer leaders, academic colleagues and above all trusted intercessors, and after my wife, Doris, agreed to assume the chief administrative duties of the Prayer Track for the balance of the decade, I sensed that it was God's will that I accept the invitation. In order to structure the legal and financial aspects of the task, Doris and I incorporated Global Harvest Ministries as a non-profit organization.

At that time I was well into the research which provided the material for what would later be published by Regal Books as the four volumes of the "Prayer Warrior Series," namely *Warfare Prayer, Prayer Shield, Breaking Strongholds in Your City,* and *Churches That Pray.* My international travels, designed to help me become personally acquainted with prayer leaders and prayer movements in different parts of the world, were very revealing. I began observing a segment of cutting-edge Christianity of which I had been only marginally aware. Through friends, many of them new friends, such as Cindy Jacobs, George Otis, Jr., Edgardo Silvoso, Gwen Shaw, John Dawson, Ted Haggard, Jack Hayford, Dick Eastman, Harold Caballeros, Kjell Sjöberg, Roger Mitchell, Gary Bergel, Dean Sherman, Jean Steffenson, Bob Beckett, Larry Lea, Roger Forster, Bobbye Byerly, Dick Bernal, Brian Mills, Alistair Petrie, and many others who could also be named, I gradually became aware of some forms of prayer for the nations of the world and for unevangelized people and for unreached people groups which were new for me. There seemed to be some significant things that the Holy Spirit was saying to the churches that I had not learned in seminary nor had my colleagues and I been teaching them in the Fuller Seminary School of World Mission.

While these forms of prayer for the nations may not have been new to some, they were to many in the circles in which I had been ministering such as Fuller Seminary, the Lausanne Movement, the National Association of Evangelicals, the World Evangelical Fellowship, and the Conservative Congregational Christian Conference where I hold my ordination credentials. Beginning with Lausanne II in Manila, I found myself cast into the role of attempting to communicate some of these new ideas regarding prayer, strategic-level intercession, identificational repentance, spiritual mapping and spiritual warfare to my friends of a more traditional mindset. The principal vehicles I used for this were my seminary classes, seminars in various parts of America and the world, my adult Sunday School class in Lake Avenue Congregational Church, articles in journals and magazines, and the above-mentioned books.

As could be expected, some of these new concepts tended to raise questions in the minds of many. A bit of controversy developed and at times I found myself functioning as a "lightning rod" as one of my friends put it. Some of the personal criticism that I had been receiving began to be projected through me and through the United Prayer Track to the A.D. 2000 Movement as a whole. It was then that Luis Bush asked me to develop a philosophy statement which would help clarify for inquirers the issues of prayer and spiritual warfare currently being advocated by the Prayer Track.

In order to implement this I asked three trusted and experienced colleagues with reputations of high integrity in the Body of Christ and who were rooted in ecclesiastical traditions similar to mine to come alongside as consultants. I was honored when David Bryant of Concerts of Prayer International, Tom White of Frontline Ministries and Clinton Arnold of Talbot School of Theology in Biola University all agreed to sustain a dialogue on these issues with me. After the four of us interacted over several months, I drafted a statement which they critiqued, and which I then revised accordingly. None of the three would have written the paper as I have done it, nor is any of the three in total agreement with the document. Nevertheless the imprints of all three are evident and I am deeply grateful to them for a substantial investment of time and energy. The statement is ever so much better now than it could have been otherwise.

To continue the process, I sent copies of the revised statement to 95 leaders of the Prayer Track worldwide with a response device. A short time later I mailed a draft which had been further revised from feedback from Prayer Track leaders to some 550 other A.D. 2000 leaders at the request of Luis Bush. A total of 73 responses from every continent have been extremely helpful and have allowed me to polish and improve this final draft considerably.

Finally, I want to mention that the entire process was undergirded with serious intercession on the part of Doris and my personal prayer partners who were kept continually informed as to every detail. I therefore have a reasonable degree of confidence that the document, while far from perfect and certainly not to the total satisfaction of all, is nevertheless one which will bring glory to God, which will edify and encourage the Body of Christ, and which will be used to advance God's Kingdom in our days.

For further information or additional copies of this document, write:

United Prayer Track
215 N. Marengo Ave., #151
Pasadena, CA 91101
Fax: 818-577-7160

1. THE MANDATE

The United Prayer Track of the A.D. 2000 and Beyond Movement was established in 1991 with the mandate of mobilizing and enabling the multiple prayer movements which God has been raising up on all continents and throughout virtually all branches of biblical Christianity to focus their prayer ministries at least in part on accomplishing the task of establishing a Church for every people and making the Gospel available for every person by the year A.D. 2000.

With such a mandate, the United Prayer Track has been called to fill a specific niche within the broad and growing prayer movement of today's world. The definition of what this niche consists of begins with a recognition, with praise and honor to Almighty God, of a widespread interest in and enthusiasm for prayer throughout the universal Body of Christ unprecedented at least in living memory, if not in the history of the church.

2. THE ROLE

In a spirit of humility and submission to God, the worldwide prayer movement could be pictured as a spiritual jewel with many facets, all of which glorify the Triune God in many different ways. The role of the United Prayer Track should be seen as only one of the many facets.

3. THE ESSENCE OF PRAYER

The essence of all prayer is a personal relationship with God made possible through the redemption purchased by the blood of Jesus Christ on the cross and enjoyed by those who have put their faith in Jesus Christ as Savior and Lord and been regenerated by the Holy Spirit.

In one sense, all prayer can be seen as an end in itself, the end of establishing and deepening relationships with God the Father. In fact, such a relationship of intimacy with the Father, which involves both speaking to and hearing from God, is nothing short of a prerequisite for all effective prayer in every facet of the prayer movement. It is an end in itself, because it pleases God.

When understood from this point of view, it is clear that prayer must not be regarded as a way through which human beings can manipulate God. To imagine that it is would quickly debase Christian prayer to the level of magic or sorcery. Rather, prayer serves to tune us in as individuals and groups to the love, grace, will, purpose, and timing of God. We also recognize that the fulfillment of God's purpose for particular circumstances in history is, more often than some imagine, contingent, by His own design, on the effectiveness of believing prayer. As one prayer leader has said, "History belongs to the intercessors."

4. PRAYER AS PERSONAL SPIRITUALITY

Through the centuries the saints of God have enjoyed the privilege of prayer as a way of deepening their personal holiness and spirituality. For many, nothing more was required. Countless classics of Christian literature on prayer have emphasized this contemplative "practicing the presence of God." Many have felt that their primary service to God consisted of a lifetime of personal waiting upon Him and bringing Him pleasure through praise and worship. A number of these have found a permanent place in Christian history as role models for the ages. They continually remind us of the holiness and power of God.

5. DIVERSITY OF INTERCESSORY PRAYER

There is such a great breadth to intercessory prayer that some understandably are not comfortable with categorizing its many facets. Others, however, feel that such categorization can help produce clarity but only with the proviso that the intimate and complex interrelationships between all forms of communication with God are acknowledged at all times. All forms of intercession are rooted in the biblical conviction that prayer releases God's power and grace in the lives of those prayed for. For example there are many ministries of intercessory prayer which should be practiced by all Christians but which are, in fact, beyond the specific mandate of the United Prayer Track. Husbands should pray for their wives and vice versa; parents should intercede for their children; believers should pray for their pastors and their churches; citizens should pray for those who rule over them; Christians should pray for God to work through the lives of unbelievers; just to name a few of some of the more obvious ministries of intercession. In today's prayer movement, many prayer leaders are called to specialize in one or more of these ministries, while affirming their relationship in the Spirit to those called to other prayer assignments. Valuable contributions to the literature on prayer are being made in all these and many other areas of prayer.

6. The Primary Assignment

The intercessory prayer ministry of the United Prayer Track is centered on prayer which will enable the lost to be saved, the unevangelized to be evangelized, the unreached to be reached, the unchurched to be churched (Mt. 9:38; 24:14; 28:19), and churches to be multiplied throughout the world. This is not seen as an elitist or an exclusive mandate, but it is indeed a primary assignment for us. Clearly, many outside the United Prayer Track also pray for the lost to be saved. Many within the United Prayer Track also pray that families will not break up, for safer streets in our cities, and for honesty, wisdom, and justice in our federal and local governments (1 Tim. 2:1-8), and for many other good things. Nevertheless, the activities of the United Prayer Track as a component of the A.D. 2000 and Beyond Movement are designed to mobilize the kinds of prayer which will specifically help open the way for the reality of a Church for every people and the Gospel for every person by the year 2000. Other equally valued segments of the Body of Christ are engaged in mobilizing intercessory prayer for any number of other worthy purposes and we applaud them all as part of our mutual desire that God's Kingdom will come and His will be done on earth as it is in heaven.

7. Prayer for Revival

A goal of the United Prayer Track is to mobilize as much of the universal Body of Christ as possible to pray effectively for world evangelization. We recognize, however, that many churches in their present state are not in condition to make a significant contribution to this united effort because they have left their first love and find themselves in a relatively powerless state. Because of this, prayer for what has been called revival or church renewal or awakening is essential. A desperate need of the hour is for massive spiritual revival within the churches throughout the nations. God's people themselves must be awakened to the urgent need to pray for the lost. To fill this need, powerful facets of the worldwide prayer ministry focus on intercession for church renewal. This type of prayer is made on behalf of the people of God. The United Prayer Track embraces this anointed ministry of prayer and indeed could not fulfill its own mandate properly without it.

8. PRAYING CHURCHES AND PRAYER MINISTRIES

At the same time there are many churches on all continents which, while not perfect, are indeed alive, adhering faithfully to their first love, impassioned for reaching the lost, hearing what the Spirit is saying to the churches, and experienced in vital prayer for evangelism. Likewise, God has raised up large numbers of prayer ministries, related in differing degrees to local churches, which have sensed a special calling and anointing to pray for lost people to be saved. It is such churches and prayer ministries which naturally provide the initial candidates for active components of the United Prayer Track. Others may, if so directed by God, join when the prayers for church renewal are answered and a passion for praying for the lost is restored in those churches.

Because spiritual power being released throughout the whole Body of Christ is so important, strategic-level prayer for evangelism (see No. 12) must never be carried out apart from uniting in revival praying, because, to the degree God wins the battle inside the church and removes strongholds there, to that degree will all other prayer for the 10/40 Window ultimately prevail.

9. IDENTIFYING AND NETWORKING PRAYER MINISTRIES

It should be noted that the United Prayer Track does not assume the responsibility of stimulating prayer or creating new prayer ministries. This is the work of the Holy Spirit and the church. Our task is rather to identify those prayer ministries targeted to world evangelization which God has already raised up and interconnect them in ways which will enhance the possibilities of each of them becoming all that God wants them to be. As such, we desire to provide a worldwide network of information and resources on prayer for the entire Body of Christ, serving also to broker the various prayer ministries throughout the network.

10. DEGREES OF EMPHASIS

The prayer ministries associated with the United Prayer Track exhibit differing degrees of emphasis on prayer for the lost. For some prayer evangelism may be only one of many good emphases. Others may be burdened chiefly, if not exclusively, for prayer for the unevangelized or the unreached. Some will be in between or will vary their emphases from time to time according to need or in obedience to divine guidance. Prayer summits, solemn assemblies, national days of prayer, monthly "First Friday" prayer and fasting, and a network of prayer rooms are a few of the many examples of prayer ministries for which evangelism is an important, but not necessarily the primary focus. Examples of movements more exclusively targeting prayer for the lost are YWAM Cardinal Points, Generals of Intercession, Every Home for Christ "Jericho Chapters," Campus Crusade World Prayer Strategy and others. There are roles in the United Prayer Track for all these and many more, regardless of the degree of emphasis.

It should be noted that each one of the other tracks (resource networks) and task forces of the A.D. 2000 and Beyond Movement has developed its own internal prayer dynamic. These, of course, differ in various degrees from one another and from that of the United Prayer Track. The A.D. 2000 Movement welcomes as wide a range of approaches to prayer for revival and world evangelization as possible. At the same time, the United Prayer Track seeks to stand in the gap for all other segments of A.D. 2000 in its intercessory prayer ministry.

11. STRATEGIC-LEVEL INTERCESSION

Some of the prayer ministries associated with the United Prayer Track, notably but not exclusively, the International Fellowship of Intercessors, Generals of Intercession, and Youth With a Mission, began in the decade of the 1980s to practice a type of prayer for the lost now called by some "strategic-level intercession." Especially since the Lausanne II Congress in Manila in 1989, this ministry under additional identificational labels such as "territorial spirits," "strategic-level spiritual warfare," and "warfare prayer" began spreading through broader segments of the Body of Christ. It took organizational form with the creation of the International Spiritual Warfare Network in 1990.

It bears emphasizing that strategic-level spiritual warfare is not to be seen as an end in itself. The end is the salvation of lost souls and the coming of God's Kingdom to our cities, to our nations, to our unreached people groups, and to human communities wherever they might be found.

12. BIBLICAL PREMISES

Two fundamental biblical premises underlie the various approaches to spiritual warfare as it applies to evangelizing the lost. They can best be stated by quoting relevant biblical texts:

(1) The devil directly and explicitly attempts to obstruct the evangelization of the lost: "But even if our gospel is veiled, it is veiled to those who are perishing, whose minds the god of this age has blinded, who do not believe, lest the light of the gospel of the glory of Christ, who is the image of God, should shine on them" (2 Cor. 4:3-4).

(2) Our weapons designed by God to help remove these obstructions to evangelism are spiritual weapons. "For the weapons of our warfare are not carnal but mighty in God for pulling down strongholds, casting down arguments and every high thing that exalts itself against the knowledge of God..." (2 Cor. 10:4-5).

13. THE SPIRITUAL WARFARE NETWORK

When the United Prayer Track was formed in 1991, the leadership of the A.D. 2000 and Beyond Movement agreed that the first and potentially largest sub-network associated with the United Prayer Track would be the pre-existing International Spiritual Warfare Network (SWN). Since then many meetings of the SWN have been held on national, regional and international levels, surfacing some issues associated with strategic-level intercession on which there seems to be quite broad consensus and others on which there remain varying shades of opinion. In a statement of the philosophy of prayer of the United Prayer Track, these issues should be recognized.

14. THE LAUSANNE COVENANT

To begin, it should be pointed out that there is virtually no disagreement among those in the A.D. 2000 Movement on the importance of spiritual warfare as an essential part of the task of world evangelization. The A.D. 2000 Movement has officially reaffirmed the Lausanne Covenant. In it, Article 12, "Spiritual Conflict," states in part: "We believe that we are engaged in constant spiritual warfare with the principalities and powers of evil who are seeking to overthrow the Church and to frustrate its task of evangelization."

15. THREE LEVELS OF SPIRITUAL WARFARE

In the work of the Spiritual Warfare Network a useful distinction has surfaced between three levels of spiritual warfare: (1) ground-level spiritual warfare dealing with demonic deliverance of individuals; (2) occult-level spiritual warfare dealing with the powers of darkness operative through such as New Age, Satanism, Eastern Religions, witchcraft and the like; and (3) strategic-level spiritual warfare (which some prefer to call "cosmic-level" spiritual warfare) in which territorial principalities and powers are confronted. Since all three operate together in the unseen realms of darkness, it must be kept in mind that they are interrelated and that spiritual warfare on any one of the levels can and usually does affect the demonic forces on all levels.

16. OUR SPHERE OF AUTHORITY

One of the most prominent unresolved issues among members of the Spiritual Warfare Network is on which, if any, of the three levels we are given biblical authority for intentional ministry. We appreciate the fact that much more dialogue on this matter is in order. Some feel that because the principal biblical examples we have of spiritual warfare involve casting demons out of individuals, we should not advocate engaging spiritual forces which may be occupying geographical areas or buildings or animals or human social networks or churches or physical objects such as trees or mountains or idols. For them it is not advisable to do strategic-level warfare and name, rebuke or otherwise address so-called territorial spirits. Others prefer to give a literal interpretation to such sayings of Jesus as "Behold, I give you the authority...over all the power of the enemy" (Lk. 10:19) and do confrontive spiritual warfare on all levels (see Col. 1:16-20; Jn. 16:15). All desire to see the captives of the Enemy set free.

17. TYPES OF ENCOUNTER

It is recognized that several types of encounter with the Enemy are described in the Bible. Two of the most discussed are (1) the "power encounter" illustrated by Paul's confrontation with the sorcerer Bar-Jesus in Cyprus (see Acts 13:6-12); and (2) the "truth encounter" illustrated by Paul's preaching justification by faith in Antioch of Pisidia (see Acts 13:38-39).

18. SEEKING A BALANCE

Among SWN members there are differing points of view as to how to keep the two of these in balance. All agree, however, that we must avoid overstressing one to the detriment of the other. Some have suggested, for example, that those who stress the power encounter may not be remembering that it is the truth which sets us free. Others suggest that relying too heavily on the truth encounter may shirk the responsibility of wrestling with principalities and powers. Practically speaking, some would interpret positive results in specific attempts at evangelism as a result of both of these approaches. Admonitions from both sides help to avoid potential excesses all around.

19. INHERENT DANGERS

Members of the Spiritual Warfare Network attempt to identify inherent dangers in strategic-level spiritual warfare and suggest antidotes to them. They realize that it may be possible to become overly preoccupied with the demonic and thereby exalt the Enemy; that some could naively adopt negative aspects of an animistic world view; that it could foster an unbalanced "the devil made me do it" attitude; that technique and methodology could substitute for the power of the Holy Spirit; and that Satan would like to seduce the church and lead it astray. All realize that mistakes can and will be made in engaging the Enemy on any level, and we agree that they should be identified and corrected whenever they happen.

20. PRECEDENTS FOR STRATEGIC-LEVEL SPIRITUAL WARFARE

Some are concerned that as yet few precedents for strategic-level spiritual warfare for evangelistic purposes have been uncovered either in the history of missions or in the history of dogma. While recognizing this, others argue that it would not be contrary to the nature of God to do a new thing and provide relatively new spiritual approaches particularly for the unprecedented challenges to evangelism presented by the powers of darkness dominating the 10/40 Window. All are agreed that ongoing efforts need to be made to clarify biblical and historical concerns.

21. SPIRITUAL MAPPING

One of these relatively new spiritual approaches is spiritual mapping. By creating a Division of Spiritual Mapping, the United Prayer Track is committed to an attempt to provide the best possible spiritual intelligence information in order to help target the prayers of God's people for the lost. Paul seems to indicate that such a thing would be helpful when he says, in the context of resolving personal relationships, "Lest Satan should take advantage of us; for we are not ignorant of his devices" (2 Cor. 2:11). Satan uses his evil devices in many ways. Spiritual mapping attempts to expose the devices Satan has used to curtail effective evangelization and allows God's people to aim their spiritual weapons against them more accurately. The challenge before us is to do our spiritual mapping in a responsible, balanced way using agreed upon field methodologies with full accountability to the Body of Christ.

22. IDENTIFICATIONAL REPENTANCE

Responsible spiritual mapping will frequently uncover sins of a nation or city which have been committed in the past, sometimes generations ago, and which have become strongholds of the forces of darkness, allowing them to keep multitudes in physical misery and spiritual captivity. When we corporately confess those sins of our nation through what many are calling "identificational repentance," they can be remitted through Jesus' blood shed on the cross, and the strongholds can be removed. God's people then can take back the place we have given to the Enemy, God's Spirit of grace can bring healing, and unsaved people can be open to receiving the "light of the gospel of the glory of Christ" (2 Cor. 4:4). No aspect of warfare prayer is more important than identificational repentance.

23. INTERDENOMINATIONAL STANDARDS

When we arrive at behavioral issues we find that our range of A.D. 2000 constituents including many who come from liturgical, traditional evangelical, dispensational, Pentecostal, charismatic, postdenominational, Third Wave, and other traditions requires all of us to make adjustments which will not be offensive to the rest. The United Prayer Track has developed a statement attempting to set forth agreed upon standards for interdenominational prayer events.

As our overall Track philosophy, we are using a statement developed by Every Home for Christ with the permission of Dick Eastman:

Remember that the moment two or more of us unite in prayer we become a symphony. As such:

- *We blend together in unity respecting the fact that we represent all of Christ's body;*
- *We realize that, like a symphony with its different instruments, there is a wide variety of traditions when it comes to prayer;*
- *We commit ourselves to accepting one another as we are, while disciplining ourselves to use wisdom and caution if we think anything we might do would offend a brother or sister.*

We want all those who participate to be themselves. We must not quench the Spirit. There are no restrictions at all on prayer styles in prayer groups of like tradition. Yet some of these styles may not be appropriate in groups of mixed traditions.

Here are some of the specific areas in which wisdom, caution, spiritual discernment, and good manners need to be used:

24. BODY LANGUAGE

Body language is an important part of prayer. Raising hands, kneeling, and lying prostrate on the floor are different physical expressions of prayer. Some pray with eyes closed and some with eyes open, some raise their chins, others lower their chins. Special discernment is needed with using such body language as dancing, falling in the Spirit or other visible manifestations associated with some revival movements in the past or present. Blowing, hissing, and physically "travailing" should generally be avoided. At the same time, spiritual travail in prayer, at times with "groanings which cannot be uttered" (Rom. 8:26), may be expected from time to time.

25. PROPHECY

We encourage the art of learning how to listen to God in prayer. Prudence in communicating words from God in an interdenominational meeting will avoid such phrases as "thus saith the Lord" or using the first person for God. Prophecies can be prayed back to God: "God, we hear you saying..." or expressed to the group with statements like "I think God may be saying to us..." and expecting others to agree if it is a true word.

In all cases, care must be taken that prophetic gifts are not publicly used apart from the covering, permission and spiritual authority of the person designated to preside over the particular session. Prudence dictates that, particularly when the prophetic word has directional content (as opposed, for instance, to devotional content), explicit permission be sought from the presider before the word is given.

26. TONGUES

It is no secret that a very sensitive issue is tongues. The A.D. 2000 Movement seeks to balance 1 Corinthians 14:39 "do not forbid to speak with tongues" with the next verse "let all things be done decently and in order" (1 Cor. 14:40). In our interdenominational Prayer Track meetings we feel that individuals may use tongues in a whisper or even in a louder voice when all are praying aloud in a concert and no one person's voice stands out above the others. But we feel it is not usually prudent to use tongues when one is audibly leading the whole group in prayer. We also need to agree that messages from God in tongues with interpretations are best left to those settings where such practice has been traditionally taught and accepted. Since it would perhaps foster confusion for some, careful discernment is called for.

27. CONCLUSION

A grassroots, networking structure like the United Prayer Track has both strengths and weaknesses. It stands or falls on personal relationships rather than on bureaucratic controls. Therefore good will is an essential personal characteristic for all who participate. This is a day in which we are seeing a visible spiritual unity of the Body of Christ which is unprecedented both in quantity and quality. We are bold enough to believe that it is an answer to Jesus' prayer "that they all may be one that the world might believe" (Jn. 17:21).

Pasadena, California
November 16, 1994

Index

Holy Spirit, 69, 121, 133-134, 149,
    151-152, 166-167, 232, 250
Holy Spirit, filling of, 166-167
Holy Spirit, fruit of, 41
Houston House of Prayer, 29
humility, 68
hypsoma, 238-240

I

identificational repentance, 13, 30-
    31, 33, 79-80, 91, 96, 159, 239,
    260
idols, 205
India, 170, 172
Indonesian revival, 114
intercession, personal, 178-180
intercession, strategic-level, 256
intercession teams, 17-18
intercessory prayer, 253
International Fellowship of Inter-
    cessors, 256
intimacy with God, 37, 48, 68, 252
Irenaeus, 115
Isaiah 43:19, 95
Isaiah 47, 62
Italy, 108-110

J

Jacobs, Cindy, 54, 74, 79, 250
James, 177, 230-232
James 4:7,8, 230-232
Japan, 137, 205, 239
Jennings, Ben A., 16, 18
Jeremiah 2:11, 174
Jeremiah 4:30, 174
Jeremiah 31:31, 95
Jeremiah 44:17-25, 174
Jeremiah 50:2, 174
Jesus, 121-138, 141-159, 186, 225
Jesus Seminar, 57, 58

Jesus, name of, 137-138
Jesus, temptation of, 131
Jesus, two natures of, 129-133
John, 220-223, 227-228
John 1:1, 52
John 5:19, 132
John 5:22, 132
John 7:38, 39, 128
John 8:12, 187
John 10:10, 178
John 10:35, 42
John 12:31, 123, 145
John 14:12, 128
John 14:14, 137
John 14:30, 123, 145
John 16:7, 133
John 16:11, 145
John 16:15, 258
John 16:33, 145
John 17:15, 141
John 17:21, 37, 247, 262
John 21:25, 92
1 John 2:14, 227
1 John 3:8, 122, 227
1 John 4:4, 180
1 John 5:19, 227
John the Baptist, 121
Johnstone, Patrick, 65-66
Joshua 1:3, 27
Jude 9, 137, 228-230
Jupiter, 109
justification by faith, 164, 189-190,
    233
Justin, 115

K

Kali, the goddess, 172
Keil, C. F., 173, 183
Kek Lok Si Temple, 61
Kendrick, Graham, 27

Matthew 10:7,8, 127, 165
Matthew 10:8, 215
Matthew 11:11,12, 229-230
Matthew 11:12, 138
Matthew 12:22-24, 58
Matthew 12:24, 146
Matthew 12:28, 132, 149
Matthew 12:29, 152
Matthew 13:13, 58
Matthew 16:13-19, 153-155
Matthew 18:18, 154
Matthew 24:14, 254
Matthew 28:18,19, 138
Matthew 28:19, 254
Matthew 28:19,20, 159
Matthew 28:20, 127
Maximon, 217-220
Maynard, Theodore, 109, 118
Mercury, 108
Merodach, 174
Messianic Jews, 84,169
Metzger, Bruce, 210, 224
Michael, 173
Mills, Brian, 250
ministry and theology, 44-46
missiological syncretism, 35
missiology, 163
Mitchell, Roger, 250
Mithra, 109
Monte Cassino, 109-110
Morales, Mario Roberto, 224
Murphy, Ed, 124, 126, 139
Muslims, 29, 186

N

narratives, 57-61
National Association of Evangeli-
   cals, 250
National Prayer Committee, 12
Native Americans, 199

Nehemiah 1:6, 79
Neill, Stephen, 72
Nepal, 170
Nero, 183
New Age, 22
new birth, 60-61, 67
Nightstalker, 123
nikao, 144-145, 151, 152, 157, 226
Numbers 22:41, 174

O

Old Testament, 78-80, 126, 230
oracle of Delphi, 196
Origen, 103, 183
Otis, George Jr., 46, 74, 206, 224,
   236, 250
overcoming, 143-148, 168, 188

P

Pan, 205
paradigm shift, 49, 53
paradigms of historians, 112-116
Paul, 44, 52, 92-93, 128, 135, 137,
   177, 179, 185-201, 203-223,
   232-247, 258
Paul, conversion of, 185-188
Pentecost, 80-81, 166
Pentecostal movement, 96, 97
people groups, 187
Peretti, Frank, 73-75
personal intercession, 178-180
Peter, 135, 161-182, 227-228
1 Peter 2:20,21, 181
1 Peter 4:13,16, 181
1 Peter 5:8, 127, 180
1 Peter 5:8,9, 227
1 Peter 5:10, 182
2 Peter 1:20,21, 42
Peterson, Eugene H., 224
Petrie, Alistair, 250

Revelation 20:10, 122
Revelation 21:5, 95
revival, 24-25, 26
rhema, 52-55, 62, 64, 155
Riscajche, Mariano, 218-220
Romans 8:26, 261
Romans 10:14, 186
Ronald Reagan, Mrs., 191

S

Saddam Hussein, 191, 236
Salvation Army, 88
Samaria, 167-171
1 Samuel 30:24, 37, 247
2 Samuel 21, 79
San La Muerte, 239
Satan, 121-138, 141-159, 229, 235-236
Satan, devices of, 235-237, 260
Schuster, Idlephonce Cardinal, 110, 118
scientific proof, 58
Second Adam, 131
Sergius Paulus, 191-193
seven sons of Sceva, 137-138, 215-216
Seventh-day Adventists, 85
Severus Sulpitius, 107, 118
Shaw, Gwen, 250
Sheppard, Glenn, 16
Sherman, Dean, 250
Silas, 195, 197
Silvoso, Ed, 35, 74, 250
Simon Magus, 135, 163, 170-171, 174-177
Simon the Sorcerer, 170-171
Sjöberg, Kjell, 28, 30, 38, 250
slavery, 84, 87, 162
Smalley, William A., 65, 72
Smith, Alice, 29

Smith, William, 117
Socrates, 205
Spirit Christology, 129
spirits, names of, 200-201
spiritual gifts, 36, 96-98
spiritual mapping, 13, 30, 33,91, 96, 236-237, 260
spiritual technology, 30, 91, 96
Spiritual Warfare Network, 20-21, 34, 62, 102, 194, 239, 256, 257
spiritual warfare, casualties of, 48
spiritual warfare, criticism of, 31-33
spiritual warfare, ground-level, 21-22, 169-170, 191,195, 213-215, 258
spiritual warfare, levels of, 21-22
spiritual warfare, occult-level, 22, 191, 215-216, 258
spiritual warfare, strategic-level, 22, 30, 258
Springer, Kevin N., 72, 248
Stedman, Ray, 96
Steffenson, Jean, 250
Stone, Barton W., 97
Stott, John R. W., 191, 202
strategic-level intercession, definition of, 13
strongholds, 159, 209, 237-238
strongman, 111, 138, 149, 152, 157-158, 171, 217
Succoth Benoth, 174
Sudan, 182
suffering, 180-182
Sun Goddess, 239-240
Sunday Schools, 32
Switzerland, 158

T

Talbot School of Theology, 22, 251
Telfer, W., 117

Learn to Fight on Your Knees.

There's a battle raging, an unseen struggle in the heavens that affects the way we live as Christians. But how can you fight against a force which can't be seen, an invisible enemy desperate to foil God's plan? The answer is prayer. That's because the battle against Satan has already been won, paid for by the price of Christ's blood. You can discover the truth behind spiritual warfare and what you can do to advance the cause of Christ around the world through these factual, biblical guides from Regal Books.

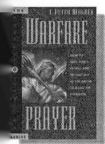

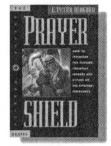

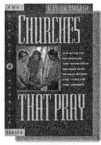

Warfare Prayer
Book One of the "Prayer Warrior" Series
C. Peter Wagner
A biblical and factual guide which will help you seek God's power and protection in the battle to build His kingdom.
ISBN 08307.15347

Prayer Shield
Book Two of the "Prayer Warrior" Series
C. Peter Wagner
Here is a tool to help you teach lay people how to intercede in prayer for your ministry.
ISBN 08307.15738

Breaking Strongholds in Your City
Book Three of the "Prayer Warrior" Series
C. Peter Wagner
Learn how to identify the enemy's territory in your city, along with practical steps to help you pray against these dark strongholds.
ISBN 08307.15975

Churches That Pray
Book Four of the "Prayer Warrior" Series
C. Peter Wagner
Take a comprehensive look at prayer and how new forms of prayer can break down the walls between the church and the community—locally and globally.
ISBN 08307.15983

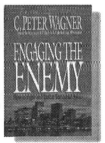

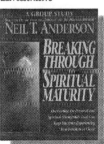

Engaging the Enemy
Edited by
C. Peter Wagner
John Dawson, Peter Wagner and 16 others provide guidance based on their experiences with territorial spirits.
ISBN 08307.15169

Victory over the Darkness
Neil T. Anderson
Dr. Neil Anderson shows that we have the power to conquer the darkness, once we know who we are in Christ.
ISBN 08307.13751

Breaking Through to Spiritual Maturity
Neil T. Anderson
Take possession of the victory Christ freely offers and mature in your faith with this 13- to 24-week course. Based on best-sellers *Victory over the Darkness* and *The Bondage Breaker*.
ISBN 08307.15312

Wrestling with Dark Angels
Compiled by
C. Peter Wagner and F. Douglas Pennoyer
Spiritual warfare is going on all around us. This collection of essays gives readers the understanding they need to fight back.
ISBN 08307.14464

These and all Regal Books are available at your local Christian bookstore.

Regal Books
A Division of Gospel Light